ANATOMY *of a*
MIRACLE

ANATOMY *of a* MIRACLE

*The End of Apartheid
and the Birth of the
New South Africa*

PATTI WALDMEIR

Rutgers University Press

New Brunswick, New Jersey, and London

To Holman of Africa

First published in hardcover 1997 by W. W. Norton & Company, Inc.

First published in paperback 1998 by Rutgers University Press, New Brunswick, New Jersey

Excerpts from *Long Walk to Freedom* by Nelson Mandela copyright © 1994 by Nelson Rolihlahla Mandela. Reprinted by permission of Little, Brown and Company.

Library of Congress Cataloging-in-Publication Data

Waldmeir, Patti.
   Anatomy of a miracle : the end of apartheid and the birth of the
new South Africa / Patti Waldmeir.
     p.   cm.
   Originally published: New York : W.W. Norton & Co., c1997.
   Includes bibliographical references and index.
   ISBN 0-8135-2582-9 (pbk. : alk. paper)
   1. South Africa—Politics and government—1978–1989. 2. South
Africa—Politics and government—1989–1994. 3. South Africa—Race
relations. I. Title.
[DT1967.W35 1999]
968.06′4—dc21   98-15628
                                              CIP

British Library Cataloguing-in-Publication Data is available.

Manufactured in the United States of America

Contents

PART THREE

LIFE AFTER APARTHEID, 249

Preface: African Mysteries

WE COULD NOT HEAR THE RIOTING, but we could see the fires burning all around, as we stood on the roof of the stadium. Black smoke spewed forth from looted shops and houses, blocking the streets and filling us with the vicarious thrill of violence. Snipers, aiming down into the urban gully of the freeway, had cut off our escape route. Already, they had killed one white woman.

We chose instead a circuitous route that took us past the heavily barricaded police headquarters. This was before the troops arrived and police said the situation was "completely out of control." In the days that followed, we could hear the drone of troop transports overhead, as five thousand soldiers were flown in to restore order. Gatherings of more than five people were banned. There was a nighttime curfew. Troops patrolled in tanks.

The year was 1967, the city was Detroit, and I was three days shy of my twelfth birthday. That was my introduction to the politics of race: the Sunday afternoon when I was caught with my father and brother watching baseball in the middle of Detroit's race riots. The issue of race defined my childhood, as I grew up in a pure white suburb of this overwhelmingly black city. It would dominate most of the next thirty years of my life.

This time we could hear the sounds of violence, as we stood on the highway overpass looking down into the squatter camp. The noises were surreal: the gentle pop of gunfire, the crackle of the fires; none of it sounded lethal. But there were victims, black men hacked to death by other black men, or killed by white police. It was nearly twenty years since my initiation on the Tiger Stadium roof, and I was once again playing voyeur to violence, this time in South Africa.

For the better part of ten years—from 1985 to 1995—I was a spectator to the political drama that was the death of apartheid. I came to the theater bearing the baggage of my childhood in Detroit, marked by vicious battles over the forced integration of Detroit area schools through busing. I came armed with a child's outrage at discrimination, and with adolescent dreams of revolution nurtured by voracious reading of the words of Malcolm X. The question of race had always held a romantic fascination for me. But the romance really bloomed when I went to live in Africa.

I went first to black Africa, that part of the continent north of South Africa, most of which had been independent of white rule by then for two decades. My first African home was Ghana, on the western slave coast of Africa, where I went to live in 1980. I arrived to teach English literature at the University of Ghana, and quickly succumbed to the charms of a continent that became my home off and on for fifteen years. Like other whites before me, I was overcome by the warmth and hospitality of black people, who welcome white visitors as honored guests in their country. Human intercourse is so much more direct in Africa, where there is no First World cloak of sophistication and mistrust to shroud it. Africa is a seductive continent; for a girl from Detroit, raised in a world of racial hatred, its warmth proved addictive.

I soon learned that Africa is also a continent of extremes. If Ghanaians took their virtues to extremes, they did the same with vices. About a year after I arrived, I started to do freelance journalism, and went to visit the scene of a tribal massacre in the north of the country. There, in the dusty main street of a nameless village, the local authorities showed me the partly decomposed body of a man half buried in a shallow grave. There were other bodies in surrounding huts, but this was my first one. It was the first dead body I had ever seen, except in a funeral home.

This struck me at the time as barbaric—the death was the result of fighting between two tribes that had been enemies for decades—but it was to prove only a mild prelude to South African atrocities. Ghanaians are a mostly peaceful people. The real tragedy of Ghana was not physical brutality but an entirely more subtle form of abuse: the incompetence and corruption of Ghana's leaders.

By the time I arrived, Ghana had lived under a series of military and civilian black governments for nearly a quarter of a century. They had reduced the country to utter penury. Even as a privileged lecturer living in a university apartment, I had running water only sporadically. To flush the toilet, I had to collect water by bucket from a tap several hundred yards away. The electricity supply was erratic, so I could seldom use the ceiling fan to dispel the oppressive heat of the tropics. Meat was exceptionally hard to come by: every year, the university issued its staff with one chicken for the Christmas meal. (These were live chickens. I took mine home, locked it up in the kitchen, and went off to seek the wisdom of Africa to deal with the situation.)

Medical care was virtually nonexistent. When my Ghanaian boyfriend fell ill and was admitted to the University Hospital, the authorities told me to bring bed linens and food, and to buy medicine for him on the black market. That was by then the only source of many basic necessities—canned fish, toilet paper, condensed milk, beer. The prices were far out of reach of most Ghanaians.

Yet Ghana had been one of the richest countries in colonial Africa, before independence in 1957. It used to be called the Gold Coast, because of its rich reserves of the metal, and of diamonds. Older Ghanaians had a great nostalgia for the days of white rule, and said so. They blamed black rule—and the confused socialism of Ghana's early rulers—for ruining their wonderful country. Thousands of miles away in South Africa, it was exactly that African nightmare which disturbed the white man's sleep.

None of what I had seen in Ghana was any excuse for apartheid. I had no doubt about that. So when I arrived in South Africa for the first time in 1985, I came bearing the certain knowledge of good and evil that was the baggage of every foreigner. The Afrikaner was demon and the African saint; there were no mixed tones in the black and white morality of the times. I relished the idea of having a front-row seat at the twentieth century's best morality play.

I soon realized that the characters in my drama were not drawn exactly according to script. The main story line was fairly accurate: the white government kept blacks in oppression, denying them the vote, and detaining, harassing, sometimes even killing those who resisted. Blacks responded, by and large, with nobility, patience, and a breathtaking generosity of spirit. Black South Africans refused to indulge the racial hatred which would have been so much more rational than tolerance. They welcomed me to their townships and their homes, as the Ghanaians had done. The old African potion began to work on me, again.

Still, there were unaccountable departures from text. On my first visit to a township, to attend the funeral of four guerrillas of the African National Congress, a black bystander was nearly burned to death by the mob. The crowd thought he was a police informer and sentenced him to death on the spot. He was spared after the intervention of a clergyman. But I wondered whether I had got my casting quite right. I found it hard to grasp the hatred that could spur such a deed, hard to condone the glee that filled the eyes of those preparing to carry it out. These were not the saints of Central Casting.

The sinners, too, proved disturbingly sympathetic. For many of the same reasons that Africans had won my heart, I found myself drawn to the white tribe of Africa, the Afrikaners, a tiny nation of 3 million people whose language, Afrikaans, was spoken almost nowhere else on earth. They were people of the South African soil, often descendants of the original handful of Dutch, French Huguenot, and German settlers who colonized this harsh and distant land in the seventeenth and eighteenth centuries. Afrikaners had no automatic right of refuge in Europe: South Africa was their homeland. They feared for their language, their culture, and their prosperity under black rule. Afrikaners were fighting for ethnic survival, and they were battling the Ghana syndrome. I felt a kind of guilty sympathy for their plight.

One knew immediately that Afrikaners were not modern people, any more than their black compatriots. Both dressed like fashion refugees from the 1960s American South, with their absurdly bouffant hairdos (in the case of whites) and their veiled churchgoing headgear (in the case of blacks). This was part of their appeal: they lacked the sophistication to hide their flaws. Both were as simple and straightforward in good as in evil. Chillingly brutal and heartwarmingly kind by turns, they taught me confusing lessons in the nature of the human spirit.

They also taught me that in Africa, politics is about power, and it was a lesson I would not forget in the years to come. The attitude of African and Afrikaner to power was like their approach to everything else—straightforward. Power in Africa is naked, like the hard stone and harsh scrub of the African bush. It is elemental, and it can be frightening. Democracy will not easily tame it.

The Afrikaner was not so much evil in fighting to maintain that power as blind to the consequences of the battle. By then, I had begun to worry about my eyesight as well. I had thought my moral vision perfect when I arrived in South Africa in 1985. By the time I left at the end of my first short visit, I could no longer see things in quite such stark relief.

The main purpose of my 1985 visit was not journalistic but commercial. I had been posted by the *Financial Times* to Lusaka, in neighboring Zambia, from which base I spent two years covering the whole of black Africa. But Zambia was another African economic cripple, and I could not buy a car there. So I flew to Johannesburg, bought a slightly used Volkswagen, and drove 1,200 kilometers across the African bush back home to Zambia.

Lusaka was also home to the African National Congress (ANC), the main liberation movement fighting white rule. By then, many of its leaders had been in exile for twenty-five years. My home was a simple cottage at 14B Twin Palm Road, in the verdant Lusaka suburb of Kabulonga. It was to prove a choice location: my landlords, Harry and Marjorie Chimowitz, were South African exiles who were not only immensely kind but politically well connected. One of their closest friends was Joe Slovo, the white Communist who commanded the ANC's guerrilla army, *Umkhonto we Sizwe,* or "Spear of the Nation." A few houses away lived Mac Maharaj, a brilliant, ebullient Indian South African who had been Mandela's confidant in prison, and was now a senior leader of the ANC. In another part of Kabulonga was the house of Thabo Mbeki, who is now deputy president of South Africa.

These men exploded most of my remaining South African stereotypes. Slovo was the first real revolutionary I had ever known. Yet he was not grim, obsessive, and charmless, a textbook terrorist; he was a rotund, grandfatherly Communist, with an impish sense of humor and a disarming openness of manner. No doubt, he was also a killer—for that was his job. But I knew him as the portly gentleman who did laps in the Chimowitz swimming pool. I often silently cursed Slovo for waking me—he swam before 7:00 A.M.—and worried that his regular visits might attract the murderous attentions of South African intelligence. But I never found him frightening.

The ANC were careful to court the international press, which was not widely represented in Lusaka. So I had time to get to know the men who would one day rule South Africa. They gave me courses in their philosophy of non-racialism, which decreed that the ANC's enemy was not whites themselves, but the system whites had built—apartheid. And I thought, if the ANC can look beyond black and white, how dare I refuse to do so?

I returned to South Africa in July 1989, at what seemed to me the country's darkest hour. After an absence of nearly three years, I was posted to Johannesburg as bureau chief by the *Financial Times.* I found the township revolt of the mid-1980s crushed by a brutal state of emergency. Nelson Mandela was finishing his twenty-sixth year in prison and some fifty thousand ANC activists had been detained. I felt certain South Africa would never escape its twisted past.

The years that followed were the most exhilarating of my life. Almost from the moment I returned, the political landscape began to shift beneath my feet. Soon there were grand figures to people the new landscape—Nelson Mandela, freed from prison, and F. W. de Klerk, the new white president. There were vignettes of remarkable African warmth and scenes of unspeakable horror. There were brains in a basin on the floor, amid the blood-soaked detritus of a township massacre; but there was also the inspiring refusal of the relatives to attack my white skin, though they blamed whites for the carnage. This was drama writ large, with characters to match. Apartheid brought out the best in people, or it brought out the worst; it left scant room for mediocrity.

You will read, in the pages that follow, a strange and wonderful tale of collective liberation, the story of how the African was freed from apartheid and the Afrikaner released from the bondage of his fear. I would ask you to remember throughout that though both sides will say this was a struggle for democracy, it was also a battle for power.

More than anything, it was a compelling mystery story, one of the great political thrillers of the late twentieth century. Why did the Afrikaners do what so few ruling groups had ever done in history, voluntarily relinquish power? How is it that they, too, felt liberated when Nelson Mandela ascended the throne built by them? Why did the Boers give it all away?

I spent much of my seven years in South Africa looking for the answers to those questions, seeking to explain the miracle of a peaceful transition to majority rule. It was a study in the psychology of capitulation; a journey into the mind of South Africa. This book is my record of that journey, which took me to the listless "platteland," the white rural areas of South Africa where the prejudice of centuries dies hardest. It took me to the hills of Natal and the townships around Johannesburg, to witness scenes of barbarity and small epiphanies of joy. I spoke to the great and the humble in my quest to understand; I went to the heart of South Africa's humanity and its inhumanity; and the trip left me changed forever.

Perhaps I will never be the same again, but neither will South Africa. Just after the first all-race elections in April 1994, South Africans cherished a sense of infinite possibility. They thrilled to the notion of creating a new country, complete with symbols and systems and languages, entirely from scratch. It was like a new marriage, or the beginning of a new life. Inevitably, that exhilaration has faded.

No one knows how the ANC will react to having power. The demographics of South Africa—Africans represent a vast and growing majority of the population—are likely to keep the ANC in a position of dominance for a decade, perhaps much more. Until Africans decide to vote against blood and tribe, for some future party whose appeal is based on economic and social policies, the ANC will face no effective opposition. Parties which hold power unchallenged inevitably abuse it.

But the future is another country that I cannot hope to visit. The present is quite extraordinary enough. For a girl who learned her race politics on the top of Tiger Stadium, South Africa was a dream impossibly come true. It was a powerful rebuke to the memories of my girlhood, a chance to do what South Africans had taught me: To liberate myself from my past.

Chronology

1652	Jan van Riebeeck lands at the Cape of Good Hope, to establish the first European settlement
1899–1902	Anglo-Boer War
1910	Union of South Africa formed from the former Boer republics of Transvaal and Orange Free State and the British colonies of the Cape and Natal
1912	South African Native National Congress formed, later renamed the African National Congress
1914	National Party formed
1918	Nelson Mandela born
1936	F. W. de Klerk born
1948	National Party comes to power
1950	South African Communist Party banned
1955	Congress of the People adopts the Freedom Charter
1958	Hendrik Verwoerd becomes prime minister
1960	Sharpeville massacre; ANC banned
1961	South Africa declares itself a republic
1962	Mandela arrested, given five-year sentence
1963	Police raid headquarters of *Umkhonto we Sizwe* at Rivonia farm, arrest many ANC leaders
1964	Mandela sentenced to life imprisonment
1966	Verwoerd assassinated; John Vorster replaces him
1976	Soweto revolt
1977	Death of black consciousness leader Steve Biko
1978	P. W. Botha becomes prime minister, later president
1979	Black trade unions legalized
1982	Right-wing whites break away to form Conservative Party
1983	New tricameral Constitution denies power to blacks; United Democratic Front formed to fight it
1984–86	Township uprising; states of emergency declared (1985 and 1986)
1985	*August:* the Rubicon debacle and the unilateral debt moratorium *November:* Nelson Mandela and Kobie Coetsee begin secret meetings
1986	Thabo Mbeki and Pieter de Lange meet secretly in New York; National

Party holds crucial Federal Congress
1987   Mells Park House talks begin
1988   Niël Barnard team begins meeting Mandela in prison
1989   *February:* F. W. de Klerk elected National Party leader after P. W. Botha
        suffers stroke
        July: Botha and Mandela meet at Tuynhuys
        September: de Klerk elected president, legalizes ANC Cape Town march
        October: Walter Sisulu and ANC leaders released from prison
        December: de Klerk meets Mandela
1990   *February:* de Klerk legalizes ANC and SACP and releases Mandela
        May: talks begin at Groote Schuur estate in Cape Town
        August: ANC suspends armed struggle; violence escalates
1991   *January:* Nelson Mandela and Chief Mangosuthu Buthelezi meet
        July: ANC holds key policy conference in Durban
        December: start of formal multi-party talks, the Convention for a Democratic
        South Africa (Codesa I)
1992   *March:* whites-only referendum endorses reform
        May: Codesa II collapses
        June: ANC supporters killed at Boipatong
        September: Bisho massacre, followed by conclusion of the Record of Under-
        standing between the ANC and government
        October: Joe Slovo publishes article offering "sunset clauses"
1993   *April:* Chris Hani assassinated
        July: agreement on election date, Inkatha walks out
        August: Mandela secretly meets Constand Viljoen
        November: agreement on interim constitution
        December: Transitional Executive Council, the multi-party interim govern-
        ment, begins to operate
1994   *March:* overthrow of Bophuthatswana, rout of the white right
        April: Inkatha enters elections
        April 26–28: ANC wins South Africa's first democratic elections
        May: Mandela inaugurated, government of national unity formed
1995   *June:* South Africa wins Rugby World Cup on home turf
1996   *May:* New Constitution adopted, to take force in 1999
        June: National Party withdraws from government of national unity

Prologue

ON A BRILLIANT WINTER'S DAY in 1994, the vanguard of apartheid's air force swooped over a hilltop in Pretoria and tipped its wings to the force's new commander in chief, Nelson Mandela. The same Impala and Mirage jet fighters that bombed black guerrillas during South Africa's liberation war pledged their allegiance to apartheid's most hated enemy on the day he became their president. It was an event of great national catharsis, the moment when white hands finally let go their 350-year grip on power. Africa and the Afrikaner were reconciled at last.

Until the first planes appeared on the horizon, trailing smoke in the garish colors of the new South African flag, this sight would have been unimaginable. Every spectator knew, rationally, that white rule had ended; but reason alone could not grasp the enormity of this truth. This simple signal of white loyalty to black rule made South Africa's unlikely revolution seem finally real. It was a transcendent moment, and I was not alone in hiding tears once it had passed.

Emotion was a constant companion in those days when the South African morality tale reached its storybook climax—especially for someone who had spent a decade following each twist in the tortured plot. Hastily, I donned sunglasses to mask unprofessional tears when Nelson Mandela placed hand over heart in sign of reverent respect for the singing of *die Stem,* the anthem of his oppression; when white army sharpshooters, deployed to guard a black president, proved as fervent in their protective duty as ever they were in persecution; when white lips struggled to form the unfamiliar syllables of South Africa's new anthem, *Nkosi sikelel'iAfrika,* paying homage to Africa at last.

Theirs is an implausible tale of collective liberation, one that might have ended so tragically otherwise: Afrikaners might have fought to keep Africa at bay until well into the new millennium, and left the new black rulers to inherit a wasteland. Africans might have merely changed the complexion of South African oppression, replacing white hegemony with black domination.

Those who believe in a God or gods—which includes most South Africans—rely on the rhetoric of divine intervention to explain their narrow escape from such a fate. But they do scant justice to the very human personalities and the very real historical forces that drove the apartheid drama to its end. For those who observed the protracted demise of white rule, it was like living a political thriller. The combined forces of history, economics, demography, and morality hastened apartheid on its way; but the outcome remained uncertain until the last plane disappeared over the horizon on the crisp bright day of Nelson Mandela's inauguration.

Disaster may yet descent on the "rainbow nation." Zhou Enlai said, when asked what he thought of the French Revolution, "It's too soon to tell." It is too soon to pronounce on South Africa, either way. But the plot thus far is gripping by any standard. History provides few enough examples of the triumph of common sense over ethnicity, or religion, or the myriad other forces which divide human populations; how rare the opportunities to savor what Nelson Mandela calls the "poetry of the triumph of the oppressed."

So how is it that white South Africans—scarcely renowned for their good sense in the decades of apartheid—managed finally to accept the dictates of reason? How could black South Africans subdue hatred and reject revenge to defy the logic of a tortured past that might have doomed them to ceaseless conflict? Why did the Afrikaner hand over power? What was it that catapulted this dour, Calvinistic, Old Testament people so abruptly into the modern world?

That story begins nearly thirty years ago, when doubt first began to enter the Afrikaner mind; in the decades that followed, Afrikaner thinking was transformed, by reformist leaders, timorous churchmen, troublesome academics, vocal editors, and ultimately, by the nagging sense of being out of step with history. Eventually, Afrikaners knew that they were wrong; but even before that, they knew they could not carry on. This is the story of their revolution, a study in the psychology of capitulation. Why, after all, did the Boers give it all away?

No single human being, no single historical force, provoked this reversal. But standing on the inaugural podium that day, May 10, 1994, and later appearing in a giant, bulletproof glass cage to greet tens of thousands of well-wishers, were the two men who did more than any others to drive South Africa's transformation: Nelson Mandela and F. W. de Klerk, black victor, white subordinate, their roles reversed by fate, and by their own courageous vision.

History will surely claim these two men as its heroes. They have guided South Africa as it grappled with the grandest questions of the political life of nations: how to order the relations between man and the state; how to balance rights and responsibilities, the demand for equality with the quest for freedom; in short, how to invent a new democratic nation from the ruins of a state built on institutionalized injustice. To South Africans, democracy is not the old and devalued friend familiar to citizens of mature nations; it is the promised land. And whatever their flaws, the two men who led South Africa to that haven will dominate its history for years to come.

They have never been friends—indeed, they are so different as to be almost incompatible—but at last they are compatriots, jointly devoted to the land of huge and empty beauty which is their common fatherland. It is that shared patriotism which carried the two men through the years of negotiated struggle; it is that reality which Nelson Mandela recognized at the pinnacle of his triumph, when he declared that F. W. de Klerk, taking the oath of office beside him as deputy president, was "one of the greatest sons of Africa."

A capricious history brought the forefathers of these two very different "sons of Africa" to live on this disputed tip of a troubled continent, in separate worlds of race, language, ethnicity, and ideology. But eventually they learned to recognize, if not a common destiny, at least a common danger: the risk of mutually assured destruction. None could live without the other. Now they would no longer try.

The fact of racial interdependence had been self-evident for many decades. White capital drove South Africa's mines, but black hands hewed the rock which held the precious metal; white farmers brought skills and machinery to till the African soil, but blacks did the hardest labor; whites managed the banks, but the tellers were mostly people of color; white matrons built a society of comforts for their men, but black domestics made comfort a reality.

Yet for just as many decades both Afrikaners and Africans denied those obvious facts. The story of how they came to accept the central reality of mutual need, how Afrikaners set out on their last Great Trek to a new multi-racial fatherland, begins with another flyover, and yet another burst of patriotic color from the exhaust trail of more jet fighters. But if the planes were the same, the colors were radically different—as was the complexion of the man they served. For this was the apartheid state at the height of its self-delusion, the nadir of its cruelty. This was the land of Hendrik Verwoerd, the man who dreamed the dream that became South Africa's nightmare.

PART ONE

————◆◆◆◆————

APARTHEID AGONISTES

I can only tell you the things that happened as I saw them, and what the rest was about only Africa knows.

Herman Charles Bosman, *Mafeking Road*

THE WIRY, BARE-FOOTED FARMER *shouted out to me not to worry: "He's not color-blind," he said of the bull terrier who had pinned me in my car. Translation: The dog bites only blacks. Canine South Africa, trained from birth in racism.*

The farmer was clad only in shorts, and one shriveled arm hung limp at his side. His mother wore a battered khaki sunhat, streaked red with the African dust. The wife, plump and shapeless, and the dirty, tow-headed four-year-old, completed this portrait of poor white Afrikanerdom. Verwoerdian man, relic of the land of apartheid, out of place in the new South Africa.

The snapshot was taken in 1992, when apartheid was shuddering toward its final demise. But Buks Viljoen's belligerence and fear were of an earlier vintage. Born an Afrikaner, he grew up in the wildest and worst-ruled black states to the north, where his father drilled boreholes. After white settlers were massacred in the Congo in the 1960s, the family returned to Verwoerd's South Africa.

Now black rule threatened his homeland, and Viljoen was having none of it. He, his seventy-three-year-old mother, Anna Maria, and wife Katerina were determined to remain poor but pure to the last. Just like the ideologues of apartheid said they should be. They used no black labor on the farm. They kept cattle, sheep, chickens, and pigs, and bought nothing but sugar, coffee, salt, and cattle dip in town. When I happened into their farmyard, in brutal midday heat, I found them digging. Buks had decided they needed an icehouse, to keep slaughtered meat for the siege.

He lived with a dark fear of being swamped by Africa. For him, prejudice was a matter of survival. The Bible forbade racial mixing: the children of Israel must not lie down with the children of Ham. The Church taught him this, and the state hammered home the lesson that white dominance was needed to ensure it. Viljoen's experience of life confirmed the need for separation: "I never met a munt who didn't smell," he assured me, chosing the crudest of

Afrikaans labels for blacks. Then he added: "I smell to him, too, probably." Personal hygiene was not really the issue. The farmer was using it as a metaphor for all that frightened him. Buks Viljoen did not want to live amongst those of another odor. He was terrified of alien smells.

1

The Myth of the Monolith

F. W. DE KLERK WATCHED, and admired, as the apartheid military celebrated the sheer naked power of the white state he would one day dismantle. All the hardware of white dominance passed before him— tanks, heavy guns, armored cars, jet fighters. It was 1966: apartheid was invincible.

De Klerk, model Afrikaner, stood on the podium that crisp bright day in May as his nation marked the fifth anniversary of the creation of an independent South African Republic. Amongst the dignitaries were Hendrik Verwoerd—the man who made South Africa famous for racial segregation— and F. W.'s father, Jan de Klerk, a minister in Verwoerd's government.

It was a moment of intense patriotism for de Klerk, no less so than the day nearly thirty years later when he would hand over power to Nelson Mandela. At least as many people attended these celebrations held at the Voortrekker Monument in Pretoria, sacred shrine of Afrikanerdom. The same Impalas and Mirage jet fighters swooped overhead streaming patriotic colors, to the fervent acclaim of a crowd which—however implausible it may seem to outsiders—was also celebrating national liberation.

The creation of a republic independent from Britain in 1961 was a decades-old dream come true for Afrikaners, revenge for their 1902 defeat by the British in the Anglo-Boer War. The war had made Afrikaners the second-class citizens of South Africa (Africans did not even rank on the class scale). And the all-consuming national conflict of the years that followed was between Boer and Briton, not black and white. The declaration of a republic in 1961 was a liberation just as sweet and true for Afrikaners as the inauguration of Mandela was for blacks.

On Republic Day, May 31, 1966, the new Afrikaner nation appeared impregnable. All the levers of control were in its hands. Top policemen, generals, bureaucrats, and judges were Afrikaners; they had inherited a white monopoly of political, economic, administrative, and technological power stretching back more than three hundred years. It was impossible to believe things would ever be otherwise.

"The white minority has a monopoly of force which it does not hesitate to use, and of power which it will not voluntarily yield . . . for the foreseeable future, South Africa will be able to maintain internal stability and effectively counter insurgent activity." That was U.S. Secretary of State Henry A. Kissinger's assessment of the apartheid state in 1969, at its zenith; that was the image created by Afrikaners to protect their vulnerable young nation.

The apartheid state had spent huge sums nurturing the myth of the monolith: the government budget for munitions manufacture rose a hundred-fold from 1960 to 1964 alone. And behind that image of military power lay the equally daunting edifice of the national will, granite-hard in defense of white hegemony. By the end of the 1960s, the psychology of white supremacy was firmly entrenched—in black minds as much as white.

That image—of the Afrikaner trapped forever in a prison of ethnic fear and loathing, ready to fight to the last man to defend the apartheid laager—would ultimately prove deceptive. But in 1966 it was a fair reflection of the national psyche. Afrikaners were aggressive because they were fearful, belligerent because they were insecure. That only made them all the fiercer.

The word *apartheid* means "separation" in Afrikaans, but segregation had been a fact of South African life long before Afrikaners took power. From the day when the Dutch sailor Jan van Riebeeck founded a victualing station at the Cape in 1652, blacks and whites lived separately. But when radical Afrikaner Nationalists triumphed in the 1948 elections, they created a vast legal superstructure to enforce separation. From then on, "apartheid" governed every aspect of national life: it assigned every baby from birth to a rigid "population group," which determined where he could live and go to school, what lavatory he could use, and whom he could marry. Many Afrikaners believe that was their greatest mistake, to set in stone what others (including whites in the contemporary American South) were content to observe as custom.

The American situation was different. Whites were a majority in America, whereas white South Africans were a small and declining minority in their country. Afrikaners were terrified that blacks would do what the English had done: render them a subject minority in the land of their birth. Their answer was apartheid. Its aim was to guarantee the prosperity and security of Afrikaners, through white domination. Apartheid was in large part an economic ideology, tailored to develop the largely poor, rural, undereducated Afrikaner nation of the 1930s into a prosperous bourgeoisie. In that, it succeeded. After the National Party took power in 1948, government employment became virtually an Afrikaner preserve: lucrative government accounts went to Afrikaner banks and contracts to Afrikaner businesses; huge state corporations, run by Afrikaners, were soon making everything from iron and steel to heavy weapons.

Verwoerd, who became prime minister in 1958, turned that policy into an ideology of national salvation, known as "grand apartheid." And he gave it a moral dimension, which made it that much easier for decent Afrikaners to accept. Verwoerd fed them what they wanted—a moral justification for white domination. As it was wrong for whites to continue ruling blacks, they would stop doing so. Black South Africans would be sent to live in their own tribal homelands, where they could govern themselves and live as they pleased. Whites would retain the bulk of the land, while blacks would be "removed" to a patchwork of ethnic states covering only 13 percent of the landmass. (Eventually, some 3–4 million people were forced to move to the homelands.) Blacks remaining in white South Africa would be treated as "foreigners" and tolerated only as migrant workers. The races would be separate; but they would be equal.

Verwoerd used the Bible to defend this policy, known as "separate development." He based his defense on the biblical injunction, "Love thy neighbor as thyself." As he told a Cape Town church congregation in the 1960s, "We have a very fine position in South Africa, we've got land, we've got a country and we are obliged by the love commandment to provide exactly the same to black people." (The clergyman who recalled this event for me in October 1994, Reverend Johan Heyns of the Dutch Reformed Church, was murdered by an assassin's bullet two days afterwards in the same room where we had held our conversation. The police believe that Heyns, who led his church away from apartheid, was killed by the kind of right-wing Afrikaner who still clings to that Verwoerdian vision of thirty years ago.)

Verwoerd gave the authoritarian state a conscience, a sense of right and wrong—however perverse—which would eventually prove one of its most fatal flaws. Had the rest of the edifice remained strong, had economic collapse, international opprobrium, terrorism, and the sheer weight of numbers not sapped the will of the Afrikaner to rule, this flaw might have remained latent forever. But in the end, morality did play a role: apartheid was abandoned not only because it failed but because its very failure made it immoral. Afrikaners could no longer rationalize their desire to rule and their belief in justice. That, as much as anything, made it possible for them to embrace the new South Africa.

Make no mistake. To the Afrikaners of the 1960s, the question of right and wrong was less important than their will to survive as a nation. But the twisted beauty of apartheid was that it appeared to them to fulfill both imperatives. Some embraced it purely cynically, as an excuse for white privilege. But others hoped it would provide a path to what the Afrikaans poet N. P. van Wyk Louw called "survival in justice." Among them was F. W. de Klerk, that most loyal child of the apartheid state, a textbook Afrikaner.

"We, my father, my uncle [former Prime Minister Hans Strijdom], have been pictured as almost hard-line criminals, willfully saying, 'I'm filled with hate, I'm a racist, I think nothing of blacks, I'm prepared to be part of a system which oppresses them.' It was never like that, and I am not prepared to admit to sins of which I am not guilty. . . .

"The people who structured apartheid and put it on the law books were not evil people. . . . Apartheid was, in its idealistic form, a plan to make all the people of South Africa free."

The passion evident in F. W. de Klerk's defense of apartheid has not waned with the years, nor can political expediency dissuade him from voicing it, even in the new South Africa. He leaned toward me as he spoke, insistent, irritated that this vital point had been so often misunderstood. I had come to know de Klerk's body language over the years, but these were signs I scarcely recognized: the gaze so intense, the tone rising high in appeal, the tension in the neck. De Klerk was not going to rest until he had made his peace with history.

It was November 1994, six months after he handed over power, and the former president was installed in his new office of deputy president. He was trying to explain how he had ended up there, shielded by tinted bulletproof glass that was never necessary to protect him when the white state was strong.

He traced the roots of his actions straight back to the ideology of apartheid, drawing an unwavering line of moral conviction from "separate development"—whose goal was "to bring full political rights to all South Africans via nation states"—to democracy. And then, in his eagerness to defend himself in the eyes of Afrikaner history, he reached even further back into the collective consciousness of his people, saying, "The Afrikaners fought the first anti-colonial war in modern history in Africa, against Great Britain. So Afrikaners have a deep understanding of the need of a people to be free."

It is a precarious argument to make before a foreigner, who is asked to accept that the architects of apartheid were not evil but merely blinded by fear, and that their motivation was not greed but the highest morality. De Klerk knows this, but he is not put off because he genuinely believes it to be true, and because he cannot bear to be seen as the man who betrayed his people's history. In his eyes, the quest of his forefathers was the same as his own—the search for "survival in justice."

He picks up the story of the creation of apartheid, one of the most ambitious social engineering projects in human history: "a dramatic process of decolonisation swept across Africa from the beginning of the 1960s. . . . South Africa found itself increasingly isolated and out of step with the rest of mankind. . . . It was clear that white South Africans would have to respond to this new situation—but how could we do it without at the same time losing the right to our own national self-determination which had been the central theme of our history? . . .

"The response was to embark on a process of internal decolonisation . . . we would lead the rural homelands to independence just as the colonial powers to the north had done. The goal was to bring justice to all by transforming South Africa into something like Europe—national states working together in respect of common interests."

Here again, de Klerk is on fragile ground, a man of the future who insists on defending the anachronisms of the past. As always, there is a tension in him between the modern, cosmopolitan leader—he is a politician of consummate skill, to rank with any of his Western peers—and the Calvinist Afrikaner born of a world that owes more to the nineteenth than to the twentieth century.

Still, the body language is entirely plausible. With head cocked to one side, the pose he adopts characteristically for maximum persuasion, de Klerk yearns to be understood, explaining, "There was a great degree of idealism in this vision. I know because my father was a member of the government which formulated it, and he was a good man. I as a student and youth leader was committed to liberate all South Africans in this way." Perhaps history demanded such a man—child of his time, creature of apartheid—to launch South Africa on a very different path to national liberation.

"The Afrikaner youth of the time were absolutely *hypnotized* by the ideology of apartheid because it was marketed as the ultimate solution of different countries for different peoples. The grand apartheid concept sounded so logical. . . ."

Willem de Klerk, elder brother to F.W. and son to Jan, muses on the early character of the man who made the de Klerk family famous. In later life, the two brothers parted company politically. Ironically, it was the elder brother who became the liberal, while F.W. clung to the conservative beliefs of their forebears. But in 1966, Willem and F.W. stood side by side on their father's Republic Day podium, united in admiration.

Framed by portraits of bearded de Klerk ancestors and a bronze profile of Calvin on his study wall, Willem (popularly known as Wimpie) recalls the state of mind of the Afrikaner nation in 1966: "We thought we were on top of the world. We had conquered the English, we had sorted out the black situation via apartheid, we had affirmative action, all the generals were Afrikaners. So the mood was, at last we have *arrived.*"

The de Klerk family felt very much part of the national triumph. When the National Party won power in 1948, "it was a wonderful day." The whole family celebrated, including twelve-year-old F.W. Politics was in his genes. One great-grandfather was a senator, his grandfather Willem was a Cape Rebel during the Anglo-Boer War; his father Jan was a member of cabinet in three apartheid governments, and president of the Senate. It was the perfect pedigree for change. Perhaps no one but a third-generation politician, whose loyalty to the National Party could be measured in decades, could have been trusted to mastermind the revolution.

"We were all Nationalists, we were all on the same side, what do you debate?" Jan Mentz, now a frail octogenarian, was once F. W. de Klerk's Latin teacher, mentor, debating society coach, and fellow spectator at the 1966 Republic Day parade.

Mentz says he had a premonition of evil that day when the parade commander collapsed and died on the spot. What he means is that he had a premonition of black rule. For this elderly gentleman's political views are like his courtly manners and exquisite hospitality, relics of a bygone age. He describes himself as an "Aryan," and remains convinced of the mental inferiority of the darker-skinned races.

Mentz has left me for a moment, sipping tea and wondering whether it would be greedy to sneak another of the delicious homemade oatmeal-and-fruit pastries from the plate by my side. This old man, with his crude talk of racial inferiority, has provoked in me a familiar dilemma: How can I sympathize with Afrikaners who hold such views, however legitimate their fears for the future? Can I eat their pastries, and accept their hospitality, without feeling somehow complicit?

My life in South Africa has been one long struggle with this dilemma, one long battle to come to grips with the paradox at the center of the Afrikaner soul. At once pious and cruel, brutal and paranoid, Afrikaners yearn to be loved, but have done so much that is both unlovable and unforgivable. Jan Mentz was just such a paradox: a bigot, but one who accepted the new order with ease; a white supremacist who expressed an irrational pride that the man who gave away white power had been his pupil.

Mentz returns to the room (noting with pleasure my consumption of a second pastry) and remembers that time of greatest Afrikaner blindness, the decades of the 1950s and 1960s. He recalls that race was never even the subject of debate at Monument High School in Krugersdorp, which gave

F. W. de Klerk his diploma in 1953. Those were the days before the slightest shadow of doubt had come to darken the Afrikaner mind.

Blacks were firmly under white control. They had no political rights, no labor rights, were barred by law from skilled professions, and kept in fenced townships built out of sight of white South Africa. Afrikaner society, too, was cohesive. No one would have needed to teach the young F.W. that every race group had its place in a hierarchy ordained not by man alone, but by God. These were the implicit truths of Afrikaner life.

During this period of greatest Afrikaner certainty, there was nothing to debate, and no sign that the young F.W.—universally described as a boy of agile but not brilliant mind—would be the one to revolutionize the politics of centuries.

Jan Mentz recalls that the future president loved Latin, because of its analytical nature. But he also loved Mentz's lessons in logic: "I taught him that he must always approach a matter in a balanced way, not be overruled by emotion, take a logical approach to everything and weigh things in an objective way." All who knew F. W. de Klerk, child and man, agree that this was his greatest strength—the courage to think rationally when fear would crowd out logic; the clarity of vision to recognize facts.

None of this sounds particularly heroic; indeed, no one who knew the future president as a child remembers premonitions of greatness. They recall a nice, decent boy, with a winning smile and a way with girls, not the type to pursue greatness with single-minded obsession. One friend remembers F.W. singing these lines from an Afrikaans folksong: "If I become president of South Africa one day, / We will drive to the capital, / The two of us in a wagon." Nobody thought he was making a prediction.

This, then, was the monolith: a nation that coupled frightening unity of vision with fearsome military force.

But at the very moment that Verwoerd and F. W. de Klerk were celebrating its strength at the Voortrekker Monument in 1966, a plot was afoot to reduce the monolith to myth. Within the walls of the maximum-security prison at Robben Island, Nelson Mandela was scheming not to overthrow but to outsmart the state. He was planning a monumental act of seduction, aimed at wooing Afrikaners away from apartheid by proving to them not only that it was wrong—but that it was unnecessary.

It took Mandela and his African National Congress (ANC) colleagues something like thirty years to find the cracks, widen them, and watch the monolith implode. But though the vast majority of ANC energy went into a military challenge to the monolith, the final victory was more psychological than physical. The journey down the road to capitulation began at Robben

Island, a barren expanse of rock off the shores of Cape Town, which was home to Nelson Mandela for nearly two decades.

To this day, Mandela can shock an audience by publicly pining for Robben Island. It is an idiosyncrasy he shares with many other former inmates of this, South Africa's Alcatraz. They all agree that incarceration on "the Island" provided one ingredient that proved essential to their struggle. "Time to think," as Mandela puts it. Time to mature politically, time to plot. Captured in 1962 and sentenced to life imprisonment in 1964 for sabotage, Mandela had plenty of time to prepare himself to rule.

Mac Maharaj was one of Mandela's closest colleagues in prison. He traces the psychological conquest of Afrikanerdom back to those distant days on Robben Island when Mandela first learned to play mind games with the Boer. The secret was Mandela's mastery of the Afrikaans language. He even used Afrikaans to refer, affectionately, to the younger Maharaj—Mandela called him *neef,* or nephew, while Maharaj returned the compliment with the Afrikaans honorific *oom* (uncle) for Mandela. The older man's choice of the Afrikaner language—detested by blacks as the language of the oppressor—was not accidental. He considered a knowledge of enemy tongues an essential weapon in battle. Throughout his imprisonment, he read Afrikaans voraciously—history, poetry, philosophy. He insisted his colleagues do the same.

Maharaj is a volatile man, who fought apartheid with powerful energy and intellect. He went on to become one of President Mandela's most trusted ministers. But in 1965, he was the angriest of young men. He recalls his outrage when, in that year, Mandela suggested he learn Afrikaans. "He said, 'Neef, we are in for a protracted war, which is going to be a combination of armed and political struggle. Slowly the armed struggle is going to become the dominant form. But to wage it, you must understand the mind of the opposing commander. You can never outmaneuver him unless you understand him, and you can't understand him unless you understand his literature and his language.'

"That's where I collapsed, and I took up Afrikaans."

In the years to follow, Mandela would exploit this psychological advantage to launch his Afrikaner interlocutors on the road to conversion. Dr. Niël Barnard led a government team which negotiated with the imprisoned Mandela in the late 1980s; he recalls that the ANC leader always greeted him in Afrikaans, and allowed him to conduct his side of the talks in his mother tongue. By volunteering to speak the language so detested by his followers, Mandela sent signals of good faith that did much to calm Afrikaner fear of cultural annihilation. Such concessions were cheap at the price. They were to prove a major down payment on peace.

Mandela spent his twenty-seven years in prison preparing mentally for the day when the oppressor would sue for that peace. He made sure his fellow prisoners did the same, launching a series of debates—over pick and shovel at the Island limestone quarry, or during mealtimes—on issues ranging from the merits of guerrilla warfare to whether there are tigers in Africa (there are not).

In this way, the ANC guaranteed unity among its leaders on key issues. The government had thought it could kill off dissent by exiling political opponents to Robben Island; instead, it merely succeeded in consolidating the opposition. But perhaps Pretoria gained, perversely, in the end, for generations of young hotheads got a sobering political education at what was known as "the University of Robben Island." Those who entered the prison hating whites—probably a majority—emerged hating the system which whites had built, but not the race itself. A case of unintended consequences, of which many more were to follow.

"One of the things that we discovered is that men are not the same, even when dealing with a community that has a tradition of insensitivity toward human rights. Because the moment we arrived at Robben Island, a debate started amongst Afrikaner warders, some saying, let's treat these people harshly so they respect white supremacy, others saying, their side in history will ultimately win, we must treat them in such a way that when they win, it should not be a government of retribution." Nelson Mandela is outlining the lessons in human nature that he learned at the University of Robben Island.

"We established a very strong relationship because we adopted a policy of talking to the warders and persuading them to treat us as human beings. And a lot of them did, and there were a lot of things we could talk about.

"And the lesson was that one of our strongest weapons is dialogue. Sit down with a man, if you have prepared your case very well, that man, after he has sat down to talk to you, will never be the same again. It has been a very powerful weapon."

I had asked Mandela to reflect on the genesis of multi-racial power sharing, the model for his first government. He traced its roots back to Robben Island. And as always, he showed no bitterness when recalling his Island incarceration. The seventy-five-year-old man sitting stiffly on an armchair opposite me had no time for extraneous emotion: he had been president of the new South Africa for less than eight weeks, and there was a huge task of racial reconciliation ahead. Everyone knew he had suffered. He wanted us to focus instead on what he had learned.

Mandela is a slow speaker, agonizingly slow. I always found his prolonged pauses unnerving. He would sit, with mouth closed and head held unnaturally still, until I was convinced he had forgotten the question. Then, when reason had extinguished passion in his breast, he would speak, most often in a flat monotone that betrayed little. There are no cheap glimpses into Mandela's soul. He is too disciplined for that.

There are insights into his thinking, however, and he offered some that day, as we took tea in the Office of the President. My mind's eye gave the place such capital letters, to mark the momentousness of the occasion. For this was what I had never thought to see in my lifetime, a black man in charge in the Union Buildings, the seat of government. And unlike Mandela, I had not had twenty-seven years in prison to learn how to conquer my emotions.

What Mandela was saying that day was just as implausible to me as his very presence in the Union Buildings: that South Africa's negotiated revolution began on Robben Island in the days of Verwoerd. But Mac Maharaj and other Islanders provide a wealth of detail to verify the point. One story concerns a meeting in the mid-1960s between Mandela and General J. C. Steyn, commissioner of prisons. The subject, ostensibly, was prison conditions.

"In this war, there has got to be a victor and a vanquished, but even over the ashes of our country, the victor and the vanquished will have to sit down and talk," Mandela told the general. "You may think you're going to win, we think we're going to win. But don't make the mistake of robbing us of the chance to respect each other as worthy adversaries. Give us the chance, while we disagree with you and are your enemies, at least to respect you." Mandela went on to use that logic to argue for better prison conditions. No one will ever know whether General Steyn understood him, but someone heard his plea. Over the years, conditions improved dramatically; and somehow, the two sides maintained that respect which was crucial, in the end, to a settlement.

But of all the lessons taught at Robben Island, none is more poignant than the case of Colonel Piet Badenhorst. He arrived as prison commanding officer in 1970, preceded by his reputation as one of the most brutal and authoritarian of officials. In the time-honored fashion of Afrikaner warders, Badenhorst swore at the prisoners, enjoined Mandela *"jy moet jou vinger uit jou gat trek"* ("pull your finger out of your arse"), and made unfavorable comments about Mandela's mother's anatomy.

None of this was unexpected. But what amazed Mandela was Badenhorst's demeanor when he left Robben Island the following year—" 'I just want to wish you people good luck,' " Badenhorst said. Mandela writes about the incident in his autobiography, *Long Walk to Freedom:*

I thought about this moment for a long time afterwards. . . . Badenhorst had perhaps been the most callous and barbaric commanding officer we had had on Robben Island. But that day, he had revealed that there was another side to his nature. . . . It was a useful reminder that all men, even the most seemingly cold-blooded, have a core of decency, and that if their hearts are touched, they are capable of changing. Ultimately, Badenhorst was not evil; his inhumanity had been foisted upon him by an inhuman system. He behaved like a brute because he was rewarded for brutish behaviour.

Few passages better capture the generosity of Mandela's spirit and the nature of the understanding that prompted him to seek peace.

Reflecting, finally, on all twenty-seven years of his captivity, Mandela then distills this lesson: "A man who takes away another man's freedom is a prisoner of hatred, he is locked behind the bars of prejudice and narrow-mindedness . . . the oppressed and the oppressor alike are robbed of their humanity. The oppressor must be liberated just as surely as the oppressed." It was through just such a feat of simultaneous liberation that Mandela defeated the monolith, and saved Afrikanerdom from itself.

He had been looking for ways to do so even before he reached Robben Island—and before he and other ANC leaders adopted the strategy of armed struggle which landed them in jail. In 1960, Mandela outlined an early vision of power sharing in testimony to the court which tried him and 156 others for high treason (they were acquitted). Mandela knew whites were not then ready for majority rule. But even if they gave Africans only 60 out of 160 seats in Parliament for, say, five years, "that would be a victory," he told the court, "a significant step towards the attainment of universal adult suffrage for Africans." Mandela wrote to Verwoerd to call for a national convention on a new constitution. He never received a reply.

But the most striking statement of the ANC leader's early moderation was the one he made from the dock in the 1964 "Rivonia" trial, which sent him to Robben Island. In it, he promised never to allow a black monolith to be built where the white one had fallen. "I have fought against white domination and I have fought against black domination. I have cherished the ideal of a democratic and free society in which all persons live together in harmony and with equal opportunities. It is an ideal which I hope to live for and to achieve. But if needs be, it is an ideal for which I am prepared to die."

Over a quarter century would pass before Mandela met a man capable of understanding this message. When he did, he immediately sought to play on the similarities in political genealogy between himself and F. W. de Klerk. Both were, effectively, princes of the South African political scene, both descendants of families with power. Perverse as it may seem, Mandela respected de Klerk not despite his political antecedents but because of them. The white president came of a powerful lineage, and Mandela understood power.

He had learned about it as he grew up, in the household of the regent of the Thembu people, Jongintaba. Mandela's father was a "headman" or councilor of the Thembu, who are part of the larger Xhosa tribe. The ANC leader still pays homage to the Thembu regent as the source of his own later notions of leadership.

In his autobiography, Mandela paints a picture of an early, Thembu prototype of the consensus-style government he would adopt as president more than sixty years later. He is describing a tribal gathering at the regent's residence, the "Great Place," Mqhekezweni.

At first I was astonished by the vehemence—and candour—with which people criticised the regent. . . . But no matter how serious the charge, the regent simply listened, not defending himself, showing no emotion at all. . . .

The meetings would continue until some kind of consensus was reached. They ended in unanimity or not at all . . . democracy meant all men were to be heard, and a decision was taken together as a people. Majority rule was a foreign notion. A minority was not to be crushed by a majority.

Only at the end of the meeting, as the sun was setting, would the regent speak. His purpose was to sum up what had been said and form some consensus among the diverse opinions. But no conclusion was forced on people who disagreed. If no agreement could be reached, another meeting would be held. . . .

Mandela would follow the same principles when he became a leader of men. "I always remember the regent's axiom: a leader is like a shepherd. He stays behind the flock, letting the most nimble go on ahead, whereupon the others follow, not realising that they are being directed from behind."

Like de Klerk, Mandela had politics not only in his heart but in his blood. But both men would have to serve a long apprenticeship to power before they stood on that Pretoria hilltop and vowed solemn allegiance to the new South Africa. Both, in their very different ways, had a long way to go to disprove the myth of the monolith.

SOMETIME IN THE 1880s, *two baby boys were born on a farm in a lush green valley near the spot where white men first settled in the Cape. They grew up there, at the foot of a dramatic pass that crosses the craggy mountains to the east. When they were old enough, they went to primary school together in the little town nearby.*

After a few years, they were separated. The one boy, who was white, went to a white school in a larger town, while the other, who was of mixed race, or "coloured," went to the coloured school in a town set aside for his population group. The coloured child completed eight years of schooling, and then returned to the farm. The white boy finished secondary school, and returned as well. At age thirty-five, the white man made the coloured man his foreman, and they farmed together for the next forty years.

At age seventy-five, they both retired. The farmer bought retirement homes both for himself and for his foreman, one in the white town and one in the smaller town set aside for coloureds. The foreman visited the farmer weekly. Then the coloured town was declared "white," and the foreman had to move. He built a house in another town, and then that too was declared white, and the two men were both over eighty by this time. The colored man came to say goodbye to the farmer, and he asked, "Why are you allowing this to happen? I can no longer be friends with you."

The farmer was in a state about it. He had been a Nationalist all his life, and now this was what the Nationalists were doing. For the first time, it really got to him. Before, apartheid was something that was happening to other people. His life had gone on normally, he was once removed from it. But that really shook him—the immorality of it! How could he accept it, in conscience?

2

The Age of Contradictions

PRIME MINISTER Hendrik Verwoerd lay dead in the aisles of Parliament. The endgame of apartheid had begun.

On September 6, 1966, a demented white parliamentary messenger murdered Verwoerd in the legislative chamber, in full view of all the members. The two men who were to lead South Africa away from apartheid in the quarter century that followed—Balthazar John Vorster and Pieter Willem (P.W.) Botha—gave chase to the assassin, but too late.

The death of the architect of apartheid marked the beginning of the end of ideology. Without the man who had dreamed the twisted dream of a separate-but-equal utopia, the vision that had bound the Afrikaner nation in unity began to disintegrate. Increasingly, Afrikaners awoke to the reality of the massive contradictions—economic and practical, political and moral—which apartheid had created. As a total ideology, which proposed a total solution to the problem of the white man in Africa, apartheid could not tolerate such contradictions. It was meant to fit together like a Rubic's Cube, as one geometrically perfect whole. But reality would not allow that.

"I remember looking at the children in their school uniforms and wondering how long they would stand up to the police. Suddenly a small boy dropped to the ground next to me . . . they were shooting into the crowd. More children fell. There seemed to be no plan. The police were merely blasting away. . . . Out of the blur of dust and fleeing children, stones began to fly at the police."

The actions of police that day—June 16, 1976, when black schoolchildren rioted in the township of Soweto outside Johannesburg—gave South Africa a worldwide reputation for repression. Black journalists, like the one quoted above, publicized the event locally. But a single snapshot flashed apartheid's wrongs around the world: the picture of a man running down a Soweto street clutching the lifeless body of thirteen-year-old Hector Petersen. The man's head is thrown back in grief, his face contorted. Hector's body, small and slight, lies limp in his arms; there is blood around the mouth. The boy's sister runs beside the man, screaming.

The cause of the rioting that killed Hector Petersen was the government's insistence that black children be taught in Afrikaans, a language they understood poorly and resented. It was all part of the Afrikaner state's social engineering, but it backfired. The uprising lasted for almost eighteen months, leaving nearly six hundred dead. By the time it was finally suppressed in 1977, an estimated fourteen thousand young blacks had fled to join the African National Congress in exile, and one of the most prominent of young black leaders, Steve Biko, had been beaten to death in police custody.

Pretoria put down the revolt with ruthless force, and the heightened political consciousness of the time soon waned. But psychologically, Soweto had planted the idea in black minds that resistance could achieve results. After the riots, Soweto schools were permitted to drop Afrikaans as a teaching medium. The generation politicized by the riots grew up to form the nucleus of ANC leadership inside the country. And at least as importantly, Soweto brought apartheid's problems to international attention. Within months of the uprising, the United Nations imposed a mandatory arms embargo on the Republic. By 1978, South Africa found itself unable to raise new long-term loans, and began to pay premium rates on short-term lending. The cost of apartheid, in international terms, was slowly becoming apparent.

One veteran ANC leader, Govan Mbeki, believes the riots gave Pretoria a salutary shock. As he told me in an interview, "The rethinking started after 1976, because before 1976 the government was convinced it had the Africans flat on the ground; 1976 showed even [Prime Minister] John Vorster that they were not all flat. He started therefore trying to find ways to make apartheid work with the acceptance of the Africans. And the white intelligentsia came to realize that the way the government had been trying to push apartheid was no longer working, and was not going to work."

Mbeki overstates the degree to which white society was shaken by the rioting. The state had built the monolith to withstand any number of rocks thrown by children, and most whites had faith in it. They carried on their lives largely in ignorance of the uprising, which took place in distant townships they never visited. But Prime Minister Vorster could not ignore it, so he appointed a commission of inquiry under the judge president of the Transvaal, Mr. Justice Petrus Malan Cillie. The commission pulled no punches: apartheid was a big part of the problem, it said. Cillie fingered "influx control," the system used to limit the number of blacks in urban areas. Under this system, every adult black had to carry a "passbook" at all times, to prove he or she had the right to live in an urban area. Africans were accosted in the streets, or hauled out of their beds, to demand the *dompas*. In the year before the riots, over a quarter of a million Africans were arrested for violating influx control. Many were beaten, or imprisoned.

"Influx control and related matters were . . . contributory factors," the Cillie Commission concluded. "An attitude of mind has been created which could make many [Soweto residents] resort to rioting. . . . [D]iscrimination . . . has engendered not only dissatisfaction but also a great hatred in many. This dissatisfaction and hatred were some of the main factors that created the milieu and the spirit of revolt. . . ."

From a government-appointed commission headed by an Afrikaner judge, one might have expected a whitewash. But this, surprisingly, was never the National Party's way; throughout the 1970s and 1980s, government was advised by commissions that told a fairly accurate version of the truth. The Cillie Commission presented apartheid, for the first time, as part of the South African problem, and government accepted this diagnosis. Nearly a decade would pass before Pretoria would act on Cillie's analysis; nonetheless, it sowed doubts.

Cillie had put his finger on the central fact which made apartheid untenable—not the stones cast at it by Soweto schoolchildren, nor even the bombs the ANC would later teach them to plant. Apartheid had failed because of economics. Ironically, it was Foreign Minister Pik Botha who outlined the economic dilemma of apartheid most vividly, in a speech to the UN Security Council in October 1974: "An African bishop, a wise man, once compared the blacks and whites in South Africa with a zebra. If the zebra were shot, it would not matter whether the bullet penetrated a white stripe or a black stripe—the whole animal would die." Whites and blacks were far too economically interdependent to live apart; not even Verwoerd could separate the zebra's stripes.

The goal of apartheid had been to do just that: not just to create separate homelands, but independent black economies, which would trade and cooperate with the white state's economy as sovereign states do in Europe. But South Africa is not Europe. The dry, often mountainous, overfarmed, and scarcely fertile black homelands had no centers of industrial activity to make them economically viable. Verwoerd refused to provide the investment needed to guarantee their viability. Indeed, in one of the mad twists typical of apartheid, he even forbade private-sector white industrialists from investing in the homelands, on the grounds that this would prevent the growth of independent black capital and perpetuate colonialism. With no one to bankroll "separate development," the system was doomed from the start.

Homeland residents needed jobs to feed the families who could not subsist in the overcrowded homelands, so they streamed to the cities. "It was thousands and millions of people moving to the cities where the real job opportunities were, where the economic growth was, where the investment continued to take place . . . that created the demographic and economic realities that made separate development impossible," according to F. W. de Klerk. "It was the feet walking into our cities and into our factories . . . which played the major concrete role."

Ironically, de Klerk gives much of the credit for ending apartheid to the ordinary people of South Africa rather than to the politicians. His main aim is to denigrate the role played by militant political opposition to apartheid, rather than to underplay the importance of National Party action. But he was right. During his apprenticeship to power—which began under Prime Minister John Vorster—Pretoria was lagging rather than leading the process of change. The human, demographic, and economic forces of population growth, urbanization, mass education, and industrial development had far more impact than deliberate government action.

What the government did achieve was, in any case, far more accidental than intentional. For if the National Party had a game plan for South Africa's future, it died with Verwoerd. From the days of Vorster until the advent of de Klerk, even hindsight can discern few clear links between the party's intentions and the consequences.

The battle for white supremacy turned out to be, in the end, a game of numbers. By the early 1970s, it had become clear that this was a battle whites could not hope to win. Apartheid's planners had got their arithmetic hopelessly wrong, underestimating black population growth by some 50 percent. During the 1960s, the black population *grew* by more than the total size of the white population, placing intolerable pressure on black homelands and forcing even more people into the cities. Afrikaner politicians urged their white compatriots to breed for the nation, but it did no good. The balance of demographic forces had turned permanently against whites.

At the same time, the economy began to outgrow its traditional pool of skilled workers: whites. A shortage of 2 million such workers was anticipated by 1980, as a result of the declining importance of primary industries like agriculture and mining, and the rise of manufacturing industry, which demanded more skills and capital. And as the structure of the economy began to change, the cost-benefit analysis of apartheid changed with it.

By the end of the 1960s, apartheid had become an obstacle to growth. The economic historian Merle Lipton has chronicled the history of apartheid's relation with South African capital. She argues that measures which ensured a large supply of low-paid and docile workers—such as the influx control laws, which limited black labor mobility; the "color bar," which kept blacks out of skilled jobs; and the prohibition of black trade unions—were good for the kind of labor-intensive, primary-sector growth on which the economy depended until the end of the 1960s. But as skill-intensive manufacturing grew, apartheid became an ever greater burden. The color bar kept white wages high by preventing blacks from competing for skilled jobs; apartheid retarded the development of the black consumer market, and depressed demand; international opposition began to restrict South African access to export markets, foreign capital, and technology; and after the 1976 Soweto riots apartheid was increasingly seen to threaten domestic stability, which also hampered growth. The economy was proving it could no longer sustain the contradictions of apartheid.

That left the Afrikaner nation with perhaps the most important choices of its history: whether to remain poor but ethnically pure, or rich and racially mixed; whether to allow blacks to do skilled jobs that could no longer be filled by whites; whether to become a modern, industrial economy, or stick with the feudal economic relations that alone were compatible with apartheid.

Afrikaners decided they were simply not willing to pay the price of their prejudices. They sacrificed purity for prosperity, and their nation passed a point of no return on the road to black rule. Lipton believes that point was passed when, in 1973, Prime Minister Vorster conceded that blacks would be allowed to do skilled work in white areas with the agreement of white unions. Soon, blacks began to work in skilled jobs whether or not the unions concurred. Previously, one white businessman recalls, "you couldn't make blacks heavy-metal crane drivers, because blacks had no depth perception." But the moment the law was changed, "blacks acquired depth perception overnight." The economic absurdities of apartheid were becoming clear for all to see.

Government also scrapped the principle that spending on black education be pegged to revenue raised by direct taxes on Africans themselves. As a result, spending on black secondary education rose dramatically: it had doubled between 1961 and 1969; between 1969 and 1974, spending trebled again.

These were two crucial breaches in the dyke of apartheid—relaxing the job color bar and extending black education. But the government of the day seems to have had little inkling of the long-term consequences of these changes. Spending on mass black education—by Verwoerd, ironically, as much as by Vorster—produced generations of politicized students to man the barricades during both the Soweto uprising and the upheavals of the

1980s. And as the far right warned at the time, jobs could not ultimately be shared with blacks without sharing power as well.

Vorster failed to detect future consequences because he was focusing on a more urgent problem, the immediate skills shortage. He believed South Africa had an economic problem susceptible of an economic solution. There is no evidence that he realized his actions would breach the political bastion of white supremacy as well. He did not foresee that permanent residency, citizenship, and eventually voting rights would have to be granted to the black workers who took over skilled white jobs. The relentless logic of politics would demand no less.

Vorster thought it possible to give ground on the periphery without touching the core of white interests; but each concession at the margin stripped away another layer of defense, until issues nearer and nearer the center also seemed marginal. He took the first steps toward leaving the core, itself, undefended.

"I think '73 was as important if not more important than [Soweto] '76, because it wasn't in the townships, it was in the cities, it was in the factories, it was hitting at the core of white power, which was economic power," says Jay Naidoo, formerly the country's leading trade unionist, reflecting on the illegal strikes by black workers in his home city, Durban, in 1973.

The strikes shocked both government and business, prompting Harry Oppenheimer, then head of the giant Anglo American Corporation gold and diamond empire, to call for trade union rights for blacks. As he said, without unions there was "no one to talk to" when problems arose. Apartheid was not up to the task of ordering work relations in a modern industrialized society.

Business could not prosper with an unstable labor force, and migrant apartheid labor was inherently unstable. One group of unskilled laborers was pretty much interchangeable with the next; they could be replaced on a moment's notice, if they caused trouble. But once business had invested in training these workers, it could not just dismiss them and start again. Business needed a relationship with a particular group of black workers—and it needed ways to resolve disputes with that group, short of dismissal.

In 1977, the government set up a commission of inquiry to look into the problem, the Wiehahn Commission. Professor Nic Wiehahn, a labor lawyer and academic, recommended the legalization of black trade unionism, and in 1979 the new prime minister, P. W. Botha, followed his advice. It was one of the most important steps ever contemplated by a National Party government. The new black unions formed the nucleus of anti-apartheid resistance in the 1980s; union activists used the economic power they gained through legalization to fight for political power as well. And the ideological shift implied by the move was profound. Legalization marked the point when government, implicitly if not publicly, began to accept that black workers must be allowed to live permanently in white areas. Philosophically, this was a major departure from the apartheid concept. It was a short step in logic—if a long step in time—from there to majority rule.

I asked P. W. Botha in 1995 whether he had foreseen the political ramifications of the move. He just brushed the question aside and said that it was "necessary." Bobby Godsell, industrial relations director of Anglo American Corporation and the man who helped pioneer new labor relations in the 1980s, believes Botha's decision simply demonstrated that a new pragmatism had replaced the age of ideology. "Once you had a society without a great utopian goal," Godsell says, "things were viewed increasingly as technical problems. Wiehahn did not see labor relations as a political issue. He wanted a technical set of labor laws that were modern, coherent, and scientific. So, instead of an ideological vision, you have kind of grudging accommodation of reality."

The importance of the move, Godsell argues, cannot be overemphasized. "Without the trade union movement, I don't think F. W. de Klerk would have ended up with a sense of the compelling inevitability of sharing power with black South Africans. For it was really in the workplace that power was shared and not just given." To the amazement of nervous whites, society did not fall apart just because blacks were granted the industrial franchise; every such reform that did not lead to disaster increased their tolerance for more.

Even more important, collective bargaining between black labor and white business provided a model for the peaceful resolution of conflict in the political arena as well. For it was in the world of industrial relations that South Africans designed, tested, and perfected the negotiating paradigm which eventually delivered a new South Africa. The government learned, says Godsell, that there were "ways of bridging a blunt transfer of power from one group to another"—always the Afrikaner's greatest fear. And young ANC leaders within the union movement learned that it is sometimes better to talk to the enemy than to fight him head-on. Mandela had known that for decades; but those who remained outside had to learn the lesson in their own way, in their own time—and in their own laboratory, the unions.

Jay Naidoo, who graduated from the trade union movement to become one of the most powerful ministers in Nelson Mandela's first government, remembers his union days fondly for what they taught him about the real world of power politics. When he first went to the table to negotiate with employers, he recalls, he refused the tea and food they provided throughout long hours of talks. "Then at lunchtime some of the workers came to me and said, 'Listen, they are offering you food. Eat it, because it is paid for by our labor.'

"I was a complete idealist," he concludes sheepishly. Collective bargaining taught both sides the limits of idealism.

So the capitalist system did much to defeat apartheid. Ought capitalists themselves to have done more? Certainly, business fought much harder for economic than for political change. Even the most liberal South African businessmen seemed ambivalent about multi-racial democracy until the township violence of the mid-1980s persuaded them that nothing else would guarantee stability. Few businessmen supported a universal franchise until very late in the day, and most feared that majority rule would harm their profits. White businessmen, who were overwhelmingly English-speaking or Jewish South Africans, were content to make money and leave the Afrikaner to make politics, as author Anthony Sampson put it. Many liberation politicians will never forgive them for that.

Capital did make clear its opposition to some aspects of economic apartheid, including restrictions on labor mobility. That, after all, was the business of business. Many businessmen concede that, in a perfectly moral world, they ought to have done more to end apartheid. Derek Keys, the veteran businessman who was the new South Africa's first finance minister, says he blames business "against the standard of the New Testament." But few businessmen anywhere in the world would pass that test; and if South African capital fails it more dismally than that of other nationalities, perhaps that reflects the more acute nature of South Africa's moral crisis. Elsewhere, for the most part, business and morals occupy separate spheres which seldom intersect. In South Africa, collisions are constant.

Harry Oppenheimer—the octogenarian patriarch of South African business—disputes the notion that business could have held government to ransom for political change. After all, if Anglo American had stopped paying taxes to government, Pretoria would have stopped buying its gold, he says. Oppenheimer argues that the true balance sheet of capital's relationship with apartheid does not depend only, or even primarily, on the deliberate actions of business to bring about political change. Business did perhaps most good by having existed at all: by driving the industrialization of the South African economy through the 1950s and 1960s, by spearheading the modernization process that eventually made the feudal political relations of the past an economic impossibility.

"One mustn't underestimate the things that were done by the opposition around the world, and by the direct and violent activities of the ANC. But I would have thought that without what happened with the development of the economy, these things probably would not have worked," he argues, adding, ". . . by the things that business does, and the way that they do them, they can produce data that government has to pay attention to."

The influx of black South Africans to the towns was "the main factor in defeating apartheid," says the gnomelike old gentleman, who, though retired, remains a formidable presence both at Anglo American and in the wider business community. But he believes morality also played a role. "Of course a thing like that [apartheid], if it doesn't work, *becomes* immoral, it really does, because if you say we are justified in not allowing black people to vote in South Africa because they are going to vote somewhere else, you might believe that, but if you cease to believe it's possible to do that, then to continue to prevent them voting in South Africa becomes immoral. I think people began to realize that a bit.

"And of course it's mixed up with the very important factor of people not liking to be disliked . . . I think if you're disliked and don't like being disliked, you're inclined to say—in your heart, even if you don't say it publicly—why are we disliked? Why are we so universally disliked? And I think people in South Africa did do that."

But for many years there was simply no sense in putting the argument against apartheid in overtly moral terms. As Oppenheimer, who was a Liberal member of Parliament from 1948 to 1957, and later a major financial backer of the white Liberal Party which opposed apartheid, recalls, "Many of us quite consciously put moral arguments in economic terms because we thought this was the way to make people listen. I used to ask Afrikaners, trying to put my views in the most acceptable way, 'Do you seriously think that you are prepared to pay the cost of what you want to do?' And they were all very doubtful, I think. Even when apartheid was in full flood, if you had private talks with Nats [members of the ruling National Party], they were very pessimistic, curiously so," he muses. "They simply were faced with the awful choice between the unacceptable and the impossible. They opted without hesitation for the impossible."

By the mid-1970s, Afrikaners had begun to recognize the impossibilities foisted on them by apartheid. They were motivated, at least in part, by morality. Gently, almost imperceptibly, apartheid had begun to prick the Afrikaner conscience; the spiritual comfort vital to the national psyche had been disturbed.

What had disturbed it was not the Soweto rioting, or the dire plight of blacks in the homelands. It was the situation of the mixed-race people known as "coloureds"—the plight of those like the coloured farm foreman whose story begins this chapter. For Afrikaners and coloureds share a cultural affinity far greater than that between Afrikaners and Africans. Some coloureds are the issue of illicit liaisons between the races; others are the children of the Khoi-khoi and the San, the original light-skinned natives of the Cape, and of Malay and Indian slaves. But almost all share the Afrikaner's language, his religion, and cultural rituals based on the consumption of cold beer and grilled meat. In all these ways, coloureds were—as Afrikaners had always affectionately if patronizingly known them—*ons mense,* our people. Only naked racism could keep them apart.

So coloureds became the moral Achilles heel of apartheid. They disproved the argument that it was not racism, but irreconcilable differences in culture, language, and religion, that made separation inevitable. Apartheid, which claimed to be a "total solution," had no answer to the problem of the coloured man in South Africa. He could not be dealt with as an African and sent back to some putative homeland because none had ever existed, even in the mad mythology of the time. He was too close to be exiled in conscience.

So another government commission—that unlikely but effective instrument of change—was set up to study the problem. And in the very week that Soweto began to burn, it issued its report. Professor Erika Theron's commission recommended that the National Party restore to coloureds what it had taken away in the heyday of apartheid—direct representation in Parliament.

No one, not least Professor Theron, was suggesting that whites would have to live with, or learn with, coloureds. The Group Areas Act, which legislated residential segregation, would remain in force. White state schools could not admit coloureds, though private schools would have that option. Still, Theron had opened another breach in the ideological bastion of apartheid. And within eighteen months, the National Party strode through that breach, publishing a 1977 election platform which effectively abolished the white parliamentary monopoly of power. It called for the creation of three separate branches of Parliament: one for the 4.3 million whites; one for the 2.4 million coloureds; and one for the 700,000 Indians (descendants of those brought from the Indian subcontinent as indentured servants). Each chamber would legislate for its own people alone. There would be no chamber for the 19 million black Africans, who were still expected to satisfy their political aspirations through the homelands. The three chambers would legislate on some matters together, and when they did, whites would have an effective veto. But if this was not integration, it was a major step away from apartheid. Whites would no longer govern everyone else on their own.

The decision to set up a "tricameral" Parliament appears to have been taken as much for strategic as moral reasons. Vorster saw the coloureds and

Indians as numerical allies against the majority black nation; if they made common cause with whites, minority groups would have a better chance in the numbers battle. But hindsight reveals a breathtaking lack of clarity in this vision. For as right-wing whites said at the time, apartheid was all or nothing; where brown-skinned people were admitted, blacks would surely follow. And to allow coloureds and Asians into the white citadel, while slamming the door in black faces, could surely only provoke African fury.

John Vorster did not see it that way; the big picture once again eluded him. The two major reforms foreshadowed during his time in office—legalization of black trade unions and extension of voting rights to coloureds and Indians—were only introduced by his successor, P. W. Botha. But he opened the gaps in the apartheid edifice through which Botha would later stride. His pragmatism marked the end of ideology.

The story of the National Party's decision to share power with coloureds—one of the most critical in its history—cannot be told purely from the point of view of pragmatism and ideology, however. Life in South Africa is never that simple—or that dull. Its history has as much to do with personal chemistry, with the bonds of shared experience, as with reason.

No one was more involved in the coloured question than P. W. Botha. As a junior member of cabinet in the early 1960s, he was minister of coloured affairs; he chaired the cabinet committee that proposed a coloured Parliament. As a Cape Nationalist, Botha was not unusual in caring more about the coloured than the black problem, for until the 1980s, blacks were excluded from the Western Cape, which was designated a "coloured preference area." To many Cape Nationalists, blacks were a Transvaal phenomenon, alien to their universe. Their problem was coloureds.

If every Cape Afrikaner has some story to tell about a childhood spent playing with coloured children—many of them romanticized and sentimentalized beyond all plausibility—few can tell as dramatic a tale as P. W. Botha.

This is his story.

"My mother lived on a farm, a lovely farm in the Eastern Free State. Her husband was serving with the Boers, he was captured, taken to Ceylon, and died. But my mother lived on at the farm with her younger sister and their children, one of whom was six months old. And there was a coloured family living on the farm, tending to the fruit and vegetable gardens, because there was much water there. . . ."

Botha, whose voice betrays his advanced age, shares a habit common to many elderly Afrikaners. He thinks like a farmer, and readily hearkens back to the days when Afrikaners lived a marginal existence in a harsh and arid land, where water was more precious than gold. He takes up his mother's story:

"One night she was asleep when a black soldier clad in a British uniform pushed open the door of her room, and told her he was going to kill her. And she said, 'My God will protect me,' and he said, 'We will see whose God is the stronger,' and when she tried to move, he threatened her with a knife. And the children were crying.

"And then she thought of a brilliant idea, because she was intelligent. She looked to the door behind him and she said, 'Hello, come in,' and he looked back, and when he looked back she jumped on him, she knocked him to the floor, and her sister and the little coloured girl who was there with her children, they tackled him and he fled.

"She ran to the coloured family. They helped her escape from the farm that night, and she went to live in a cave in the mountain nearby. She stayed in that cave for three months, until the British troops eventually found her and arrested her, and took her to a concentration camp, where two of her children died. And the coloured family stayed behind and looked after the farm. . . .

"[As prime minister] I went out of my way to deal with the coloured problem."

So a debt incurred even before he was born (Botha's mother met and married his father only ten years after the Boer War ended) influenced P. W. Botha's political agenda for life. His gratitude went only so far: Botha always made clear that, whatever their position in Parliament, coloureds were not to be confused with whites. Still, he obviously felt a bond with coloureds that did not extend to blacks; and that ancient bond, formed in the very different world at the turn of the nineteenth century, would do much to shape the Afrikaner's future at the end of the twentieth.

If the fate of apartheid was influenced by this tale of nineteenth-century loyalty, it had even more to fear from exposure to the increasingly modern world of Afrikanerdom in the 1970s. That world was largely made up of prosperous, urbanized Afrikaners who had learned to identify as much with class as with ethnicity. Afrikaners coming of age in the late 1970s no longer used the Boer War as their chief historical point of reference. Their parents had not been interned in British concentration camps; they had not been jailed (like Vorster) for siding against the British in World War II.

Afrikaner college students at the end of the decade were the first to come to political consciousness—after the independence of Mozambique and Angola (two of South Africa's closest black neighbors), after the Durban strikes and the Soweto riots. They knew white hegemony was doomed; and the politically ambitious among them were looking to develop a new, multi-racial power base.

Ironically, it was apartheid itself which produced this new psychology of confidence among the young. By the late 1970s, this poor man's ideology had created a large and prosperous Afrikaans middle class. Chester Crocker, formerly U.S. Assistant Secretary of State for Africa, and a persuasive analyst of modern South African history, says apartheid was, for many Afrikaners, "a power trip into the land of Mercedes." By the end of the 1970s many Afrikaners had made it to that promised land. Only a tiny proportion remained on the farms; well over two thirds were in white-collar jobs; and opinion polls showed their overwhelming worry was that black rule would threaten order, security, and prosperity. Less than 15 percent voiced traditional concerns about ethnicity, language, and culture.

Leading Afrikaans opinion formers began to adopt a much more sympathetic attitude to change. Writing in 1976, the Afrikaans columnist Dawie captured the uncertainties of the time: "from our own history we know that a people worth its salt will not in the long run submit to alien government, and because we are aware of this we have not really got the heart to try it." And for the first time, Afrikaans culture came under outside influence, through the "Sestigers" (school of the sixties), a group of radical Afrikaans writers who had studied in Paris during the previous decade.

The new political divisions—between what Wimpie de Klerk termed the *verkramptes* ("narrow ones") and the *verligtes* ("enlightened ones")— largely followed class lines. Those with a direct interest in the continued exclusion of blacks—petty bureaucrats, blue-collar workers, farmers—remained supporters of apartheid. But academics, professionals, businessmen, the new Boer yuppies, all wanted change. For their worries were no different from those of the middle classes around the world: security, standards, the preservation of income. Economic interests did not entirely displace ethnic concerns; Afrikaners still responded to the call of the tribal drum. But they were no longer obsessed by it.

In the end, apartheid succeeded too well to survive. By promoting the economic advancement of the Afrikaner, it rendered itself obsolete. As Afrikaners began to balance class and ethnic interests in a more modern way, their support for overtly racist policies declined. They were beginning to overcome the inferiority complex of decades—the complex which had turned them, like other intrinsically weak peoples round the world, into bullies.

Bullying was, in any case, starting to look difficult. In military terms, the monolith was as strong as ever. But that was no longer enough. "It became clear to all of us that a long-drawn-out war was completely possible from the military point of view," says General Constand Viljoen, former head of the South African Defence Force. "Because of the military strength of South

Africa, we could carry on indefinitely. But from the country's psychological point of view, it was not possible, and one had better find a solution."

General Viljoen is a trim and handsome man, with the correct manners and upright bearing befitting the Afrikaner nation's top soldier. When he was its military chief he disdained the ANC as a fighting force, dismissing its guerrilla army, *Umkhonto we Sizwe* (Spear of the Nation) as "the weakest of enemies." But he had a healthy regard for its ability to undermine the legitimacy of the white state.

In the seventies, that state was becoming ever more isolated. By mid-decade, a left-wing coup in Portugal had precipitated Mozambique and Angola to independence under African Marxist rulers. The cordon sanitaire of white rule around South Africa had been breached, and would be demolished altogether once Rhodesia became Zimbabwe in 1980. "I can remember at least four occasions when we had formal briefings for the cabinet, between 1975 and 1985, in which we warned them that militarily we can carry on for a long time but politically, year after year, the strategic options keep narrowing," Viljoen recalls. He counseled early action, otherwise "you end up in a much weaker position than if you had tackled the thing politically at the right moment."

Viljoen learned that lesson from Rhodesia. "In 1980, when the final collapse took place, I had some Rhodesian officers on a staff course at the army college, and I asked them to analyze for me the mistakes made by the Rhodesian security forces and the government. . . . Mr. [Ian] Smith [the Rhodesian prime minister] eventually settled for much less than he could have got if he had settled earlier. . . . I presented that paper to the government and I said, 'Now, there you have it. These are the lessons that you can learn from Rhodesia. Please apply those lessons in South Africa.' "

The Afrikaner government refused for nearly two decades to heed Viljoen's warning that, in the war of the weak against the strong, South Africa could never win.

By the end of the 1970s, pressure was building deep within the monolith. Prime Minister Vorster continued to defend the apartheid principle, but adjusted his practices to accommodate the real world. The economy was suffering from apartheid labor and economic policies; black political opposition was finally rising from its long depression; the international community was increasingly hostile; Marxist regimes in neighboring countries posed a threat to state security; and Afrikaners had begun to recognize and act against the political and social contradictions implicit in apartheid. The crisis would not mature until well into the next decade, but it was beginning to trouble the Afrikaner mind.

The ideal of a territorially separate white nation faded under Vorster;

but Afrikaners remained terrified of the alternatives. Foreign Minister Pik Botha summed up the mood at the end of the Vorster years in an interview recorded in 1978: "A political system of one-man one-vote within one political entity means our destruction. It's a statistical fact, not a political one. I am not aware of any nation in the history of the world having knowingly committed that sort of suicide."

"That sort of suicide" was committed in the end. The story of how Afrikaner leaders were tricked, cajoled, coerced, and seduced into doing so spans the whole of the next decade. Forces larger than man had doomed apartheid to failure; but only a revolution of the mind could force Afrikaners to accept that fact with equanimity.

SOMEHOW, *the man broke away from the mob, and collapsed screaming at the feet of the bishop. The man's neighbors said he was a police informer, and they were preparing to burn him alive. You will have heard that many people died this way in South Africa. Perhaps you will have seen pictures of their bodies. They are gruesome beyond words.*

But this was not to be a day of charred bodies. The bishop used the moral authority of the cassock, and his own impeccable political pedigree—for he was Archbishop Desmond Tutu, father confessor to the ANC—to save the man from incineration. The "spy" was horsewhipped and beaten to within an inch of his life, but not beyond. The funeral pyre prepared for him was allowed to burn out.

It was my first week in South Africa, and my first trip to a township. I had gone to attend the funeral of four ANC guerrillas. At that time—July 1985—political funerals were like football games; you could count on at least one every Saturday. They were even held on the local soccer field, being the only township public space large enough to hold thousands of mourners. This one took place in the township of Duduza, but it might have been anywhere else. The format was always the same. The closed caskets, draped illegally in the black, green, and gold flag of the banned ANC; the wailing women, the fiery speeches; the haunting melody of the ANC anthem, Nkosi sikelel'iAfrika ("God Bless Africa"); and the dust, the township dust, rising from thousands of angry feet doing the toyi-toyi, the ANC war dance.

It was during the procession from the soccer field to the cemetery that the spy met the mob. Driven half-mad by impotent fury at the deaths of their four "comrades," township youths turned on this sellout, this traitor to the cause, and prepared for his execution. Strong young arms overturned his car and set it alight; soon a cloud of oily black smoke defiled the flawless blue of the winter sky. Angry flames flared ready to receive their victim. It was a tableau of purest evil: the four futile caskets of those who ought not to have died for apartheid; the scapegoat, whose true guilt or innocence was a matter of scant interest to the mob; and in the background, the sound of police armored troop carriers careening through the streets in a show of bravado. Soon there would be tear gas, and rubber bullets, and more blood.

Suddenly, Bishop Tutu was there, pleading for the man's life, making the impossible argument that the oppressed must not sink to the level of the oppressor: Pretoria could murder its opponents, but Duduza must show them mercy. The spy was reprieved, and another purple-skirted bishop sped away with him to a nearby hospital.

The crowd, suddenly subdued, trudged on to the cemetery. A middle-aged lady from the Duduza Parents' Committee, her feet clad in house slippers, pledged to carry on the struggle, unarmed, while a lone plaintive voice cried out for help: "Where are you, Umkhonto we Sizwe, we are waiting for you. . . ."

3

To the Rubicon, and Beyond

"MR. MANDELA ARRIVED, and he was given refreshments, which he accepted."

P. W. Botha, the man who held Nelson Mandela captive for over a decade, is sketching the scene of an encounter implausible even by the standards of South Africa's unlikely history: The day he first entertained Nelson Mandela to tea in his own sitting room.

The setting is Botha's secluded retirement home at the Wilderness, on the Indian Ocean coast in the Eastern Cape. It is April 1994—a matter of days before the first all-race elections—and the aging Freedom Fighter has come to ask the Old Boer president for help to ensure a peaceful poll. He has asked Botha to intercede with right-wing Afrikaners who have been planting bombs and strafing taxi ranks in an attempt to make voting impossible. "If the election date is postponed, the people will slaughter us," Mandela told his unlikely confidant. Unless Botha intervened, Mandela said, "all his work"—by which he meant everything the old president had done for South Africa—would be destroyed.

Thus did Nelson Mandela willingly acknowledge the role that Botha had played in bringing about peace. Never one to let political correctness stifle genuine sentiment, Mandela says Botha is "a first-class gentleman"; every year on his birthday, he phones the old president to wish him many happy returns of the day.

Mandela credits Botha with taking the essential steps that led to his eventual release from prison; with opening channels of communication shut for decades; in short, with laying the groundwork for the new South Africa. His views run counter to the conventional wisdom regarding the Botha years: that the changes wrought by the dour and abrasive National Party leader were meaningless; that Botha strengthened the mold of apartheid, which only F. W. de Klerk would find the courage to break. But convention does not interest Mandela. He prefers to judge the man.

"You respond to individuals in accordance with how they interact with you," Mandela once told me. "I have heard a lot of stories about P. W. Botha, and I don't challenge them. But my own attitude must be determined by how he responded to me and the problems I put to him."

Botha, by temperament more grudging, also displays respect for Mandela as a man and a Thembu aristocrat. But he will go to his grave opposed to black rule. Despite Mandela's plea, he had no intention of urging the right to participate in a poll that would strip whites of power. "Oh, no, no, no," says Botha, horrified at the very idea. "I didn't agree with majority government. I wanted to explain what they should do instead of the road to ruination they are proceeding along at present."

But it was Botha, more than any other Afrikaner leader, who put South Africa on just that road. He does not acknowledge that now, and did not realize it then. He wanted to get Mandela out of jail before the prisoner died, but he never meant to make him president. Like his predecessors, he only wanted to modernize apartheid.

If Botha was a reluctant revolutionary—an unwilling, unwitting, sometimes almost unconscious one—he was a revolutionary, nonetheless. His strength, in arms and repression, gave the Afrikaner state the confidence to risk political compromise; his reforms prepared the Afrikaner mind for change. In the end, he took the Afrikaner nation beyond the Rubicon, without even noticing that he had crossed it. He charted the track that de Klerk would follow, to the new South Africa.

P. W. Botha is a deeply religious man, and one who betrays an old man's altogether natural obsession with eternity. Talking to him is like conversing with an Old Testament prophet. He inhabits an intellectual, emotional, and spiritual universe which I find it difficult even to visit.

To listen to Mr. Botha—as I did, for almost four hours in March 1995, about a year after Nelson Mandela's inauguration—is to remember the old South Africa. Not the belligerence and arrogance of the old days, when Mr. Botha terrified opponents and colleagues alike with his wagging finger and fierce dark scowl; the elderly gentleman who entertained me to tea no longer bothered with aggression. But the bitterness, the pessimism, the hatred, and the fear that informed every sentence and tainted the whole, were relics of a bygone age, of the days when I thought South Africa would never escape from apartheid's vortex of madness. It depressed me to think that, somehow, Mr. Botha had been left behind in the whirlpool.

It had taken months to persuade the former president to see me; Botha made clear that he was no longer interested in mortal assessments of his character. Finally, he gave in (though only after I had made myself an expert on his life by poring over hundreds of pages of his personal papers, in

Afrikaans, at a closed university archive). I set off for his retirement home, in that "fairest Cape in all the world," cradle of apartheid.

Mr. Botha met me at the outside door of his study, where he loomed large in the dark doorway, several steps above where I stood in the semi-tropical garden. I was nervous, expecting a vintage Botha harangue. But I had forgotten the golden rule of hospitality observed in every Afrikaner home. Mr. Botha would not shout at me while I drank his tea; that would not be proper.

Instead, the elderly gentleman's behavior—indeed, the occasion it-self—was a model of propriety. Tea was served with an extravagant attention to detail scarcely fashionable in the 1990s. My china teacup, in an elaborate floral pattern, was perched on its own lace doily, with an organdy-flowered, lace-edged napkin beside it. The saucer held a gold-plated spoon and the creamy blossom of a fresh frangipani flower, which added its heavy scent to the aroma of Earl Grey steaming in the cup. *Boere rococo,* at its best.

Tannie (Auntie) Elize Botha, the matriarch who presided over the state banquets of her husband's presidency, personally served the tea, and urged on me a large slice of warm home-baked *melktert,* the pastry cliché of Afrikanerdom. We both carefully played the parts decreed for us by Afri-kaner society: she self-effacing, but assiduously attentive to our needs (as-sisted by a uniformed coloured maid, who smiled and smiled, but never said a word). I, dressed in a floral summer frock carefully chosen to convey an image of innocence, eager to get my body language right—inclining to Mr. Botha when he spoke, in deference to his age, and obediently consuming my slice of *melktert.*

But if the tea service was Mrs. Botha's preserve, the study was her husband's territory, its decor unashamedly African. At his side, a footstool made from the amputated leg of an elephant, complete with three huge toenails. Near the door, a collection of ceremonial tribal walking sticks, one adorned with the teeth of the African warthog. The study floor and chairs were covered with the smooth skins of wild animals, including the national symbol, the springbok, shot by P. W. Botha in his active days as a hunter. On Botha's desk sat a small South African flag in the orange, blue, and white of the old, discredited Republic—a relic of the days when that banner was flown mainly behind barbed wire at embattled police stations.

The tea ritual completed, I settled down in Mr. Botha's time capsule, in this oasis of the old South Africa, and asked him to guide me through the decade that sealed his nation's fate (Botha ruled South Africa from 1978 to 1989, first as prime minister and then as president). Why did he make the many concessions of his days in power, from legalizing black trade unions to repealing the hated pass laws? Why did he open secret talks with Nelson

Mandela? Why give coloureds and Indians the vote, but exclude blacks? What was the pot at the end of his rainbow of reform? And a final question of personal interest: Why did I awake one morning in 1986 to find that P. W. Botha had bombed the city which was then my home, Lusaka, Zambia?

Mr. Botha's answers were peremptory. He showed supreme disinterest in the issue of why he had bombed Lusaka, except to say that he always reserved the right to attack terrorists (his planes hit only a UN refugee camp). Asked why he had repealed the hated law barring interracial marriage, he informed me that Moses had married a non-white woman, and what was good enough for Moses could not be bad for ordinary South Africans. He explained many of the rest of his actions with one word answers only: they were either necessary, unavoidable, or simply overdue.

I wondered whether my questions had bored Botha. Was it was simply too late to explore the inner workings of the mind that had caused South Africa such heartache? Then I realized that the old man was telling me the simple truth as he saw it. He could not provide what I sought, a grand plan to explain his presidency, for no such plan had ever existed. Botha was the supreme pragmatist: changes were made on an ad hoc basis when they could no longer be avoided. No ideology, no vision, guided them. Though Botha took down the signs that screamed of segregation, he maintained the barricades that kept blacks out. Botha passed apartheid's death ʿentence, but refused to execute it. To him, that was simply a bridge too far.

For P. W. Botha was a child of the old, old South Africa, his political consciousness shaped in the days of Afrikaner inferiority, when the Boer War defeat, and the concentration camp wounds inflicted on Afrikaner women like his own mother, were still fresh in the national mind. At the time that Botha entered politics, Harry Truman was president in America and Clement Attlee was British prime minister; by the time he left, the youngsters Bill Clinton and John Major were on the horizons of power. Botha's hero—as he constantly reiterated to me during his four-hour peroration—was General Barry Hertzog (whom he described, without a trace of irony, as the "George Washington" of South Africa); the first Nationalist prime minister, Hertzog fought alongside Botha's father in the Boer War. P.W.'s mentor was D. F. Malan, the man who brought the National Party to power in 1948, ushering in the era of apartheid. Malan's owlishly bespectacled face peers out from the Bothas' wedding photo on the study wall.

But Hertzog and Malan were giants of a much earlier age, and I began to realize, as I listened to Botha revere them, that he was not so much a child of his time as of a much harsher, more distant past. Perhaps it was foolish to expect such a man to recognize, let alone embrace, the political realities of the late twentieth century. Still, I was disappointed at the vitriol of his condemnation of the new South Africa. I had gone to the Wilderness hoping that he, like so many conservative Afrikaners, would have found the 1994 elections strangely liberating. After all, he had entertained Nelson Mandela to tea in this very house, only days before the voting began. Surely this implied a change of heart?

But no. Botha was caught in a time warp from which not even Nelson Mandela could free him. As he put it, "There is a gradual buildup of two forces in the world. The one is the final return of Christ to this earth and the other is the eventual destruction of Satan himself. I told Mr. Mandela when he came here, I told him here downstairs in our house where my wife received him very well, I told him, 'Mr. Mandela, I warn you, these forces are going to destroy you.' He didn't reply."

Botha refused a personal invitation to attend Mandela's inauguration, and kept the television firmly switched off on that remarkable day. Where did he spend the inaugural hours, I asked? At his farm, well away from all risk of jubilation. How did he feel? "Precisely as I do today—that they're heading for destruction." True to form, Mr. Botha drew these portents of doom from a biblical context: "You read of the spirit that went into the pigs while Jesus was preaching, and they ran down the cliff and they all died. I am afraid we are also busy rushing to disaster."

Musing on my long and exhausting encounter with the "Groot Krokodil"—a nickname that scarcely needs translating—I reflected on the question, why did the Boers give it all away, and concluded that P. W. Botha, at least, had done so mostly by accident. Yet the momentum built up during those years did carry the Afrikaner across the Rubicon in the end. And for that, South Africa must thank P. W. Botha, one of history's most unlikely revolutionaries.

"I am not able to recall many of the details of the Mxenge murder, but it should be remembered that this murder happened quite some time ago."

Dirk Coetzee was a member of the South African security police, and the commander of one of apartheid's death squads. In 1989, he fled to ANC protection overseas, and began to publicize the activities of these hit teams. He oversaw the 1981 murder of anti-apartheid activist Griffiths Mxenge, one of the first of a number of high-profile assassinations to take place under Botha.

Coetzee commanded a unit known as "Vlakplaas," after the isolated farm where he converted former ANC guerrillas into police informers. Their task was to mingle in the townships, to finger ANC members for arrest and detention. They were also trained as assassins.

"One morning, Brigadier Van der Hoven [security police commander in Durban, where Mxenge lived] gave me background information on a certain Griffiths Mxenge and said we should 'make a plan with him.' He explained that Mxenge was an ex-Robben Island convict [who] acted as an attorney in many trials of activists and ANC members," Coetzee recounts. "[He] said that we should not shoot or abduct him, but that we should rather make it look like a robbery.

"I was in charge of this operation . . . I obtained a chunk of meat, cut it into four pieces, and treated it with strychnine. . . . This was intended for Mxenge's dogs." Coetzee gives a detailed account of how the strychnine was disguised in the meat to prevent the dogs from vomiting. Mxenge found them dead on the morning of his murder.

Coetzee left the details of the murder to be worked out by two Vlakplaas members, and arranged to meet them in a local bar when it was done. "One rainy Thursday night, when I stopped at the bar at approximately 10:00 P.M., I found them. [One] was wearing Mxenge's jacket and watch." These items were destroyed the next day, and Mxenge's car doused with gasoline and burnt. Coetzee concludes: "The Griffiths Mxenge murder can be seen as a typical hit squad operation."

Such activities were part of Botha's "total onslaught" against what he saw as a Communist-inspired offensive upon white Christian civilization in South Africa. It involved repression at home coupled with military operations against neighboring states to dissaude them from harboring the ANC.

Botha presided over a white state obsessed with security. During the 1970s, when he was defense minister, he had fortified the monolith beyond the maddest dreams of Verwoerd. Fighting strength had tripled, the defense budget had grown in geometric progression, and South Africa had developed a world-class arms industry. When he became prime minister, the State Security Council—comprising the heads of all security services, key ministries, and government departments—supplanted the cabinet itself as the focus of state power. Botha also set up something called the National Security Management System, which militarized the whole of civilian administration down to township level.

But Botha's aim was more sophisticated than mere repression. To match the "total onslaught," he had a "total strategy" for maintaining white supremacy. Military action was only a part of it. Politics, psychology, economics, and technology were also roped in. Under his plan, the security forces would provide stability—in the townships, and in the Southern African region—to give him the time and space he needed to sort out the politics. Hearts and minds would be wooed in the townships through socioeconomic development, on the principle, stated by Defense Minister Magnus Malan, that once blacks had toilets, they would not want democracy. And Botha sought to pacify the Southern African region by signing a series of non-aggression pacts—most spectacularly, with Marxist Mozambique in 1984—promising to look after those countries which threw the ANC out.

The centerpiece of the total strategy was political reform, and in this, Botha went well beyond his predecessors. In 1983, he made the first decisive break with the concept of a white nation when he introduced the new "tricameral" Constitution. The new Constitution created the three-chamber Parliament, with separate houses for whites, coloureds, and Indians, according to a ratio that roughly mirrored the country's demography—4:2:1. Whites continued to dominate the system, both numerically and through strong new powers granted to the (white) state president. But if Afrikaners would continue to rule, they would no longer rule alone; and they would get used to the sight of dark-skinned peoples in the corridors of power.

The introduction of the tricameral Parliament was a moment of truth for whites. It provoked the first major split in Afrikaner politics since World War II: right-wing members of Parliament broke away to form the Conservative Party in 1982. But it proved a moment of equal or greater truth for blacks, enraged by their continued exclusion. For P. W. Botha, the consequences could hardly have been worse: whites were divided by it and blacks united against it. For both communities, it proved the major watershed of the Botha years. What began as a plan to deal with the contradictions inherent in apartheid—especially those affecting Botha's favorite non-white community, the coloureds—served only to highlight the greatest contradiction of all, the total exclusion of the majority from power.

When Botha opened the new "rainbow" Parliament in 1984, he put this problem at the top of his political agenda. By August 1986, at the National Party's Federal Congress, he was ready to lead his party in abandoning forever the concept of black homelands—the final and most important break with apartheid. That Congress resolved that all South Africans, black and white, would be citizens of one state, whether or not they lived in areas designated as "homelands" (except those living in the four tribal areas which had already accepted independence from South Africa—Transkei, Ciskei, Bophuthatswana, and Venda). And blacks would be granted political representation "up to the highest level," Botha said.

This did not imply one multi-racial Parliament or cabinet. Each racial group would have its own legislature and executive; there would be universal suffrage, but within segregated structures of government. Decisions of so-called common interest would be determined jointly by a racially mixed "Council of State." But whites would have an effective veto in that council—

because it could take no decision without the consensus of all groups, including them. Still, the 1986 Congress marked a radical departure from the notion that blacks would never have any power at national level.

Crucially, the ANC was excluded from this plan. The aim, instead, was to lure moderate blacks into state structures (including the newly formed black local authorities, which were to be elected directly by township residents), and thus to build a buffer against militant blacks. It did not work; even the leading moderate, KwaZulu homeland leader Chief Mangosuthu Buthelezi, refused to participate.

By the inverse logic that always applies when a tyrant sets out to mend his ways, every small step toward compromise proved a big step backward for political stability. In the end, Botha could not overcome the central dilemma of his presidency: He had to yield some power to blacks in order to maintain white control. He opened up ever larger areas of political space for blacks in hopes that moderates would colonize them; instead, radicals seized every bit of such territory. They organized campaigns of assassination against all those blacks "co-opted" into the system, whether as elected township officials, homeland politicians, or township policemen. By mid-decade, the black areas were in revolt. Botha's decade of reform soon became a decade of ungovernability.

By the time I visited South Africa for the first time in 1985, Botha's unwanted revolution was in full swing. From Duduza on the industrial East Rand to the townships of the Eastern Cape, there was a convulsion of black anger. Every form of mass resistance was used—school boycotts, political strikes, rent strikes, consumer boycotts, and massive rallies and marches coupled with escalating sabotage by the ANC. Armed guerrillas attacked township police stations and government offices, and murdered many who were considered "collaborators" with the white regime. The uprising lasted for two years, from 1984 to 1986, rendering many of South Africa's townships "ungovernable."

The African National Congress provided both a name and a unifying ethos for the revolt. But this was largely a case of the ANC leading from behind, for by the time a "call to ungovernability" was issued from faraway Lusaka in January 1985, South Africa's townships were already in an advanced state of chaos. But the ANC neither generated the chaos nor controlled it. Hundreds of local organizations—social, political, religious, cultural, professional, and civic groups—rose up spontaneously to fight grievances in black townships. And though almost all owed allegiance to the ANC, few took (or were even offered) orders from its leaders.

By the mid-1980s, the ANC army, the Spear of the Nation (*Umkhonto we Sizwe*, or "MK"), had scarcely scratched the surface of the Afrikaner monolith. In the decade after the Soweto uprising, MK carried out over five hundred attacks in South Africa. But most were minor; none seriously threatened the authority of the state; and the price paid by its guerrillas was high: roughly two were killed or captured for every three attacks. In the late 1980s, according to one MK commander, the casualty rate for guerrillas entering South Africa from Zimbabwe was 100 percent within forty-eight hours.

Still, this was a case where myth was more powerful than reality. Township residents must have realized that MK was never going to march on Pretoria and liberate them. But armed activity, however negligible, gave the ANC an unrivaled profile in the black community; the political dividend derived from it far outweighed the cost. So, if the ANC was mad to keep sending MK members to attack the monolith where it was strongest—in the military—there was method in its madness. MK replaced what apartheid had so long drained from black breasts: inspiration, and pride, and the will to fight.

Parks Mankahlana, an angry young man who was one of the 1980s revolutionaries, tried one day to explain this to me, from behind his new desk as Mandela's presidential spokesman. "You didn't have to wage an armed struggle. What you needed was a propaganda war, military propaganda, like one bomb every six months. For in the minds of the oppressed, white domination was not really represented by the man at the white post office or administrative office—they were the peanuts of apartheid. The true symbol of apartheid was the police officer, the army officer who knocks at the door, kicks it open, and then arrests you, or the military vehicle that drives down the street, filled with soldiers aiming guns at you, and shooting.

"The knowledge that we had a military organization that could strike back—no matter how small its capacity—to know that there was someone who could shoot at them just like they shot at us, you needed that kind of moral inspiration. And that was why so many young people were willing to fight back, even with stones. For at the end of the day every young person had this vision of himself as a soldier, a member of MK, armed to fight."

Joe Slovo, my Lusaka neighbor, never tried to pretend that the legendary "MK" which he commanded was a successful guerrilla army. But he thought such a scorecard was irrelevant. "Whatever you can say objectively about the armed struggle, the people had more confidence in it than military strategists and analysts would have had," he told me when we debated the issue again, post-liberation.

Slovo was by then terminally ill (he died of leukemia in January 1995), and he was not going to allow me to insult the memory of the armed struggle.

"From the very beginning, after the ANC was completely smashed inside the country, we faced a dilemma," he explained. "We knew that without mass political organization, you couldn't get the armed struggle off the ground. But we also knew that without manifestations of armed resistance, you couldn't get the political forces motivated. What gave the people the will and the inspiration to do their bit was the SASOL attack, the Koeberg attack [two successful operations against strategic energy installations], attacks on police stations. So, though it wasn't an armed struggle in the classic way of trying to overthrow the other side by military battle, armed propaganda had a key inspirational impact without which we would not be where we are today."

Slovo may be right. The ANC undoubtedly provided leadership to the ordinary people of South Africa, even where it could not give them operational commanders. But the crucial strategic shift which finally delivered liberation—the decision to attack the state at the point where P. W. Botha had made it most vulnerable, through political reform—does not seem to have come from Lusaka. Millions of black people simply decided to exploit their power—educational, economic, industrial, if not military—to improve the daily conditions of their lives. They stopped trying to lock horns with the apartheid bull, and began to nip annoyingly at its ankles: by refusing to pay rent on government houses, staying away from school and destroying school properties, staging political work stoppages, and boycotting white-owned businesses. And for the first time in seventy years of ANC history, they began to win.

The aim was to raise up a thousand flowerheads of resistance, which could not all be mown down by the apartheid scythe. To that end, the United Democratic Front (UDF) was formed in 1983, a loose alliance of hundreds of groups united by local grievances, and by a generalized hatred of apartheid. Almost all its leaders—drawn from community organizations, civic associations, youth groups, women's gatherings, virtually every forum where blacks met to further common interests—were ANC members or sympathizers. But the UDF was far more than simply a legal front for the ANC. It pioneered a new form of struggle, based on the principle that the fight against township rents, or broken window panes, or high electricity charges, was all part of the grand battle against apartheid.

Soon, Botha lost patience with the upheaval, and crushed it in a way which removed any doubt that the authority of the state had ever truly been at risk. He imposed emergency rule, detained tens of thousands of black activists, and stepped up assassinations. But the enduring victory went to the UDF. It created realities that could not be suppressed along with dissidence;

it threatened white prosperity and undermined white morale. In the end, the revolt did not have to shake the state; it only had to shake the confidence and unity of whites. In that it succeeded, creating the first acknowledged crisis of Afrikaner power.

"We could see no light at the end of the tunnel. It was just a question of sooner or later, there is going to be a huge conflagration. We realized there had to be a total change of direction, otherwise we were simply going to fight to the last man, and whoever inherited this country would inherit a wilderness.

"And we knew that the longer we waited, the more difficult it was going to be to climb out of this hole—that it would be better to start negotiating while the government of the day still had some power, while South Africa was still a going concern."

No one could have persuaded me, as I stood at the Duduza gravesides in 1985, that South Africa was about to suffer the attack of rationality outlined above—by one of P. W. Botha's chief spies, now head of the South African Secret Service, Mike Louw. On the contrary, all the signs were that Botha would relish a fight to the finish, that he would never stop digging until the Afrikaner had buried himself alive.

But by the mid-1980s, there were voices of reason even within the Botha administration. They did not speak to outsiders; they did not talk loudly; and most of all, they spoke not of surrender to black rule, but of ways to perpetuate Afrikaner power once white hegemony had gone. This meant preparing to talk to genuine black leaders. Mike Louw, then second in command of the National Intelligence Service (NIS)—the apartheid state's KGB—was one of the first government officials to meet the enemy.

Louw is an engaging man, who welcomes me to his office with a slightly awkward joke: "Take any seat, they're all bugged." It is gentle ribbing, but well deserved. For as I sat in Louw's waiting room, fixing my hair and lipstick, I wondered uncomfortably whether some close-cropped intelligence agent was watching this spectacle on a secret screen.

Once I met Louw, I thought not, for he seems uncomfortable in the skin of a spy. Instead, he highlights his background in academia, stressing that he was trained in intelligent thought, not intelligence. And like Joe Slovo, he does not look like a thug (though the fact that they sent each other car bombs for years may suggest otherwise).

So how did Louw and his fellow spooks decide that it was time for the Afrikaner to stop digging? "The whole idea on which South Africa was built was crumbling," Louw replies. "The homelands were failing hopelessly, they were totally corrupt, billions were pumped into them and would just disappear. Apartheid couldn't work because it was not tackled with gusto, and implemented with vision—it was just little handouts here and there."

Make no mistake. Louw was a trusted servant of the government that made those handouts (he worked for the notorious Bureau for State Security [BOSS] under Vorster). He spied for Vorster, and helped, in his small way, to crush black resistance in the days when apartheid still seemed to him to make sense. But by the mid-1980s, that was no longer so. "We were left without anything to guide the country, except the pragmatic constitutional maneuverings of P. W. Botha," who Louw says was trying to create a benevolent sort of apartheid.

Louw obviously respects Botha, who turned the National Intelligence Service into his own private think tank of reform; its young director, Niël Barnard (then Louw's boss), became Botha's intellectual handmaiden, and one of his most trusted advisers. But by mid-decade, Louw and his superiors were growing frustrated with the old president's lack of vision. Speaking in 1995, after their soft landing in the new South Africa, intelligence officials were inclined to suggest that they foresaw what Botha could not—a happy multi-racial future under Mandela. But when I raised an eyebrow at this supposed prescience, they did not insist. They retreated to the safer ground of claiming that by 1985, it was clear that Botha had no answer to the country's problems. "He was like an elastic band," says Louw. Botha extended power sharing to coloureds, "but you couldn't stretch him any more than that.

"At the back of his mind, I think he still believed that the white had to maintain power. Yes, bring the black much more into government. But to hand over power to the majority—that was a bridge he wouldn't have been able to cross."

For years, Botha milled and lurked on the threshold of that bridge, getting ever more angry with a world which failed to understand why he could not cross it. "The entire world turned their backs on us; my children were growing up knowing that the world hated them, that they were welcome nowhere. The entire nation was being stigmatized," says Louw.

Members of the Botha government put up a good show of not caring about that stigma. But ordinary, decent Afrikaner people—and even some ordinary, decent people in government—grew more ashamed than angry at their pariah status. "The Boers are not angels but they are not barbarians," P. W. Botha often claimed. By the mid-1980s, Louw thought it was high time for the Boer to prove it. "So we said to ourselves, it is now time to sit down with the other party with whom we are in conflict, and thrash out something we can all live with. Because it was quite clear that the days were over when a little group of white Afrikaners could sit down and plan for an entire nation as diverse as ours."

But even sitting down with the other side—which the Afrikaner saw as the height of magnanimity—proved difficult. "You say, 'Let's consult about this plan,' say, for bettering the townships. And they would say, 'We don't have the vote, we are not free people, so we are not going to negotiate.' "

For Louw, the ungovernability campaign was the last straw—"it was clear that everything was just going down the drain." He elaborated on this point to the Afrikaans historian Hermann Giliomee: "Nowhere was the situation out of hand but it was clear that politically and morally we were losing. Everything we tried to put up—schools, water tanks, taps—were destroyed because people saw them as attempts to delay their liberation."

If the National Intelligence Service, under Louw and Barnard, grew impatient with Botha's pace, it was not leaps and bounds ahead of him. Top intelligence officials had begun to advocate talks with Nelson Mandela from as early as 1984—on the very sensible grounds that if he died in prison, there would be hell to pay. They held weekend *dinkscrums* (literally, "thinking scrimmages") to try to brainstorm a way out. But all the signs are that, until the late 1980s, NIS strategy was merely a more imaginative variation of Botha's: to marginalize radicals by wooing moderate allies. The difference was, the NIS was prepared to look for those moderates within the ANC.

So, by mid-decade, one of the key institutions created to bolster the monolith—the nation's spy service—was preparing to risk all to find a new kind of security. At the time, no outsider could have believed that this was so. But Niël Barnard can now claim, with conviction, that the outside world simply misunderstood his nation. "The Afrikaner people are much more pragmatic than people think," he maintains. "The typical idea of an Afrikaner being a dour, Old Testament, Calvinistic type of person, I don't think it's true deep down. To have been able to survive for three hundred years, under very difficult circumstances, should indicate one very important thing. We are capable of adjusting to what is happening." As the old Afrikaans saying goes, " *'n Boer maak 'n plan*" ("A farmer makes a plan"). Stuck up the blind alley of apartheid, the Afrikaner was looking for a way out.

"We were charting a road in the uncharted veld of Africa. We knew we would come to gorges, and everything would almost stop. And we would have to build bridges and so on, tunnel through mountains. Because we were embarking on a high risk road. The very shape of our *lives* was going to change."

Even today, Pieter de Lange can get quite emotional about the crusade he embarked on in 1983, to deliver the Afrikaner to safety. Niël Barnard may have had more direct impact on the thinking of P. W. Botha. But the NIS acted in total secrecy—those who knew of its initiatives could probably have been counted on the fingers of two hands.

Pieter de Lange, through his chairmanship of the Afrikaner secret society, the *Afrikaner Broederbond* (Brotherhood), had a far larger network. The Brotherhood had branches in every outpost of Afrikanerdom, from the tiniest *dorp* to the dormitory suburbs of state power around Pretoria. It was a secret conduit to the Afrikaner elite, to virtually every teacher, businessmen, clergymen, political, and cultural leader of the Afrikaner nation. De Lange used it to wage the psychological warfare of change.

If Afrikaners had not been prepared for change—overtly, by the Broederbond, and imperceptibly, by myriad forces from international isolation to economic sanctions—the gamble to end apartheid would not have succeeded. Which is not to say that de Lange willed the eventual outcome of black majority rule, with only the thinnest veneer of power sharing with whites. He did not. This soft-spoken man, whose integrity, decency, and sharp mind made him a favorite touchstone for me throughout my years in South Africa, belongs to a generation that will always see itself as Afrikaner first, rather than rainbow South African.

Still, de Lange had the courage to think the unthinkable, at a time when the Afrikaner mind had grown unused to experimental thought. De Lange's election as Broederbond chairman in 1983 marked a split in the Brotherhood, long viewed as the sinister braintrust of apartheid.

Almost immediately, he began to circulate a discussion document entitled *Basic Political Conditions for the Survival of the Afrikaner*, which maintained that "the exclusion of effective black participation in the political process is a threat to White survival, which cannot be offset with the maintenance of the status quo or of a further consolidation of power in white hands." In a momentous reversal of the logic of apartheid, the document argued that "the scrapping of statutory discrimination . . . [is] a condition for the continued existence of the Afrikaner." It even conceded that the head of government need not be white.

None of this implied an acceptance of black majority rule; indeed, the document ruled out the kind of one-man, one-vote democracy born in 1994. It spoke of special representation for (racial) groups, group vetoes, and aggressive devolution of power. For the Broederbond did not want whites to negotiate themselves out of power; nor did it advocate the release of Mandela and unbanning of the ANC, whom it considered dangerous Communists. The plan was for whites to remain in the engine room of power, even if the skipper was black.

Yet the document remained a shocking and revolutionary denial of the premise which had underpinned decades of National Party rule, that law alone could secure Afrikaner survival. "The will to survive as an Afrikaner and our drive and spirit is the greatest guarantee," it concluded. "The biggest risk which we run today is to take no risks at all."

The Brotherhood lost a third of its members when the discussion document—which was well ahead of government thinking—began to make the rounds. But de Lange brought to the task of propagating it a missionary conviction. "It was not a giving up; it was, I suppose, an act of faith that it was possible in South Africa for all these groups to live together in relative peace." Brute force could keep the Afrikaner in power until the early part of the next century, but it was not worth the cost in economic devastation. It was time to enter what de Lange calls "a totally new life phase."

"The people of the monopoly would have to transform their whole perception of reality; their definition of problems, their finding of solutions, their stereotypes, their prejudices would have to be changed. And this shift in power would take place not only on the political front, but also on the economic front, and perhaps fastest of all on the administrative side. I told them to remember what we had done when we came to power in '48—it took us a couple of years, six months in most cases, to replace the head of the SABC [South African Broadcasting Corporation], of the railways, the military, etc., etc., down the line. We just moved in."

By the mid-1980s, the Broederbond, the NIS, the whole framework of institutions set up to bolster Afrikanerdom and apartheid had begun to shake the Afrikaans community and insist it come to its senses. Even the Dutch Reformed Church, that most conservative of all the mainstream Afrikaner institutions, began cautiously to distance itself from apartheid in 1986. At last, the Afrikaner nation was on the move.

Not fast enough, however, to forestall an economic and diplomatic crisis of epic proportions, sparked by international opposition to apartheid. For where hindsight can detect a healthy, creative turmoil in the Afrikaner nation of the mid-1980s, the contemporary vision—especially that of bankers and protesters in distant Western capitals—saw only the destructive upheaval of township revolution and answering repression. International banks worried about the risk to their capital; anti-apartheid groups protested the outrage to human rights. Together, they put Pretoria under unprecedented pressure.

P. W. Botha never reacted well to pressure. He was enraged that the West seemed to single him out for censure while ignoring human rights violations in neighboring black-ruled states. Botha reacted like a surly adolescent, with irrational defiance. In a classic exchange, a belligerent Botha told U.S. Ambassador Herman Nickel in 1986, "We are a small country but I am not going to be buggered about—I'd rather fight."

Yet, ironically, it was Botha's own attempt to appease the West that provoked the biggest crisis of his presidency. In early August 1985, he gave notice that he would soon take major new steps away from apartheid: he would deliver a speech—later dubbed the "Rubicon speech"—to outline South Africa's path across the Rubicon of apartheid to the new South Africa. The international hype was unprecedented: Pik Botha, the veteran foreign minister (no relation to the president), was dispatched to Western capitals to carry the glad tidings. Top U.S. officials were summoned on short notice to Vienna, to hear Botha promise a major leap across the Rubicon.

In the end, P. W. Botha did not leap, and—thanks to Pik—his failure to do so was broadcast live to much of the Western world. The old president's twisted, hectoring visage dominated TV screens, making it difficult to listen to what he said. It was a spectacular failure of packaging. Stripped of the body language, the speech was, ironically, one of the most important Botha ever delivered. Those who could decipher his paranoiac code knew that it marked a groundshift in the land of apartheid. In it, Botha promised some kind of power sharing with blacks ("the government is prepared to share its power of decision-making with other communities"). He acknowledged that blacks would live permanently in white South Africa—the most public renunciation of apartheid up to then—and said they must be granted political rights outside the homelands. He even hinted at an offer of South African citizenship for all, fully a year before the National Party adopted that policy. ("My party and I are committed to the principle of a united South Africa, one citizenship and a universal franchise.") And he suggested that he was reconsidering the hated pass laws (they were repealed the following year).

But only those used to picking through the entrails of South African politics would have recognized these gems. And the real problem was what he did not say: He did not offer what Pik Botha had promised, a formula that would have amounted to the unconditional release of Nelson Mandela (Mandela would no longer have been obliged to renounce violence to be freed; other black leaders would give this commitment for him).

Without the hype, the speech would have been just another mild disappointment. Instead, it was seen as a major public rejection of reform. It was the worst debacle of his presidency. Every member of the Botha cabinet distributes the blame for Rubicon differently. The former president trades insults on the subject with his foreign minister, arguing that Pik Botha deliberately inflated international expectations in order to embarrass him. "That was his game; that's why he doesn't come here," Botha told me that day in the Wilderness. He dismisses the account of the episode which has become received wisdom over the past decade—that he wrote a dramatically reformist speech and discarded it at the last moment. The old president says this is nonsense. His plans for the speech never changed; only the climate of public expectation was altered.

For this, he blames Pik Botha. For the foreign minister had raised hopes of dramatic change, and soon newspapers around the globe were offering free advice on what the president should say. This enraged the hypersensitive Botha, whose handwritten notes for the speech betray his anger: "the media have already informed you on what I was going to say tonight, or what I ought to say according to their superior judgement." His paranoia becomes more apparent as the notes go on: "Of all the tragedies in the world, I think the greatest is the fact that electorates have so far refrained from electing these gentlemen as their governments. They have all the answers."

It is hard to believe that Botha ever intended to do as Pik had promised. Influential members of his cabinet—including Constitutional Development Minister Chris Heunis and Justice Minister Kobie Coetsee—certainly wished him to do so. They wrote a draft of the speech which, among other things, would implicitly have acknowledged that no deal could be reached without the ANC. But when President Botha learned that Pik had arranged for the advertising agency Saatchi & Saatchi to market that speech without the president's approval, he hit the roof. He had never agreed to it, he said, and had no intention of delivering it.

He called a snap cabinet meeting, and presented his ministers with a fait accompli—"He handed us copies of the speech" (his own, weaker version) "and he said, this is what I'm prepared to say, who's agreeing with me, who not," Kobie Coetsee recalls. "And there was definitely war in the air." P. W. Botha still gets annoyed when he remembers that meeting. "I read my speech, which I wrote out myself, to the cabinet—and all of them agreed with what I was going to say," he insists, as if daring me, after all these years, to dispute it.

Some blame F. W. de Klerk—a noted conservative in the Botha cabinet—for dissuading the president from reform. But P. W. Botha is not one of them. Though he has harsh words for his successor on almost every other issue, he gives him no role in the Rubicon debacle. De Klerk may well have agreed that the reformist draft went too far—that would have been consistent with his policies of the day—but there is little evidence that he played a leading role in sabotaging it.

Still, sabotaged it was. If Botha had set out to demolish what remained of his country's international reputation, he could not have done it more effectively. The speech inaugurated an era of economic sanctions and international isolation that would end only with Botha's departure from power.

Ever defensive, P. W. Botha remains adamant that his Rubicon speech did not provoke the economic state of emergency which paralyzed South Africa for much of the rest of the decade. And technically, he is right. Chase Manhattan Bank prompted an international crisis of confidence in South Africa's finances when it stopped rolling over loans to South African borrowers. But it made that decision at the end of July 1985, two weeks before Rubicon.

The decision was purely technical, a Chase executive told Hermann Giliomee. "We felt that the risk attached to political unrest and economic instability became too high for our investors. We decided to withdraw. It was never the intention to facilitate change in South Africa, the decision was taken purely on account of what was in the interest of Chase and its assets."

Probably other unspoken factors also influenced Chase: the feelings of black board members; the threat of depositor or shareholder resistance; the impact of nightly television footage of South African police brutality. But the move was primarily an economic response to economic conditions. South Africa was unstable, and small; small, unstable countries (unlike large ones) do not borrow money.

The Chase move was crippling, for where it withdrew, others followed. With some two thirds of the country's $24 billion foreign debt short term, South Africa was perilously exposed to such action. Even before Botha spoke, the country was facing the most acute financial crisis of its history. But the speech made matters immeasurably worse. The South African currency, the Rand, fell precipitately; capital fled by all means, legal and illegal; markets were forced to close and the government declared bankruptcy, imposing a unilateral moratorium on the repayment of foreign debt. Though these debts were later rescheduled, and Pretoria resumed payments, South Africa was shunned thereafter, economically and financially, as well as diplomatically and morally.

Soon South Africa's crisis would deepen, with the imposition of politically inspired economic sanctions, to match the sanctions of the marketplace. In August 1986, the U.S. Congress enacted the Comprehensive Anti-Apartheid Act, a package of highly visible measures including a ban on new U.S. investment and loans, on landing rights, and on imports, among them, coal, uranium, iron, and steel. The Commonwealth and European Community also imposed various sanctions. Taken together, these hurt far less than financial sanctions, which seriously inhibited Pretoria's ability to pay for apartheid, but they contributed significantly to the assault on the psyche of white South Africans.

Botha, predictably, reacted to the measures with pure belligerence. Genuinely mystified by what he considered the perverse refusal of foreigners to credit his good intentions, he gave up reform to concentrate on repression. He lost the will to change, if not the will to rule.

If sanctions had a counterproductive effect on the Afrikaner leadership, they took their toll on white morale. Afrikaners felt besieged, and the majority did not like it. They wanted their rugby and their cricket (sports sanctions were particularly hurtful); they wanted their national pride restored. And they wanted their prosperity, for the economic crisis meant that Pretoria had less and less money to spend on keeping whites sweet. Per capita gross domestic product had begun to fall at the start of the Botha years, and by the time of Rubicon, it had returned to mid-1970s levels. The economic costs of Rubicon had, at last, provoked a real moment of truth for apartheid.

There was only one rational response to the concert of political, economic, diplomatic, social, and moral pressures directed against the Afrikaner state by the mid-1980s—talk to the enemy, and try to make a deal. But there was no sign at this point that Botha was tempted to be rational.

PART TWO

NEGOTIATED REVOLUTION

I once described South Africa as a country where you hope on Monday and despair on Tuesday.

Alan Paton

SO I ASK, *getting straight to the point, why don't you hate whites? The young man from the ANC smiles indulgently at my crude question. "There is no way I can hate whites. To hate whites would be unfair." Unfair? Is this slight, soft-spoken young-ster perhaps aspiring to early sainthood? Or do I just look like a sucker for the martyrdom routine?*

"Our problem is not whites per se. Our problem is the system which made whites the culprits of apartheid."

The cynic in me sneers that this is just a recitation of the ANC dogma of non-racialism. ANC leaders have spent thirty years teach-ing, by word and example, that racism is off limits. If this young activist hopes for a future in the movement, he has no choice but to genuflect before the principle of color blindness.

Don't you resent what whites did to you? I ask, probing for the pain which must lurk beneath. When he was in high school, police put him in a canvas bag, tied the bag with rope, and dropped it to the bottom of a river. After he lost consciousness, they fished him out, and put him in a cell to dry out. Next, they took him to a graveyard, had him lie down among the tombstones, and took pot-shots at his outline in the dust. Then they put him in solitary con-finement. When his class graduated, he was in detention. He never finished school.

And you don't hate them? I ask. No, they were just following orders. They were pawns in the game of apartheid. Should they pay for what they did? No, it was not their fault.

I met this same young man again and again, in every South African township. Sometimes his name was Thabo, sometimes it was Sipho, sometimes it was Lucky or Joe. Sometimes he had been dropped in a river, sometimes he had been strung up by his ankles, sometimes he had had electrodes attached to his genitals. But al-ways, he was a true believer in the religion of non-racialism. It was there in the body language, in the earnestness of the gaze and the openness of the visage. It was there in the refusal to hate, or suspect, or resent me, lily-white and pampered, glowing pale in his dark world.

The cynic in me never understood such generosity of spirit. The amateur psychologist in me thought it had something to do with ubuntu, the African word for the best that is human in all of us; and something to do with the two main philosophies that shaped the ANC—Marxism (which focuses on class instead of race) and Christianity (which says all men are equal before God). But the journalist in me knew simply that this quality was central to the South African solution. It was the secret of the great seduction.

4

The Great Seduction

IT WAS ONLY NATURAL: when Seretse Choabe, African freedom fighter, met Pieter de Lange, Afrikaner patriot, he threatened to kill him.

Choabe was a senior official of the African National Congress, and de Lange, as chairman of the Afrikaner Broederbond, held pride of place in the ANC's constellation of demons. Their peoples were at war, their rival nationalisms locked in terminal battle. No one expected them to be friends.

In front of forty-odd witnesses attending a conference at the Ford Foundation in New York in June 1986, Seretse Choabe vowed to shoot Pieter de Lange. It was the first meeting between a representative of the apartheid establishment and exiled officials of the ANC. In coming to New York, both sides had violated the chief political commandment of the day, that the ANC should meet the Afrikaner only on the field of battle. The risks were high, the rewards uncertain—and this was hardly an auspicious beginning.

Thabo Mbeki, sent by ANC President Oliver Tambo to show the acceptable face of the ANC, drew reflectively on his pipe and exchanged a glance with his colleague, Mac Maharaj. Choabe had jeopardized their careful strategy for the talks—to seduce where they could not conquer. The New York meeting was a key step in their grand and subtle plan to breach the psychological bastion of Afrikanerdom. Mbeki, cloaked in sweet reason, charm, and fragrant pipe smoke, had been sent to New York to assuage the ethnic paranoia of decades. Death threats were not on his agenda.

So when Choabe leaped up and shouted, "I'll shoot you, you Broederbonder"—conforming exactly to the stereotype used to terrify generations of Afrikaners like de Lange—Mbeki and Maharaj knew they had to limit the damage immediately. The ANC could no longer afford to be seen as consisting of mad terrorists bent on Afrikaner annihilation. Both at home and abroad, it had to cultivate a new image. To Maharaj fell the delicate task of issuing what the subtle de Lange would recognize as an apology, without humiliating the volatile (and slightly hung-over) Choabe.

"If you want to understand what apartheid is about, and how it affects us, then listen to the raw anger of Seretse," Maharaj told the meeting. "There is tremendous anger amongst our people at what apartheid is doing to us. That's a side of it you cannot ignore." But indulging such grievances would merely trap South Africa forever in its polarized past. "We have to chart a way forward from that anger," Maharaj argued. And that meant guaranteeing de Lange's freedom of speech, whether in New York or Pretoria. "We don't agree with you, but you have the right to put your views," Maharaj reassured the Afrikaner, knowing that, as gatekeeper to the national psyche, his conversion was crucial.

But only Choabe himself could finally heal the breach opened by his outburst. At the end of the conference, in a moment that captured all the turbulence of the time, he embraced a startled de Lange and apologized. "He said, 'Remember it's our children dying in Soweto,' " de Lange recalls, still moved by the memory of the action of Choabe, now dead. "And I said, 'I know that,' and we left."

Such impossible moments of reconciliation were to be repeated thousands and thousands of times in the years to follow, as South Africans fought to reestablish the bonds of origin severed at birth by white supremacy. Again and again, they rediscovered the central facts which apartheid was designed to obscure: the fact of a common patriotism, common values, a shared dedication to God, land, and family, a common humanity. For Afrikaners and Africans—whom Nelson Mandela has described as "brothers who happen to be different colours"—the bonding was particularly intense, and absolutely crucial to peace. They are the true tribes of South Africa, rooted to its soil and shackled to its future in a way that other groups—especially English-speaking South Africans, with their ultimate refuge in Europe—are not. Neither tribe was devious by nature; when they were racist, their racism was naked and obvious, not the deep pathological hatred that twists the psyche of many divided nations; and when they were reconciled, their enthusiasm was boundless.

So in New York and Soweto, Lusaka and Dakar, South Africans met to lay the human foundations and erect the emotional buttresses for a lasting peace. In less than a decade, the ANC had pulled off a monumental feat of seduction—the conversion of the Afrikaner nation, the liberation of the white tribe of Africa from the irrational fears of centuries. In the end, the mysterious chemistry between African and Afrikaner forged a bond strong enough to defy both the logic of the past and the political correctness of the modern day. The new South Africa will stand or fall on the strength of the human bridge built during the negotiation decade, 1985–94.

When that decade began, its start marked roughly by P. W. Botha's disastrous 1985 plunge into the Rubicon, seduction was only one part of the ANC's strategy—as it was only one of the conflicting impulses in Seretse Choabe's breast. The ANC was in no way ready to abandon the violent struggle. It would continue to issue death threats—and carry them out, wherever possible—for many years to come. The campaign to render black townships ungovernable was reaching new heights of anarchic prowess; only weeks before Botha's Rubicon speech, the ANC had held an important strategy conference, its first since 1969, and announced a new drive to export violence from the townships to previously tranquil white areas.

After "twenty fruitless years of selected sabotage," the gentle and gentlemanly Oliver Tambo promised "more bloodshed than ever before." The aim was to make white South Africa feel the heat of war—even if this meant blurring the distinction, always scrupulously maintained by Tambo, between "soft" civilian targets like supermarkets and schools, and "hard" targets like the military.

Despite the tough rhetoric, the ANC never prosecuted the civilian war with gusto. Its orders were contradictory. Radio Freedom, the ANC radio station, would broadcast a call to black domestic servants to attack their white employers; then Oliver Tambo would seem to retract that order by warning against the "indiscriminate and senseless massacre of white civilians." The movement was torn between those—like firebrand guerrilla leader Chris Hani—who were intent on striking fear into white hearts, and those—like Thabo Mbeki—who preferred to charm whites all the way to defeat.

Mbeki, then head of the ANC's department of information, outlined the movement's dilemma for me one day in 1985. "We're concerned about the impact on white South Africans of attacks against whites," he told me. "Our aim is to win them *away* from apartheid, even if they don't come to us. So, attacks hurt us."

Many of Mbeki's colleagues did not agree. Even Mac Maharaj, Mbeki's sidekick at the Ford Foundation conference (and my neighbor in Twin Palm Road), saw a grim utility in white deaths, saying, "There is a psychological barrier in the white population after which such terrorist attacks will not provoke a closing of ranks, but rather a questioning of the grounds of white power."

An excited Joe Slovo (then commander of *Umkhonto we Sizwe*) echoed Maharaj's enthusiasm. He told me, just after an ANC strategy conference held at Kabwe, Zambia, in 1985, that he believed whites were losing confi-

dence in their ability to dominate forever, while blacks had begun to overcome the centuries-old African curse of impotence. Chillingly, he informed
me that Africans had finally developed the one quality without which no
revolution could succeed, "contempt for death." And Slovo, for one, was not
going to waste this last great shot at the revolution.

That ANC conference followed a confusing path between the two positions. While calling for the extension of violence to white areas, it also
hinted at an apparently contradictory strategy of engagement. The conferees
agreed that it was important to "win as many whites as possible to our side,"
noting that more and more whites were looking for a way out of apartheid's
crisis, "posing the possibility that our movement will be in contact with levels
of the ruling circles of our country that it has never dealt with before." That
gave Mbeki his opening to meet with de Lange.

By the time the two men came face to face in 1986, Mbeki was convinced that Botha's government could be terminally undermined from
within. The ANC leader, who believed in lubricating political discourse with
charm and liberal quantities of strong drink, was a great favorite of the
international press. So he arranged to give a series of newspaper interviews
to publicize the new thrust of ANC strategy, which was to form a broad
alliance of businessmen, Afrikaner intellectuals, and black homeland leaders, and turn them against Pretoria. "We are reaching out, exploring all these
forces, trying to mobilize the political weight of all of them to the point
where Botha finds that he can't go on confronting them in their totality. . . .

"Then we are talking not of overthrowing the government, but of turning so many people against it" that Botha would be forced to capitulate. He
would then say, "Okay, let's talk," and the ANC would also be prepared to
negotiate, Mbeki concluded.

First, Mbeki needed to locate the faultlines in white politics, an area
woefully misunderstood by the ANC in exile, dependent on white Communists like Joe Slovo for their analysis of a politics into which they had little
insight. The ANC had long neglected the most basic commandment of
warfare, according to Mandela: Know your enemy. Mbeki set out to correct
that weakness, to answer questions which the exiled movement had not even
thought to ask, such as, How did the ruling group think? What did it fear?
How could its internal contradictions be exploited? How could the Afrikaner
be saved from himself?

The ANC's decision to get under white South Africa's skin—motivated
largely by President Oliver Tambo, but carried out by Thabo Mbeki—was
probably the most important one ever made by the exiled movement. For
Tambo and Mbeki, unlike the romantic revolutionaries among their colleagues, were intent on delivering not just the corpse of a defeated nation,

but the mind and soul of the Afrikaner people to the new South Africa. No doubt they set out with the aim of wooing merely to weaken—their goal to sow confusion in the enemy camp, not to seek true converts in overwhelmingly hostile territory. But Mbeki, for one, was shrewd enough to understand that behind the facade of the Afrikaner bully dwelt an almost pitiful yearning to be understood, loved, and accepted by Africa. Only the subtlest of ANC minds could recognize this truth: that petting, coddling, and cajoling the Afrikaner would pay enormous dividends. And apart from Mandela himself, there was none subtler than Thabo Mbeki.

"What you needed to do—which sometimes wasn't easy—was to start off from where they were."

Thabo Mbeki explains how he persuaded Afrikaners that they did not need apartheid. He takes out his pipe and sucks on it, as I reflect on the extraordinary role that instrument played in the Afrikaner conversion. Throughout the negotiated revolution, Mbeki sported his pipe as a badge of sophistication and urbanity, and used it to suggest a cultivated reserve inconsistent with white stereotypes of primitive Africans. One of his interlocutors of the period remembers that the pipe made Mbeki look like a "black Englishman," by which he meant, of course, that the ANC leader was a sort of "honorary white man." Exiled for thirty years, with a master's degree in economics from Sussex University, Mbeki—unlike most South African blacks, including senior liberation figures—had the confidence to treat whites as equals. And that confidence was gained early in life, in ways not open to most black South Africans.

Thabo Mbeki's childhood was shaped by prosperity and by an acquaintance with business, two influences unusual among blacks, who were largely precluded from both wealth and commerce by apartheid. A child of the black middle-class intelligentsia of the Transkei homeland, Mbeki's parents were both educated at the prestigious Lovedale College, a missionary institution in the Eastern Cape which produced the country's finest black leaders. From his father, Govan, he learned the game of politics young; one of the most extreme of the ANC Communists, Govan Mbeki was a senior ANC leader in the 1950s and 1960s, and served a long prison sentence with Nelson Mandela. From his mother, Epainette, the formidable matriarch who ran the family's large general trading store, the young Thabo learned confidence in the presence of whites. Working in the business, Thabo dealt with white wholesalers and competing white traders from a position of strength, and on a basis of equality. Through both his parents, Mbeki had power, and local whites—businessmen, magistrates, teachers—respected that.

When, decades later, Thabo Mbeki set out to carry the message of non-racialism to the Afrikaner, he did it with the same quiet confidence and self-possession learned at the store. Where his interlocutors expected aggression, they found only self-assurance. "A lot of the time they were surprised that we were not confrontational," Mbeki says. Settling comfortably among the symbols of his new prosperity—Mbeki is now deputy president of the new South Africa—he recalls early meetings with the enemy. "We didn't want to be confrontational," he explains, "because we knew it was not going to produce results.

"They were racists, we were opposed to racism, but when we talked to them, we did not denounce them for that racism, we assumed it as given. They knew we were opposed to it. But we had to start off from where they were."

Mbeki's voice adopts the same low, sweet tones of reason he used all those years ago to disarm the enemy. Like the accomplished lay psychologist that he is, Mbeki made clear that nothing would outrage him: no aberration of human behavior was too great to be corrected, no fear too ridiculous to be taken seriously, no rift too deep to heal. But his greatest weapon was always his charm. Not the easy openness of character that is sometimes denoted by that term, but a personality tool wielded sharply to advantage. For Mbeki, charm is a form of self-discipline; it masks his feelings, and ensures that he never gives anything away. It was the perfect weapon for the battle to hand. Mbeki wielded it skillfully to win liberation for his people, and a formidable position of power for himself in the new South Africa.

"We would say to them, you have fears about the future of Afrikaans and Afrikaans schools, and your land, and all of this, these are legitimate fears. We may think they are unjustified, but that does not remove them, they are there, what do we do about them?

"And they were surprised. 'You mean you recognize the fact that I have a right to my language and I can indeed take up arms to resist?' And we said, 'Ja, sure we recognize that, so let's deal with the matter.' So I think in the end it was really the removal of fear, and an understanding of how you move people. We simply had to say, we sink or swim together—and persuade them that they shouldn't see change as threatening. . . ."

Mbeki had realized that the ANC alone had the power to restore to Afrikaners what they most desired—the right to be proud South Africans, proud members of the human race. And no Afrikaner had a more vehement desire to restore the good name of his people than Pieter de Lange. So Mbeki and de Lange, thoughtful and subtle sons of the same soil, met on alien turf in New York in 1986 to begin that process of restoration.

They talked for hours at de Lange's New York hotel. When the Broederbond chairman's pipelighter broke down, Mbeki was able to offer his, a gift from a recent visit to North Korea. (De Lange recalls, chuckling, that "it worked perfectly well.") When an afternoon of talks stretched on into evening, de Lange invited his wife Christine to join them for dinner. "Apparently that was the first time in his life that Thabo had had dinner with an Afrikaner woman," de Lange recalls, laughing soft and long at the memory. At that meal, the two men agreed that the Broederbond leader should work for national reconciliation on his return to South Africa.

But if de Lange left New York with what he says was "a normalized perception of the ANC as human beings," Mbeki also left enlightened. He recalls an exchange with de Lange over the issue of P. W. Botha's reforms. De Lange sought to persuade Mbeki that the repeal of both the Mixed Marriages and the Group Areas acts—the legislative pillars of marital and residential segregation—was crucial to the creation of a new South Africa. Africans dismissed such moves as meaningless. As Nelson Mandela had told a visitor to his prison cell the previous year, "It is not my ambition to marry a white woman. It is political equality we want."

De Lange acknowledged this. He told Mbeki,° "I know what I am saying is nonsense as far as your own aspirations are concerned, but you must understand the Afrikaners; we needed those laws because we thought that without them, the Afrikaner people would cease to exist. They would be swamped and perish as a people.

"Psychologically, we have built a fortress around ourselves. But when Botha repeals the Group Areas Act, and we wake up the next morning and nothing has happened, our suburb has not been swamped by black people; when he removes the Mixed Marriages Act, and the Afrikaner people remain the Afrikaner people, that will allow Afrikaners to pose the question, do we need a white government? Because we thought we needed these laws to protect us, and they have gone and nothing has happened. Do we need a white government? The existence of that government is threatening our security. Perhaps if it, too, went the way of the Group Areas Act, nothing would happen.

"It is of no meaning to you to repeal these laws, but of great meaning in terms of preparing Afrikaners for change," de Lange concluded. That is what Mbeki means when he says, "You had to start from where they were. Then you would understand."

At almost precisely the moment that Seretse Choabe (physically) and Thabo Mbeki (mentally) embraced Pieter de Lange in New York, back in South Africa the battle for power entered its darkest hour. On June 12, 1986,

---

° This reconstruction is based on an account of the meeting given to me by Thabo Mbeki.

P. W. Botha declared a state of emergency which would destroy lives and crush dissent, ruin the country's international reputation, and polarize its communities—yet create, in the end, precisely the conditions needed for peace.

Had anyone suggested such an outcome to me that day—as Pretoria's iron fist descended on black South Africa with a vengeance—I would have thought them mad. Scarcely forty-eight hours before, I had stood timidly on a motorway overpass above a burning squatter camp near Cape Town, known as "KTC," watching as police-backed vigilantes battled the radical "comrades" of the ANC-aligned United Democratic Front (UDF). The fighting eventually left sixty people dead, and a cameraman colleague hacked to pieces as he filmed it. Another burst of force from Pretoria would, I was sure, only make things worse.

Already, some twelve thousand people had been detained during an earlier, partial emergency declared in July 1985. It had failed to crush the uprising. Black township dwellers were refusing to pay rent, and black children came to school only to vandalize and burn the symbols of white authority. The ANC had created "liberated zones" in some townships, where they imposed "alternative justice" on frightened residents. Ungovernability was, largely, a reality.

Botha was enraged. So as I stood listening to the light crackle of gunfire from KTC, the cabinet put the finishing touches to a far uglier emergency. It imposed de facto military rule, giving the lowliest police officer broad powers of arrest, detention, and interrogation without warrant. Public meetings were banned, and strict media censorship was imposed.

The emergency made tyranny legal, and freed the police from any remaining psychological impediments to oppression. Some 25,000 people were detained in the first six months of the new emergency, a third of them children; many underwent physical or psychological torture. The UDF lost almost its entire national leadership, as activists were jailed, murdered, or forced into hiding or exile. By the end of 1987, shell-shocked activists were nursing their wounds, unrest had abated, and a tense calm prevailed in the townships. And in the region, the ANC had been neutralized, as Pretoria strong-armed and persuaded its neighbors to expel ANC guerrillas.

The tragic irony of the times decreed that this brutality would prove an essential stage on the road to change. For the most basic principle of Afrikaner politics has always been "act from a position of strength." The 1986 emergency fulfilled that precondition of action. It persuaded Botha that he was strong enough to contain the violence; it gave him delusions of grandeur on the political front, where he believed he could gain substantial support from apolitical blacks just by restoring order. It convinced him that he had the upper hand. It was time for a new political initiative, to complement the crackdown.

Perversely, the ANC made a similar calculation of strategic advantage. Despite the ravages of the emergency, the movement felt it had won the battle of the townships. Pretoria could contain, but not eradicate dissent; it could never rule peacefully again. The ANC felt that it, too, could now operate from a position of strength.

The township struggle gave the ANC and the state a new reading of the domestic balance of forces between them, but at the same time it vastly altered the balance as viewed from overseas. Pretoria's brutality chilled even traditional foreign supporters, like Prime Minister Margaret Thatcher in Britain and U.S. President Ronald Reagan. The international sanctions campaign—and crucially, the suspension of foreign loans—began to cramp the economic growth needed to underpin gradual reform.

At the same time, the ANC came under greater pressure to be reasonable. The revolt had boosted its international profile; regarded, for the first time, as a government-in-waiting, the movement had to begin to act like one. Every meeting with a Western government focused on one question: When would the ANC negotiate?

Meanwhile, unrelated events in the Soviet Union (the ANC's closest international ally, and its main weapons provider) were creating similar pressures. Soviet leader Mikhail Gorbachev soon made clear that his ailing country had no more time or money to devote to the South African struggle. When he met President Reagan for the 1986 Reykjavik summit, Gorbachev resolved to end all the regional conflicts that had kept the superpowers tied down in battle. He did not make peace to get rid of apartheid; that was merely a side effect. But from the moment Gorbachev declared war on regional conflicts, revolution was out of favor internationally. The ANC knew it could not afford to remain on the wrong side of the new world politics, so it fell in with the trend toward negotiation.

Perversely, it was violence that launched South Africa on the road to negotiation. And from about 1985—from the time of the first state of emergency—talking became the country's primary growth industry. Soon, the most unlikely interlocutors were sitting down together, in Western and African capitals, maximum-security prisons, township watering holes, African game parks, and English stately homes. After refusing to talk for 350 years, South Africans indulged in an orgy of communication.

The gray men from Pretoria—even, on occasion, cabinet ministers— met the angry young men of the townships, in increasingly desperate efforts to buy off the revolution. Tentatively at first, as early as 1984, they met in township "shebeens" (drinking establishments which, ironically, were illegal and often raided by police). Sometimes they sat down in the back of a government minivan, complete with well-stocked bar.

For both sides, contact was dangerous. Leaders of the UDF risked death if they were discovered talking to the enemy. And the government official involved, Kobus Jordaan, an adviser to the Cooperation and Development Ministry, risked his job. Jordaan's brief was only to probe the causes of the uprising, but even for that limited task, his superiors could not openly support him. They wanted to be able to denounce him if things turned sour. And so they did. In 1988, news was leaked that Jordaan had met the exiled ANC in Lusaka, probably the first time a government official had made direct contact. His security clearance was withdrawn and he was hounded from his job.

The security establishment opposed all such contacts, sometimes violently. Sam de Beer, in 1985 deputy minister of education and a noted liberal, was the most senior government official to talk to the powerful Eastern Cape UDF leader, Matthew Goniwe. De Beer believes Goniwe paid with his life for these talks. He was murdered soon afterward, and de Beer blames elements in government that opposed the negotiations.

Meanwhile, over cocktails and canapés in diplomatic sitting rooms, government ministers like Chris Heunis—who, as chief constitutional theorist, was second only to P. W. Botha in ANC demonology—chatted to other UDF figures, declared and undeclared. Members of the exiled ANC often condemned them for doing so, but the reality was that UDF leaders simply could not avoid contact with government. Exiles could maintain their splendid isolation; but the UDF—which was the public face of the underground ANC—collided with the authorities at every turn. It had to talk to survive.

And survival was most acutely a priority at the local level, where local power groups recognized more quickly than their national masters that they had reached a stalemate. It is one of the ironies of the time that ungovernability led as often to talks as to chaos; for activists knew that insurrection, on its own, could not deliver the goods. They had political power, but the state had control over the essentials of life—electricity, water, housing. Only negotiation could bridge the gap.

Local communities were among the first to renegotiate substantive power relations between white and black, as the local white establishment sought neighborhood solutions to immediate crises such as rent and consumer boycotts. The townships became the laboratories where ANC activists developed a whole new concept of power, rejecting the revolutionary paradigm in favor of strategic compromise. In this, they were heavily influenced by both business and labor. Business had the most to lose from the social and economic upheaval; it was far more eager than government to talk.

And since their legalization in 1979, the black trade unions had adopted a sophisticated strategy of seeking gains through negotiation. Both business and labor had already tested the negotiating paradigm and proved that it could work. Now it was time to export those lessons to Lusaka.

Within weeks of P. W. Botha's August 1985 Rubicon speech, a group of Anglo American Corporation executives and newspaper editors became the first political explorers to the land of ANC. Over the next four years, they were joined by hundreds of others, from the broadest possible range of South African life—liberal Afrikaners and their conservative brothers, clergymen and pressmen, unionists and radicals, even government officials. Negotiations were breaking out all over.

The Anglo American Corporation struck a clever blow for capitalism when it became the first to break the taboo against talks with the ANC. In September 1985, several months before the secret New York meetings with de Lange, its chairman met with Congress leaders deep in the Zambian bush. Anglo thus legitimized contact with the movement, which had been shunned by the South African political and corporate establishment as well as by most Western governments. The meeting proved a major diplomatic coup for the ANC. After waiting for decades for salvation from Eastern Europe, the ANC began to espy allies amongst their long-term enemies, the capitalists.

The meeting very nearly did not take place. Oliver Tambo feared the charge that he was selling out to capitalism; he was only persuaded to attend through the strenuous efforts of Zambian President Kenneth Kaunda, who hosted the gathering at his luxurious Mfuwe Game Lodge. P. W. Botha browbeat all but a few businessmen into canceling their trip. In the end, only Anglo group companies were represented, and even Anglo patriarch Harry Oppenheimer did not support it.

Those who attended were bowled over. "I was surprised (almost overwhelmed) by the cordiality of the meeting," businessman Tony Bloom wrote in his notes from Mfuwe. "A more attractive and congenial group would be hard to imagine. There was a total lack of aggression, animosity or hostility towards us . . . the initial round of introductions was almost like a reunion."

The gulf between the economic policies of business and those of the ANC remained huge. Thabo Mbeki promised not to nationalize white South Africa's ubiquitous swimming pools, but the ANC delegation nonetheless stuck to the policies of its 1955 manifesto, the Freedom Charter, calling for state ownership of "monopoly capital." Still, the dynamic of the day drove the two sides to look harder for common ground than for differences. The ANC was banking on the fact that, once it persuaded Anglo American its money would be safe in the new South Africa, Anglo executives would return home as powerful ambassadors for change.

Already, the ANC had an improbably close relationship with the Zambian office of Anglo American—the movement used Anglo's Lusaka headquarters as a postbox for sensitive mail. Mbeki treated the home of Anglo Zambian managing director Vernon Webber as an unofficial clubhouse for entertaining visiting South Africans. When a delegation from the liberal white opposition, the Progressive Federal Party (predecessor of today's Democratic Party), visited in 1985, Mbeki invited them to Webber's house for drinks—without giving him so much as a few hours' notice. They raided the Anglo liquor cabinet for whiskey and the fridge for snacks, while Webber and his wife diplomatically withdrew.

At the Mfuwe talks, Anglo delegation leader Gavin Relly found immediate common ground with Mbeki over their shared vice of pipe smoking. Oliver Tambo put the businessmen at their ease, calling Relly by his first name, suggesting that the groups should mingle instead of sitting rigidly opposite one another at the table—and demolishing stereotypes of godless ANC communism by insisting on saying grace over lunch.

"I think all of us expected something a lot more sinister and horrifying," Relly recalls. Instead, Tambo, a courtly gentleman in the mold of Nelson Mandela, stressed the ANC's reluctant conversion to violence. "I myself have an abhorrence of violence," he said. "I even take insects out of the bath!"

The ANC managed to convey just the right message: That they were patriots, as deeply and passionately committed to South Africa as any of their white visitors; that they were human beings—and moderate ones at that— not fanatic ideologues; and that they were counting the days to go home. Gavin Relly puts it best: "They were just a bunch of homesick South Africans."

"Kiss the ground for us," said the ANC official to his Afrikaner counterpart; both men had tears in their eyes. They were parting after another such emotional reunion, at Dakar in Senegal. There, in August 1987, the ANC worked its soothing rhetorical magic on some fifty dissident Afrikaners, the largest group yet.

Thabo Mbeki had opened the meeting with his usual audacity. "My name is Thabo Mbeki, I'm an Afrikaner," he said. He went on to assure his audience that (despite ANC rhetoric to the contrary) they were not about to be murdered in their beds. "White South Africa *knows* there is no instinct in our people to slaughter white people," he said. "White South Africa lives with black South Africa *every day*. It doesn't believe the stories that the maid will poison the madam." And Afrikaans language, culture, and history were no more threatened than Afrikaner lives.

By the end of 1987, Mbeki's message had begun to get through, and not only dissident whites were listening. The ANC was on the verge of penetrating the citadel itself, through the medium of Botha's spy corps, the National Intelligence Service. The NIS wanted to play the same game as the ANC: Know thine enemy. So intelligence officials approached returning Dakar delegates for information on the meetings. A government minister even approached one delegate proposing that he arrange direct talks with the ANC, but these did not take place.

The two sides had been in indirect intercourse for years already. At a time when Zambia was rhetorically at war with racist South Africa, Zambian officials undertook regular secret missions to Pretoria. South African aircraft even came to Lusaka to fetch them. Zambian President Kaunda and P. W. Botha held two secret summits in the South African bush, never disclosed by either side. And the heads of the NIS and South African Military Intelligence traveled regularly, sometimes in disguise, to visit Kaunda at his State House residence. They took tea with the president within yards of the residence of Oliver Tambo, who lived in a cottage in the State House grounds. Tambo was never invited—or at least, never agreed—to join them. But the two sides spoke to each other through Kaunda.

Meanwhile, the NIS was pursuing its own investigations independently of Kaunda. Its infiltration of the ANC was pervasive, and it used its own agents in Zambia, as well as Zambian intelligence (which was in close contact with its ANC opposite number) to gather information. Its goal was identical to Mbeki's: Find the enemy faultlines, and plant dynamite beneath them. P. W. Botha believed, to the end of his reign, that he could divide the moderate nationalist wing of the ANC from the Communists, failing to realize that the gap between the two was far narrower than rhetoric would suggest. So he sent Niël Barnard and his men from the NIS to discover where the rival camps divided. They soon realized they needed an insider to probe for the cracks.

One day in 1987, two National Intelligence officials went to the home of a prominent Afrikaner and made him an outrageous proposal. They asked him to spy for his country. Professor Willie Esterhuyse remembers that day, and shivers even now, "because if the thing misfired, if it backfired, I mean. . . ." Esterhuyse leaves the phrase incomplete. Such an outcome would be too ghastly to contemplate. The NIS and the ANC were at war, and anyone caught crossing the no-man's-land between them would be a target. Esterhuyse had been asked to do just that: to report to Pretoria on the internal workings of the ANC. His life as a professor of philosophy in the storybook

Cape Dutch town of Stellenbosch had done nothing to prepare him for this, and his temperament disinclined him to danger. "My wife and I, we sat for nearly a whole night talking about it," he recalls. He can smile, now, at the memory of his fear.

Professor Esterhuyse was the perfect choice for the job. He was about to take a group of establishment Afrikaners to meet the ANC in Europe—a fact that the NIS knew through its own clandestine methods. This was Niël Barnard's chance to establish a low-risk channel through which to conduct the first indirect talks with the ANC. Publicly, P. W. Botha could continue to declare that his government would never talk to terrorists. Esterhuyse would do it for him. He had taught Botha's daughter, Rozanne, and had close relations with P.W., to whom he acted as informal political adviser. Esterhuyse was an intermediary whom Botha could trust.

Botha could have achieved the same goal over three years earlier, before the township uprising which cost so many lives, for Esterhuyse received his first overture from the exiled movement in 1984. He was invited to Lusaka along with his colleague at Stellenbosch University, Professor Sampie Terreblanche. "But then we got a phone call from P.W.

"He was quite friendly; we sat in armchairs—with P.W., when he remained seated behind his desk, you knew it was going to be a thunderstorm—and we had a nice chat," Esterhuyse recalls. Botha told him that, given his close links to government, any such meeting would be seen as the start of negotiations with the ANC. And in 1984, Botha could not afford to give such an impression. "He said that, from a strategic point of view, it was not the right moment, in that period of turmoil," Esterhuyse recalls. "So of course I had no other option but to say, listen, we can't do it."

Botha was probably right; neither side was ready to talk. In 1984, each had more to lose than to gain by negotiation. Three years later, that calculus had changed beyond recognition. Violence had done its job of motivating change, and foreign pressures on both sides were becoming irresistible. So, after years of desultory, indirect contact—through spy channels, diplomatic channels, and the mediation of Kenneth Kaunda—government was ready to become the sleeping partner in talks. And those who could read the runes of ANC rhetoric knew that the movement, too, was dragging its heels reluctantly toward negotiation.

Days before Esterhuyse's first meeting with the ANC, the national executive committee of the movement, its highest policy-making body, issued a public statement ruling out an early start to talks. But that rebuttal masked a dramatic development: the ANC had received a message from Pretoria—what spies call a "signal." The Botha government was looking for a way to release Nelson Mandela from prison, without losing face; it wanted to talk to the ANC about achieving that goal. It was the first such overture from Pretoria, and the first sign that Botha knew he could no longer ignore the ANC.

The ANC replied with an impossible demand: three members of the exiled national executive should be allowed to enter South Africa to consult on the issue with the internal ANC leadership, in prison and in the townships. Pretoria did not reply. But the ANC statement had nonetheless served its purpose. Its vigorous arguments against negotiation put the question of talks firmly on the public agenda for the first time.

In December 1987, talks began in England between Willie Esterhuyse and Thabo Mbeki; but deciding to meet did not, at that stage, mean deciding to compromise. These were negotiations thrice removed—talks . . . about whether to talk . . . about talks. In the early days, both Pretoria and the ANC had a hidden agenda—and it was the same one. Engage the enemy, in order to confuse him; understand, in order to outsmart. The NIS was still bent on splitting the ANC. Its officials repeatedly asked Esterhuyse whether there were nationalists in the ANC who would renounce both violence and communism. He had to disappoint them and say no.

The ANC agenda was no more propitious. Mbeki may have begun to realize that compromise was inevitable, but that was not true of the vast majority of his colleagues. They still intended to negotiate only the mechanics of the transfer of power. So, in 1987, whites still aimed to keep power and blacks thought only of taking it; neither side was yet prepared to share.

Over the years that followed, this changed, and Esterhuyse's contacts with Mbeki—the two men held their own private talks, kept secret from other members of the Afrikaner and ANC delegations—helped soften attitudes on both sides. They developed a close personal friendship. Esterhuyse had been afraid to tell Mbeki that he was reporting to the NIS. But when he did, soon after the talks began, he was relieved to find that this was exactly what the ANC leader wanted—a reliable channel through which to feed his message of reassurance to Pretoria. Professor Esterhuyse, a congenial and cultured man with an easy laugh and open manner, was exactly the sort of decent Afrikaner whom Mbeki could respect. In conversation, Esterhuyse— true to his philosopher's roots—searched constantly for answers to the existential predicament of South African life. And Mbeki had answers to give him.

Unlike the suave Mbeki, Esterhuyse is a rougher diamond, his thick Afrikaans accent almost a badge of cultural identity. Mbeki's gift was to respect that identity. Esterhuyse did not apologize for being an Afrikaner— and Mbeki did not expect him to do so. Their relationship touched something in Esterhuyse far deeper than politics. After a year of meetings, he recalls, "I came back and I told my wife, I said I am prepared to entrust my life to Mbeki."

Esterhuyse marvels at that fact still. "This fellow was regarded as a terrorist, a Communist, etc., yet I was prepared to trust my life to him." His features are fixed in the same expression of fond wonder I have seen on the faces of so many of the early pilgrims, describing the miracle of reconciliation. For they were not convinced by Mbeki—they were converted. And none more fervently than the warm-hearted Willie Esterhuyse.

"The main reason was the way in which he understood the Afrikaners' predicament; it was incredible." Esterhuyse's deep voice rises high with surprise, even at this distant recollection. "You must remember the fellow was out of the country for so long, and he was the victim even of an attempt to kill him, and still he was able to understand the feelings of the Afrikaner. And he had no bitterness. Those were the two things: his understanding, and no bitterness."

That may say more about Mbeki's cleverness and his charm than about his true feelings. He knew resentment would get him nowhere with the Afrikaner, so he took it off the agenda. He was not about to let his own emotions get in the way either of liberation or of power. So he set about the bonding process with a vengeance. The strategy paid off. Bonds between men were to prove, again and again, South Africa's safety net. Informal networks of friendship bridged the cultural divide, and kept communications open even when rival politicians had ceased to speak. Apartheid would have ended without them: it was doomed by forces larger than personality. But only human beings could make peace. The Mbeki-Esterhuyse talks were to prove an important part of the peacemaking process.

Certainly, the setting was conducive to bonhomie. Most of the dozen meetings that took place between November 1987 and May 1990—bringing together, at different times, some twenty members of the Afrikaner political elite with ANC officials led by Mbeki—were held at Mells Park House, a stately home near Bath in western England. The participants included Attie du Plessis, whose brother Barend was P. W. Botha's minister of finance; Wimpie de Klerk, F.W.'s brother; and Mof Terreblanche, one of F.W.'s closest friends. They remember antique silver, vintage wine, and winter evenings warmed with malt whiskey consumed before the Mells Park fireplace. They also remember the South African grapes and wine provided (in flagrant violation of the British boycott then in force) by one participant, Louis Kriel. "The ANC always asked, 'Will Kriel be coming and will there be grapes?'" Esterhuyse reminisces with a chuckle. It was that sort of question which exploded Botha's stereotype of the ANC as humorless ideologues.

Formal Mells Park meetings took place during the Saturday and Sunday of the weekend sessions; but the real work was done over Glenfiddich at the fireside, and was scarcely ever complete before the early hours of morning, when Mbeki (a notorious night owl) finally put himself and his pipe to bed.

Mof Terreblanche, an oversized, jovial Afrikaner stockbroker, captures the essence of the Mells experience. "It's a civilized world there. If you have a drink with somebody, and you argue and you sit, and you sit and talk, and have another drink, it brings understanding," he explains. "Really, we became friends."

Appropriately, it was business that helped facilitate the talks. After its initial involvement at Mfuwe, Anglo American Corporation had backed away. But the British mining house Consolidated Goldfields, whose primary assets were South African, stepped into the breach. Oliver Tambo asked Michael Young, head of Goldfields' communications, to set up a dialogue with establishment Afrikaners. With the help of Fleur de Villiers, a former South African journalist then working for De Beers—Anglo American's diamond subsidiary, and a consultant to Goldfields—he did so. Goldfields agreed to keep them fed and warm at Mells Park House.

Government involvement in the talks was kept scrupulously secret. Only P. W. Botha himself, and a handful of NIS officials, knew of it; the cabinet, amazingly, did not. The ANC, too, kept all but its most senior leaders in the dark, fearing that hard-liners would otherwise denounce diplomats like Mbeki as sellouts.

Esterhuyse identifies two phases to the talks. First, the two sides had to discuss the issue of how to start negotiating. After a year or so, they moved on to the second stage, a discussion of positions and principles. When would the ANC suspend its armed struggle? Would it accept a multi-party interim government to rule in the transition to full democracy? What about constitutional safeguards for the white minority? And crucially, what economic system did it favor?

Esterhuyse remembers that the two sides departed from radically different conceptions of change. "We from the South African side tended to say, listen, there is movement, let's give it time to develop. But the ANC was saying, you can't reform apartheid, you have to abolish it. And the only alternative is a negotiated agreement."

When he accepted that, it was a major moment of truth for Esterhuyse. "If you ask me when my real political liberation started, it was when I realized that South Africa's future is not dependent on Afrikaners alone. At school and even university, we were made to believe that the only real leaders of the country were white, and preferably Afrikaans. Interacting with people like Mbeki made me realize that this country has a pool of leadership which is not defined by a color, the color white or the language Afrikaans."

He reported all this to Niël Barnard and a small team of his NIS colleagues. Esterhuyse remembers many hours of stimulating discussion in NIS "safe houses" throughout the country, with an intelligence team whose bona fides he came to accept. (The silver-haired professor also remembers, somewhat sheepishly, the efforts of NIS agents to teach him rudimentary counterespionage techniques, such as how to detect a car bomb. In the end, he had to tell them that spying was not his métier. He clearly enjoyed the excitement of the clandestine life, but was fatalistic about the risks.)

But Barnard was not the only one receiving firsthand reports from Mells. At the end of 1988, F. W. de Klerk's brother, Wimpie, began to attend. The ANC invited him because they were worried about the conservative image of F.W., viewed as a possible heir to P. W. Botha. Wimpie could not ease their fears; he was as concerned as they were. The best he could say about F.W.—who toed the tough party line scrupulously throughout the 1980s—was that he was "open-minded."

"I was not that enthusiastic that he would be the messiah of the new order," Wimpie recalls. The brothers had clashed over politics for years, as Wimpie had grown more liberal and F.W. had remained within the fold. So the elder brother was scarcely surprised when F.W. opposed his ANC contacts. "I didn't tell him about the first visit," Wimpie says. But on his return, he insisted on a meeting. "Mbeki expects me to give reports to you," Wimpie told F.W. "I was chosen because I was your brother." F.W. replied very cautiously: Wimpie could send reports of the sessions, but would receive neither acknowledgment nor reply. "So I sent him full reports—six, eight, ten pages—and he never answered me," Wimpie remembers, stressing that on the very day of F.W.'s inauguration, the new president tried to persuade his older brother to sever contact with the Mells group. He sent him to see a top NIS official, who told him the ANC was "an organisation on its knees" which "could never play a role in negotiations." F.W.'s reasons were largely tactical. He did not want well-meaning amateurs meddling in the delicate process of political rapprochement. But his resistance reinforced his image as a hard-liner.

Appropriately, the Mells Park meetings culminated in February 1990, when Thabo Mbeki and Willie Esterhuyse sat together to watch F. W. de Klerk announce the release of Nelson Mandela from prison. Together, they celebrated with Mells Park champagne the event that they had done so much to bring about.

Back in South Africa, there were still plenty of Afrikaners who would not have shared a teacup, let alone a champagne glass, with the ANC. Most kept their racism to themselves; it was just a fact of rural life, like drought and low corn prices. But a few groups chose to trumpet their prejudice, like the *Afrikaner Weerstandsbeweging* (AWB), the Afrikaner Resistance Movement, which would bluster and bomb its way through the next ten years on the lunatic right of the National Party.

At about the time that Pieter de Lange and Thabo Mbeki were meeting in New York, I attended the launch of the AWB, on a bright cold winter's day at the Voortrekker shrine in Pretoria. I reached a judgment there which I would not revise throughout the years that followed: that despite their proto-Nazi regalia and paramilitary bravado, these were not fighting men. They played at being fierce, while their wives and mothers donned pioneer costumes to serve the pastries of Afrikanerdom, *melktert* and *koeksisters.* There was a certain indisputable logic to their position that, as Conservative Party leader Andries Treurnicht said that day, "when you divide power, you lose it." I just thought they would lose it, in the end, without too much of a battle.

Lives were lost while they played at revolution. One extreme right Afrikaner, member of a splinter group separate from the AWB, murdered seven blacks in a shooting spree in Pretoria's central square. He even staged a practice run of the execution, killing two blacks in a squatter camp several days before. Right-wing farmers carried on the brutal traditions of centuries with their black laborers. Afrikaner town councils, especially in small towns, kept blacks out of municipal swimming pools and libraries. Afrikaner judges continued to hand down absurdly light sentences for white crimes against Africans. But if these Afrikaners were not yet bent on reconciliation, neither were they a real threat to peace. And they were not the only ones who preferred fighting to talking.

While Mbeki's pipe was working overtime at Mells, the insurrectionist wing of the ANC was also plotting revolution. Just as Mbeki and Esterhuyse were settling down to their first Mells supper, Mac Maharaj was walking across the border from Swaziland disguised as an African peasant, come to overthrow the government at last.

Those who knew Maharaj—a wiry, hyperactive, brilliant Indian Marxist—knew that he thrived on adventure and loved nothing better than the paraphernalia of conspiracy: secret codes, invisible ink, concealed microphones, elaborate disguises. So they would not have been surprised at his plan to engage in a bit of revolutionary adventurism. But only the most senior ANC leaders actually knew of his mission, code-named "Operation Vula"; even MK commander Joe Modise did not. Officially, Maharaj had gone to Moscow for treatment of a kidney complaint caused by prison torture; those of us who were his neighbors in Lusaka shook our heads at the evils of a system that could inflict such grievous injury.

In fact, Maharaj had been infiltrated into South Africa to have a last crack at revolution. As he tells it, ANC leader Oliver Tambo authorized his mission in 1986—as soon as it became clear that negotiations with Pretoria were on the horizon.

Maharaj was sent to strengthen the ANC's weakest link, the internal underground. His tale of secret entry to South Africa demonstrates the magnitude of the task. MK members charged with smuggling him across the border from Swaziland chose a night crossing under a full moon, a spotlit caper that South African patrols would easily have foiled. Maharaj decided instead to cross on a quiet Sunday at midday, clothed in overalls, balaclava, and the traditional stick of the African peasant. Once over the border, ANC inefficiency struck again: his reception party had gone to the wrong border, the distant one with Zimbabwe. Maharaj had to make his way to Johannesburg unassisted.

Perhaps the Vula project had the same strategic significance as Pretoria's emergency—to persuade the ANC of its own strength. Perhaps it was an insurance policy, in case negotiations failed. Maybe it was one last tilt at revolution. ANC leaders themselves still dispute Vula's meaning, an issue over which emotion clouds hindsight. No one knows what Maharaj was really up to with Vula; though he is today one of Mandela's most trusted ministers, even the wily old president would probably be pushed to explain his motives.

But one thing is clear. However successfully Thabo Mbeki was triumphing over the suspicions of his Afrikaner interlocutors, he had not yet won the battle for the soul of the ANC. The liberation camp held diplomats and strugglers, realists and romantics, hotheads and gentlemen. The fiercest battle, as always, was the battle within.

"Whenever I met with ANC leaders, the question I asked over and over was, How exactly are we going to take over?" Mohammed Valli Moosa, handsome and boyish in his new job as deputy minister of constitutional development,° was a thin, intense, and very young man when I first met him in his role as UDF spokesman in the late 1980s. By 1987, he was fed up with what he saw as the ANC's romantic approach to revolution. The Lusaka leadership carried on cheerfully plotting insurrection, but the UDF was increasingly reluctant to do the legwork.

Valli remembers a meeting between the UDF and ANC in "a nice old castle about an hour's drive from London," where the UDF proudly presented its analysis of the South African crisis to its mentors in the ANC. "We

---

° He has since become the minister.

said, we've done everything, and we can do a bit more of everything, but there is a stalemate," Valli Moosa recalls. "We were saying, something else now needs to happen. The Boers are killing us, and it's not conceivable that we are going to be able to overrun Pretoria."

Valli spoke passionately for his generation of activists, almost all of whom (including him) had been detained, harassed, and threatened by police. They were tired of fighting. *Umkhonto we Sizwe* could do little to prosecute the revolution, with its neighboring bases closed by detente and its supplies from the Soviet Union curtailed. They were not yet advocating negotiation; but they had recognized—far earlier than most exiled leaders— the existence of the essential precondition for talks, stalemate.

"We were *attacked* by the leadership for even suggesting that there could be a stalemate," Valli recalls. "We were given a lecture on insurrection and sent back to prepare for it. And of course, that's what we did." For, ultimately, no upstart UDF leader would dare to question Lusaka wisdom. The hard men of MK were their legendary heroes, Valli recalls, pulling out an album of snapshots of himself and other UDF figures dressed in combat uniform at an MK base in Tanzania. "None of us even knew how to shoot a gun!" He laughs. In the end, the UDF always deferred to those who did.

Such debates continued. Though the ANC had long stressed its readiness to negotiate, this was largely a rhetorical position; many thought, privately, that they would never be forced to face the reality of talks. Virtually until the final deal was done in 1993, deep divisions remained between the diplomats and the strugglers in the ANC. The latter always suspected a trick, doubting the bona fides of the South African side, and fearing an enemy whose shrewdness they always overestimated.

In the end, Mbeki could prove that he had read the balance of forces correctly way back in 1985, when he opted for talks. Yet he was among a lonely minority then: Oliver Tambo backed him, but most other ANC leaders were highly suspicious. Joe Slovo continued to argue for the outright seizure of power; Maharaj preferred to fight his way to the table; Chris Hani still thought killing whites was the answer. Persistent rumors that Mbeki was an enemy agent capture the intensity of suspicion against him.

None then knew that the greatest seduction of all was about to take place, not in posh New York hotels and English stately homes, but behind bars. Nelson Mandela had spent twenty years studying the psychology of capitulation. Now he was ready to put those lessons into practice.

"MR. MANDELA, *aren't you going to eat your chocolate mousse?*"

I am a nervous hostess at the best of times, but having Nelson Mandela to lunch had just about done me in. Now he wasn't eating his dessert and I was debating whether to order the hovering waiter to take it away.

"My dear," he said, with all due gravity, "I may be over seventy years old. But if a pretty woman walks by, I don't want to be out of the running." I could think of no suitable reply, except to put down my own spoon and regret that Nelson Mandela was not around more often to put me off my pudding.

Mandela likes women—young women, middle-aged women, blond women, African women, his tastes are Catholic in this regard. He is an incorrigible flirt, and a charmer. I was in a position to experience this firsthand, because as chairman of the local foreign correspondents' association, I was the natural choice to sit next to him when we invited him to lunch.

Mandela is one of nature's great seduction artists, and no target is too humble for his notice. He does not have to work at it; charm is his natural condition. I have watched him in the act of conquest hundreds, maybe thousands of times, but I still could not tell you exactly how he does it. It starts with the smile—that is the threshold. The eyes squint with the sheer energy of his delight; the fat cheeks beam and the white teeth shine with it. Who could resist such an opener?

The smile is a powerful invitation to trust, but the eyes are another. It is not just that the gaze holds no bitterness; it betrays not the slightest suspicion of harm. It is as though he is refusing to jump to conclusions, giving everyone—P. W. Botha, his captors, cynical journalists—a chance to show their best side. It is a curiously powerful form of flattery.

This is not mere benevolence but a kind of compulsion. Man-

dela is driven to reconcile, driven to bridge the racial gap, because nothing else can make sense of the life he gave up in the name of fighting separation. For him, lunch with the foreign correspondents is just another of life's many opportunities for bridge building. For me, it was my own priceless episode of the great seduction.

5

Secret Mission

IF NELSON MANDELA were a saint, his behavior would be easier to understand. Then, one would expect him to turn the other cheek, to forgive his captors and heal his tormentors. Saints do such things because God inspires them to do so. One understands their motivation.

Mandela is not a man of God; he is a politician. He is a schemer, a conjuror, a manipulator of men—and that made him a great statesman. No saint could have done as much to produce South Africa's miracle. For Mandela did not so much forgive his captors as try to understand them. He spent a lifetime studying their mental pathology, and twenty-seven years in prison devising ways to cure it. He condemned their policy without condemning them as human beings, and set them free from the bondage of a fear they could not conquer on their own.

Perhaps his greatest gift was to believe that that was even possible: to remain convinced, despite a lifetime's evidence to the contrary, that behind apartheid's mask of brutality lurked an essential humanity. He gambled everything on that belief, on his unshakable conviction that the Afrikaner would, eventually, listen to reason, and that when he did, he would prove as loyal to a new non-racial South Africa as to its apartheid predecessor.

Mandela launched his secret mission to understand the Afrikaner with the human material he had most immediately to hand, however unlikely. As a young lawyer, he sought to engage the government officials who administered the apartheid pass laws, playing on their basic humanity to gain clemency for his clients. Later, as a prisoner, he aimed to convert the only audience available to him—the prison warders who kept him behind bars.

Mandela's mission of reconciliation began long before his exiled colleagues launched their seduction campaign overseas. Substantially, it began in 1963, when he first became Prisoner 466/64, at the maximum-security prison on Robben Island.

I have long sought the roots of Mandela's extraordinary empathy with Afrikaners—believing that it explained South Africa's peace—and he has always directed my gaze to the same spot, Robben Island. Seated beneath a tree in the sunny winter garden of his stately presidential home, Mahlamba Ndlopfu, in July 1995, he reflected on his lifelong vocation in terms both practical and humane: "One had to understand the Afrikaners because they ruled this country, and the harsh policies of apartheid were evolved by them."

Mandela speaks, as always, with painful deliberation, at a fraction of the pace of normal speech, and in a tone that seldom gives anything away. His speech is like his personality, rigidly disciplined; almost nothing (except the deaths of blacks in political violence) can rouse it and him to passion.

"If one wanted to change the policy," he continues, speaking each word as though it had equal length and value, though punctuating important phrases by inclining the whole of his stiff torso, "you had to use the most effective methods of doing so. One of them of course was to rely on ourselves as blacks . . . that was the top priority," he says with a staccato burst for emphasis. "But to attain this transformation with less conflict, bloodshed, and bitterness, we had to try to interact with the Afrikaners. The Afrikaners were between the oppressed people and liberation, and we had therefore to remove them . . . and one of our tactics—apart from using our strength— was to talk to them."

Mandela began to talk to his enemies at the earliest possible opportunity, when he came to Johannesburg from the Transkei homeland of his birth, to train as a lawyer. "I joined a firm where I interacted with Afrikaners, articled clerks, typists, and some of them were very kind to me in those days when I was in difficulties."

Mandela shakes his head in wonder at the cherished small kindnesses of half a century ago, unlikely proof of the existence—in the hostile world of 1940s Johannesburg—of a common humanity denied by racism. As he would do all his life, he learned then to separate people from policy. And he gave everyone—the officials who administered apartheid, the judges who imposed its penalties, and the politicians who created it—the chance to prove themselves.

"When I became an attorney, many of them assisted me, especially when it came to cases like the pass laws . . . which could actually destroy the life of an African." Mandela expounds at length on the indignities done to blacks in the early days of apartheid, his outrage unabated by the decades. But indignation, however righteous, would do little for his clients in the short run. So this angry young man, who started the first black African law firm in South African history, learned to master his passion, and play the system to win. "I would go to a pass officer and say to him, 'Look at the human tragedy that has been caused by this system. I can't go to court because the law is clear, I'll lose. Can you, on humanitarian grounds, with-draw this?' And in most cases, they responded positively. That made an impression."

These were the people who kept apartheid ticking over, without whose acquiescence it could not have endured. Mandela might simply have hated them; instead, he hated their policy, and gave them the space to operate humanely within it. As a strategy, it was both generous and inspired.

But his true journey to the center of the Afrikaner mind began only later, after he had become the Afrikaans nation's most celebrated prisoner. He developed personal relationships with his jailors that would endure into the new South Africa—three of his former warders were even honored guests at his inauguration—relationships which allowed him both to turn the tables on his captors and to fight the spiritual oppression of captivity itself.

His memoirs bear eloquent testimony to these prison relationships:

I always knew that deep down in every human heart, there was mercy and generosity. No one is born hating another person because of the colour of his skin . . . people must learn to hate, and if they can learn to hate, they can be taught to love. . . .

Even in the grimmest times in prison, when my comrades and I were pushed to our limits, I would see a glimmer of humanity in one of the guards, perhaps just for a second, but it was enough to reassure me and keep me going. Man's goodness is a flame that can be hidden but never extinguished.

Mandela told me that day in the Mahlamba Ndlopfu garden that the simple kindnesses of warders helped inspire his mission of reconciliation. "Behind high prison walls you had warders who appreciated that we were human beings. And so we learned a vital lesson, that even among the most conserva-tive sections of the South African community, you had people who thought like human beings." That was where the negotiated revolution truly began: at the lowest level, where poorly educated warders, at the bottom rung of the Afrikaans hierarchy, met those whom Afrikanerdom held as captive animals. At that level, Mandela towered. Walter Sisulu, perhaps his oldest friend and the man who shared his prison for twenty-six years, watched these relationships develop.

"They began to like the man firstly because he has got that which they like, authority," Sisulu points out. "He was brought up in royalty, and Afrikaners like that type of thing, so although they thought he was a Commu-nist, and Communists are people you worry about, they began to look at the man differently. He was a man they could respect."

Mandela soon learned to exploit that advantage. He trained himself to stand his ground when dealing with Afrikaners; eventually, he knew, they would bow before a show of strength. Again and again, he provoked them to blink first. It was one of his greatest skills.

The warders, too, were learning, for Mandela and the other political prisoners were a revelation to them. Many of the prisoners had university degrees, or pursued correspondence courses by mail, studying in their cells for hours after their backbreaking work at the Island quarry had ended. They were sophisticated men, not the childlike, dependent figures that apartheid had taught the warders to expect.

Aubrey du Toit became a Robben Island warder in 1976, at the age of nineteen. By the time he left, in 1992, he described the political prisoners as "friends." "When I grew up I had no contact whatsoever with black people. It was a shock to meet these people and see that they were intelligent human beings," he reminisced in 1994, shortly before Mandela led a sentimental journey of former prisoners to the now-deserted Island. "Mr. Mandela was a prisoner but also a leader, anybody could see that . . . the moment he walked into a room, his manner, his way of speaking, his dress, you knew he was a leader."

Among leaders, they come no stronger than Nelson Mandela. Despite the stiffness in his gait, and his obvious difficulty in negotiating stairs, the septuagenarian president still dwarfs all interlocutors. Partly, this dominance is physical, the effect, simply, of a tall man who stands up very straight. But it is more than that. Mandela's presence is pure power. Everyone who meets him chooses a different adjective to capture that essence—regal, patriarchal, chieftainly—but they all recognize it immediately. Mandela was born to rule. He thinks so, and after a few moments, so do you.

That was the key to Mandela's popularity among the warders, and to his eventual success in wooing Afrikaans society. For Afrikaners recognize the same quasi-tribal patterns of authority that operate in the traditional black society where Mandela was raised; they have a strong herd mentality and know how to take orders; and they are loyal servants of the prevailing political system—whatever it happens to be. As Walter Sisulu once told me, "I always felt that, in the end, Afrikaners would be part of us." Mandela thought so too.

So, once Afrikaners had accepted that loyalty to apartheid was an absurdity, it was a small step to transferring their allegiance to the new multiracial order. Mandela captured their loyalty not only by stressing a common humanity but also by emphasizing the common basis of African and Afrikaner nationalism. Though he could never condone its racist policies, Mandela implicitly acknowledged the legitimacy of Afrikaner nationalism, and sought not so much to defeat it as to enlist it for his own purposes.

From the earliest days of his faltering dialogue with officialdom, Mandela ceaselessly played the Afrikaner nationalist card. He met his first government minister in 1976, Jimmy Kruger, minister of justice, police, and prisons. Kruger achieved international infamy a year later when police beat black-consciousness leader Steve Biko to death in their custody. Upon hearing the news, he commented, "It leaves me cold."

Mac Maharaj, then one of Mandela's closest Robben Island confidants, recalls that Kruger shocked the inmates by showing up one day without warning, when the prisoners had just returned from work. "And he comes to us, and he says, 'So you people want to take over the government. Now, I say to you, over my dead body.' And we are looking at this chap, who is he? And then, that's Jimmy Kruger."

Mandela suggested the minister sit down to talk. He treated him to a history of African nationalism—about which Kruger was woefully ignorant, Mandela recalls. The prisoner outlined the whole sad record of the ANC's efforts to start a dialogue with government, including his letter to Verwoerd in 1961 requesting a constitutional convention. He pointed out that he had written to Kruger himself in 1969, but had had no reply.

Then Mandela shifted tack. He made an argument for the release of political prisoners based on an audacious precedent from Afrikaner history. He used the example of two of Afrikanerdom's most celebrated political prisoners, Robey Leibbrandt, a Nazi sympathizer who led Afrikaner resistance to South Africa's pro-British stand in World War II; and General Christiaan de Wet, the Boer War leader who led a bloody rebellion against South African involvement in World War I. Both were sentenced to life imprisonment, but soon pardoned. Mandela demanded the same for black nationalists. By doing so, he was implicitly accepting the validity of the Afrikaner nationalist cause for which the two earlier prisoners had fought.

Kruger brushed aside such comparisons. He had come to offer Mandela a dramatic reduction in his sentence on condition that he retire to the Transkei black homeland where Mandela's nephew, Kaiser Matanzima, was leader. Mandela refused to accord this legitimacy to the Transkei, an apartheid creation, and nothing came of the meeting. But as Mandela notes in his autobiography, "the mere fact that they were talking rather than attacking could be seen as a prelude to genuine negotiations."

"Though I acted as though this was the most normal thing in the world, I was amazed. . . ."

Nelson Mandela is remembering the day, nearly ten years later, when the negotiated revolution was well and truly launched. In November 1985,

Justice Minister Kobie Coetsee visited the ailing Mandela, who was having prostate surgery in a Cape Town hospital. "He dropped by the hospital unannounced, as though he were visiting an old friend who was laid up for a few days. He was altogether gracious and cordial and for the most part we only made pleasantries," Mandela recorded in his memoirs.

The two men took to each other. As Coetsee told me in 1995, "He got the feeling—he has said so—and I went away too with a feeling that this could be the beginning of another chapter."

A television interviewer once asked the newly elected President Mandela who was his hero, and he said, Kobie Coetsee. Political correctness was outraged. Coetsee had been his official jailer for nearly a decade; he was a difficult man and an unpopular minister, a Nationalist who appeared to have little future in the new South Africa. But Mandela hearkened back to that unlikely hospital meeting, and to the beginning of substantive negotiations some nine months later. "In those days," when township violence and government repression were at their height, "hardly any leader of the National Party was prepared to associate himself with a move which would entail the government sitting down with the ANC—a terrorist organization—to discuss any question, including that of peace.

"The honourable President of the Senate"—Mandela named Coetsee to that post in gratitude—"had the courage, the honesty, and the vision to realise that this was the only solution." Coetsee was the one who finally heard Mandela's plea for peace.

The two men had been brought together by the most unlikely of intermediaries—Mandela's firebrand wife, Winnie. Brash and beautiful, Winnie was the inspirational figurehead of the ANC in the 1980s, as she repeatedly defied government banning orders, and banishment to a remote town in the rural Orange Free State, to emerge as a populist leader. The quality of her leadership was, to say the least, controversial. In 1986, she exhorted township youth to burn opponents alive, with her celebrated vow that the ANC would liberate South Africa "with our boxes of matches and our necklaces"; and in 1988, she was involved in the kidnapping of several young boys who were later severely assaulted at her Soweto home. (She was convicted of kidnapping and as an accessory to that assault in 1991. After a 1993 appeal, her assault conviction was set aside. The kidnapping conviction was upheld, but the five-year sentence was reduced to a fine.)

In November 1985, Winnie Mandela was meekly sitting in her economy-class seat on a flight to Cape Town to visit her ailing husband when Justice Minister Coetsee stopped by to assure her of the government's best wishes for his speedy recovery. A few minutes later, Mrs. Mandela visited the minister in his business-class seat and struck up a conversation that lasted for most of the two-hour flight. By the end of it, Coetsee had decided on his momentous hospital visit.

By that time, Coetsee says, he had been mulling over the problem of Prisoner 466/64 already for years. He once told me how it all began, and it is a story that is unlikely enough to be entirely plausible. It started when Coetsee took over the prisons portfolio in 1981. "We were inundated with court cases initiated by people from the Island as to their rights. Many of those cases were lost, and as a lawyer, I hated the idea of losing any case. I immediately started to work on it, and in that way I became exposed to the individual Nelson Mandela. And I became determined to do something about the situation.

"We made a study of all the little points that were troubling them, and we attended to them, and after that there were no further court cases. They got complete freedom to study, freedom of movement on the Island, they had sport, tennis, soccer, access to all the newspapers, television, study facilities—each one had his own desk and own little cubicle—and we increased their visits many-fold."

So, measures like allowing access to newspapers—which Mandela has always said had a profound impact on his decision to start negotiations—were taken, not for any grand strategic reasons, but to remove an immediate irritant: a flood of court cases. Other regimes, which felt less need to provide legal justification for their oppression, might simply have ignored such challenges. Not the National Party; it liked to think it lived by the law.

Then Coetsee says he started to work on a policy for releasing political prisoners, a far more difficult problem. And here again, the story is strangely plausible. P. W. Botha instructed Coetsee to work on it, not so much to deal with the problem of Mandela but because of a case much closer to his heart, the imprisonment of the dissident Afrikaans poet Breyten Breytenbach, an ANC supporter. Breytenbach's family were scions of the Cape National Party, which Botha led; the prisoner's brother was a senior military officer. Botha believed that Breyten, jailed in 1975 for nine years, was an errant idealist who should be given another chance, "so he said to me, work on that."

From this subjective impulse of P. W. Botha's grew the possibility of parole for political prisoners, who had previously been forced to serve out full sentences. This meant that the release of such prisoners, including Mandela, was now firmly on the agenda. But politics did not provide the first impetus to change. It took Botha's concern for a fellow Afrikaner to do that.

Coetsee began to prepare for the eventual release of Mandela. By this time, Mandela's imprisonment had become a major cause célèbre overseas.

By sheer force of personality, he had dominated the political scene on Robben Island, and though he did not enter prison as the acknowledged head of the ANC, he rapidly assumed that position in the minds of the movement's members. The natural mystique of the prisoner, coupled with the high-profile activities of his beautiful wife, made him the posterboy of the international anti-apartheid opposition. Botha knew he could never satisfy the West until he had Nelson Mandela out of jail.

So Mandela and three other ANC leaders were moved from what Coetsee calls the "Robben Island campus" to Pollsmoor Prison on the nearby mainland. The government felt it would be easier to talk to Mandela there rather than in a place where virtually every political prisoner in South Africa could listen in. Meanwhile, Botha was working hard to come up with a release offer that Mandela would accept. Unfortunately, he saw the problem in one-dimensional terms. Says Coetsee, "For Mr. P. W. Botha, [Mandela's] release was solving the problem of him being in jail. As for his future constitutional role, I never really came across any clear thinking of Mr. P. W. Botha on this score."

Botha always saw Mandela as part of South Africa's problem—not as part of a solution. He wanted the ANC leader out of jail because imprisoning him was more trouble than it was worth, not because he intended to hand over power to him. Botha still believed that the silent majority of blacks supported him, not Mandela. He wanted to pursue his strategy of co-opting moderate blacks into a government of limited power sharing; but the figure of Mandela in prison cast a long shadow over these efforts.

Botha made six release offers after that delivered by Jimmy Kruger in 1976, all on terms that would have involved Mandela giving up the liberation struggle. They were refused. Then, in January 1985, after a visit to West Germany where he met and discussed the issue with the Bavarian leader Franz Josef Strauss, Botha made a new offer: Mandela would be released if he unconditionally rejected violence.

The old president was delighted at the new formula; this, he thought, was an offer Mandela could not refuse. The ANC leader need only renounce violence—surely not an unreasonable demand—and he would be freed. If he refused, he would have no one but himself to blame. Botha was sure foreign governments would also see it this way.

All Botha achieved was to give Mandela a veto over his own release. In effect, he handed over control of the biggest political problem facing his government to the enemy. Mandela exploited this position: His daughter Zindzi delivered a damning rejection of the offer at a rally that gained wide coverage overseas. And for the first time in over twenty years, Mandela's people heard the words of their leader: " . . . what freedom am I being

offered while the organisation of the people remains banned? . . . what freedom am I being offered when I must ask for permission to live in an urban
area? . . . what freedom am I being offered when my very South African
citizenship is not respected? Only free men can negotiate. Prisoners cannot
enter into contracts. . . ."

Early in 1986, Mandela was installed in a three-room prison apartment
at Pollsmoor, isolated from his colleagues three floors above. As he explains
in his memoirs, he had time to take stock.

It would be too strong to call it a revelation, but over the next few days and weeks I
came to (see) my new circumstances not as a liability but an opportunity. My solitude
gave me a certain liberty, and I resolved to use it to do something I had been
pondering for a long while: begin discussions with the government. . . . We had been
fighting against white minority rule for three-quarters of a century. We had been
engaged in armed struggle for more than two decades. Many people on both sides
had already died. The enemy was strong and resolute. Yet even with all their bombers and tanks, they must have sensed they were on the wrong side of history.
It was clear to me that a military victory was a distant if not impossible dream.
It simply did not make sense for both sides to lose thousands if not millions of lives
in a conflict that was unneccessary. It was time to talk.

Divisions within the ruling group helped precipitate this judgment, Mandela
explained later in the Mahlamba Ndlopfu garden. "I became aware that
there was a furious argument amongst them," he told me. "Some said let us
tighten the screws of oppression and save South Africa from a Communist
onslaught; others said that this is not a Communist onslaught, this is a demand by people who want human dignity and who want to live in safety and
security. But of course they had said on numerous occasions, we will never
talk to terrorists, and one therefore had to consider the necessity of helping
them to retreat without losing face."

Mandela knew that the vast majority of ANC members, and even most
of the leadership, would not understand this. They saw no need to offer the
Boers an honorable retreat. He told no one: not his colleagues upstairs nor
those in Lusaka (with whom he was able to communicate by clandestine
methods). For though he pays passionate lip service to democracy—and
always tries to ensure the broadest possible support for all he does—he is by
nature an autocrat. This was one case where autocracy was the best policy.

Mandela did not let his colleagues know that he was talking to the
enemy until nearly two years later. By then, although no one could have
known it at the time, the outlines of the future deal were already becoming
clear.

It took the intervention of outsiders—something resisted at the time by
both the exiled ANC and the government—to clarify those outlines. For

after their promising start in late 1985, several months passed before Coetsee and Mandela met again. The prisoner wrote twice to the minister, proposing "talks about talks," but he received no reply. Then, in March 1986, Mandela again found his chance to be heard.

The British Commonwealth sent him some visitors—the rather pompously named "Eminent Persons Group" (EPG), co-chaired by former Australian Prime Minister Malcolm Fraser and former Nigerian military ruler General Olusegun Obasanjo. It was charged with making peace in Southern Africa. The group introduced into the public domain for the first time the idea of a negotiated settlement in South Africa—a notion that ranked alongside peace in Northern Ireland and a settlement in the Middle East as the impossible dreams of contemporary politics.

Yet the group found a fervent desire, across the political spectrum, for such a settlement. "No serious person we met was interested in a fight to the finish," it reported. So the group set out to construct a framework for peace. Top of its agenda was a meeting with the celebrated prisoner Mandela, who had seen only a handful of outsiders during the preceding twenty-three years.

Mandela was eager to exploit this opportunity to put the ANC's case, but Pretoria was equally keen on the meeting. Kobie Coetsee recalls that the government saw in it an opportunity to score a public relations coup. "It was almost heartwarming, the way [prison officials] went about preparing Mr. Mandela for that meeting, pinstripe suit, shoes perfect, the setting Pollsmoor guesthouse, him in a large chair. . . . They [the eminent persons] were completely taken aback. I could see the disbelief on their faces. And for me it was a moment of glory. I felt that I had trumped them; they expected this emaciated person, and there he was completely in control."

Coetsee reflects the sincere if naive belief which inspired Pretoria to allow the EPG group to visit South Africa in the first place: that it could win the international community over to the cause of gradualist reform. The government was keen to show the benevolent face of the evil empire—and they wanted Mandela to help them do so.

Mandela, for different reasons, also remembers the visit as a watershed. He recalls, with something akin to pride, the preparations for it, noting in his memoirs that the suit "fitted me like a glove," and that the prison commander complimented him on it, saying he looked "like a prime minister and not a prisoner."

Mandela broke the ice by asking EPG member Lord Barber, who had escaped from a Russian prisoner-of-war camp in World War II, for tips on how it was done. He discussed cricket with the Australian member, Malcolm Fraser. He was the perfect host.

Moni Malhoutra, an aide to the group, recalls that one of the first things Mandela said was that "there is nothing like a long spell in prison to focus your mind, and to bring you to a more sober appreciation of the realities of your society." The group found in him "palpable goodwill" toward other races, and a powerful desire for racial reconciliation. They were surprised to find that Mandela "recognised the fears of many white people . . . [and] emphasised the importance of minority groups being given a real sense of security." It was the first public indication of his flexibility on that most crucial of issues, minority rights.

Mandela's position on violence was also reconciliatory—"He stressed that violence could never be an ultimate solution and that the nature of human relationships required negotiation." Mandela agreed immediately when the group proposed to him their draft terms for negotiation: The government must release political prisoners, unban the ANC, and halt its violent campaign against blacks. In exchange, the ANC must temporarily suspend (not renounce) violence, and start talking.

Mandela's acceptance of the proposed suspension was the most positive development in South African politics in many years. But Coetsee was not present to hear him do so. For he chose to leave after introducing the prisoner to the eminent persons. Coetsee recalls a situation that must have seemed absurd to the foreign visitors. "Mr. Mandela said to me, 'Please stay,' but I said, 'No, this is your occasion,' and he said, 'Please, I insist,' and I said, 'I really think this is your day.'" But a government official, Jan Heunis, son of the constitutional development minister, remained for the entire session. The moderate wing within the cabinet must have found his report encouraging.

The EPG proved to be an idea before its time, however. On the very morning that the group was due to hold a crucial meeting with a special cabinet constitutional committee, the South African Air Force launched predawn bombing raids on supposed ANC bases in neighboring Zambia, Zimbabwe, and Botswana. That was the bombing raid I had discussed with P. W. Botha at the Wilderness. Though a handful of people were killed, the biggest casualty was Botha's reputation.

No one has satisfactorily explained to me why Botha chose to blast his way to international opprobrium—least of all the former president himself. When I asked him whether his timing had not been unfortunate, he replied that if President Ronald Reagan could bomb Libya, he could bomb Zambia.

Chester Crocker, then U.S. Assistant Secretary of State for Africa, offers a more plausible explanation: Botha was fed up with foreigners telling him what to do, without ever offering any credit for positive action. Botha accused foreigners of treating South Africa like a moral playground, a place where they could fight out their own domestic racial battles without worrying about the damage. His (sometimes justified) persecution complex overcame all sense of diplomacy, and he paid a high price for his obstinacy. Moderates in cabinet—Coetsee, Pik Botha, Chris Heunis, Barend du Plessis—were furious. They were not informed of the raids, which were decided upon by the president and his security chiefs without even consulting the State Security Council. Divisions within government deepened.

But far more damaging was the impact on international public opinion. The EPG mission was Botha's last chance to prove his bona fides before the Commonwealth imposed new sanctions against South Africa. When it failed, Margaret Thatcher—the sole opponent of sanctions in the Commonwealth—could no longer hold back the tide. Nor could Ronald Reagan. The Comprehensive Anti-Apartheid Act, with its package of sanctions, was imposed later that year.

All those who hoped for a peaceful settlement despaired at the bombings. Mandela recorded his disappointment: "I felt my efforts to move negotiations forward had stalled." But, ironically, his colleagues in Lusaka and in the UDF displayed something far closer to relief. Botha's bombs had got them out of a tight diplomatic corner. Pretoria was not the only party reluctant to negotiate. The ANC in exile, and the UDF, were also less than keen—and certainly less keen than Mandela. Their judgment was that the balance of forces had tipped decisively in their favor as the township revolt gathered pace; they were not ready for compromise. General Obasanjo, the straight-talking co-chairman of the EPG, tried to disabuse them of this notion. Aides recall that he told the exiled leadership, "You people are out of your minds if you think you can defeat the government." Oliver Tambo was outraged.

Still, the ANC was realistic enough to realize that the "negotiating concept" proposed by the EPG would not die a quiet death. (Indeed, four years later it would emerge unscathed, to provide an exact blueprint for F. W. de Klerk.) So, after the EPG debacle, the ANC set to work on a strategy for negotiation. Soon, the first real signs of moderation could be detected from the exiled leadership. As we sat one night in my Lusaka cottage, Joe Slovo told me privately that the ANC might be willing to accept interim power sharing with whites "as a historical necessity."

"As long as the majority had real power, we might be prepared to assuage the fears of whites in exchange for a settlement which would make it possible to avoid ten more years of violence," he asserted. That might sound like the kind of thing Nelson Mandela would say—but it was far from popular in Lusaka. It began to look as though the EPG mission might prove a milestone after all. Henceforth, negotiation was firmly and publicly on everyone's agenda.

That was scarcely apparent from Pretoria's behavior. Only three weeks after the EPG bombings, Botha made what appeared a decisive retreat into repression, imposing effective martial law with the June 1986 state of emergency. But inside the laager, something very different was going on.

"Bring him round," Kobie Coetsee told the prison officials in June 1986, and within minutes, uniformed Prisoner 466/64 settled into an easy chair at the minister's Cape Dutch mansion, Savernake. The imposition of the new emergency had prompted Mandela to write again proposing talks with the government—and this time, the response was immediate.

The two men broke the ice by talking Afrikaner history. Then negotiations began in earnest. Coetsee went straight to the heart of the matters dividing the two sides: Under what circumstances would the ANC suspend the armed struggle? Did Mandela speak for the movement as a whole? Did he envisage constitutional guarantees for minorities? It was the first time they had discussed issues of substance. The talks were kept secret, even from the cabinet; only P. W. Botha knew they were going on.

Mandela asked for a meeting with Botha, and Coetsee noted his request. Soon Mandela was back in prison, free to ponder the meaning of it all. "I was greatly encouraged," he wrote in his autobiography. "I sensed the government was anxious to overcome the impasse in the country, that they were now convinced they had to depart from their old positions. In ghostly outline, I saw the beginnings of a compromise."

But once again, his hopes were dashed. Mandela heard nothing further from the minister. Coetsee recalls that the township revolt made further progress impossible. Botha was obsessed by the violence, telling Coetsee repeatedly that he must impress on Mandela the need to stop the upheaval. But it did not stop, and Botha refused to move forward.

Meanwhile, Coetsee was pursuing his own secret plan to prepare Mandela for release. He was giving the prisoner a crash course in freedom. On Christmas Eve, 1986, Lieutenant Colonel Gawie Marx, deputy commissioner of Pollsmoor, took the ANC leader for a drive around Cape Town. It was Mandela's first outing in twenty-two years. Suddenly, the prisoner found himself with rather more freedom than he had bargained for. Colonel Marx stopped to buy a soft drink, leaving Mandela in the car—alone.

As the seconds ticked away, I became more and more agitated . . . I had a vision of opening the door, jumping out, and then running and running until I was out of sight. . . . I was extremely tense and began to perspire. Where was the colonel? But then I took control of myself; such an action would be unwise and irresponsible, not to mention dangerous. . . .

When Marx emerged carrying two cans of Coke, Mandela was delighted.

The tourist expeditions continued, to the Cape Peninsula's perfect beaches and its stunning mountains; to cafés for tea; to the apartment of one of the warders, where Mandela met his wife and children (he still sends them Christmas cards). And through it all no one recognized him. Though his name was by then famous throughout the world, no picture of him had been published for a quarter of a century.

If anyone had told me then that Nelson Mandela was touring Cape beauty spots with a prison official, I would have thought him mad. Mandela's cozy chats at Savernake, and his jaunts around the Cape Peninsula, were—and would remain—the best-kept secrets in South African history. The cabinet would have been equally incredulous; the outside world would never have dreamed it; and the UDF would decidedly have disapproved.

Nobody—with the possible exception of P. W. Botha—had a full picture of the wide range of contacts already established between African and Afrikaner. For Botha kept each initiative in its own sealed envelope. Chris Heunis was allowed to meet the internal anti-apartheid movement, but never Mandela; Coetsee ran what he called "the Mandela initiative" in almost total secrecy; and the NIS was pursuing its own clandestine agenda throughout.

Within the ANC, information was equally sketchy. Mandela kept his Lusaka colleagues in the dark about everything but the simple fact that he had met the government (he gave no details of the hundreds of hours of talks which took place); and he had to ask Coetsee for details of Mbeki's 1986 meeting with Pieter de Lange. Lusaka did not provide them.

The outside world saw only a state dedicated to ever more brutal repression, and a black community riven by internal violence. Government seemed to have lost all restraint when dealing with the opposition: death squads like Dirk Coetzee's assassinated a number of high-profile activists; others simply disappeared. No one knew who had killed them, or why. But the state had no patent on brutal violence. Hundreds died by Winnie Mandela's favorite method, the necklace killing, carried out by ANC supporters. And in Natal Province, the ANC and Inkatha, the traditionalist Zulu political organization headed by Chief Mangosuthu Buthelezi, were virtually at war. Blacks were fighting blacks, sometimes with the active connivance or criminal neglect of the police, often for their own political, historical, and economic reasons. South Africa was a mess. Only P. W. Botha could have known how good the chances then were for peace.

He was neither able to recognize that fact nor to act on it. Instead, he pursued the narrower ambition of getting Mandela out of jail. Coetsee and Mandela met several more times, in 1987—Coetsee recalls that the focus of these talks was to find an alternative to armed struggle—and then Botha proposed that a committee of senior government officials begin intensive negotiations with the prisoner.

Mandela was happy to talk. But then he discovered the name of the man he was supposed to talk to, Niël Barnard, Botha's spymaster. It was like asking Andrei Sakharov to talk to the head of the KGB. Mandela balked. But dealing with Barnard could not be avoided. As the old president's trust in him grew, the young Barnard took on the role of chief architect of government strategy. Coetsee had broken the ice with Mandela, and they continued to talk privately, but now it was time for Botha to bring in his top strategic thinker. Mandela knew he risked alienating the cantankerous old president if he refused to see Barnard.

First, he thought he had better square matters with his prison colleagues. He told Walter Sisulu that he was thinking about starting talks with government (Mandela did not dare let on how far matters had already progressed). Sisulu objected—he did not want the ANC to make the first move. Though he understood Mandela better than anyone, he did not understand his strategy. "I was not against negotiations in principle. But I would have preferred the government taking some initiative [first]," he told me nearly a decade later. "I wanted to feel that we had created a position whereby they could not ignore us."

Mandela replied, somewhat crossly, that if Sisulu had no principled objection to negotiation, what did it matter who started them? Sisulu saw that there would be no stopping his old friend, no matter what he said, and he acknowledges now that he was wrong: "I would have hesitated, I would have wanted certain things done; I might have lost the chance." Mandela did not.

At exile headquarters, Oliver Tambo was also worried. Though Mandela had sent an emissary to Lusaka—his lawyer, George Bizos—to report on the hospital meeting with Coetsee in late 1985, Tambo had only the sketchiest idea of what was going on. Tambo, who had been Mandela's law partner before his arrest, sent Mandela a message. He had heard rumors that Mandela was talking secretly with government. "What," he asked in a somewhat peremptory tone, "were they discussing?" Mandela replied tersely that he was discussing a meeting between the ANC national executive and the government. He trusted Tambo would come round.

"The first meeting was in May 1988, in the office of the Commanding Officer, Pollsmoor. We had tea, and there were small sandwiches on these big silver platters, and it was touching to see the way the Old Man was enjoying this meager fare. I felt deep down a sense of sympathy for this man in prison overall and boots, and he was *thin*."

Niël Barnard is not, by nature, a sentimental man. His persona is pure spy. The unlined mask of his face suggests the close-cropped, alien coldness of Leonard Nimoy in *Star Trek* (without the pointed ears); no hair strays from its place, no rogue emotion crosses his visage, no humor is indulged. But Barnard's voice warms to the subject of the "Old Man," and he remembers the early days of their talks with something akin to reverence.

"And then the next meeting took place in [Commissioner of Prisons] Willemse's home, and his wife prepared the meal like she would have done for anybody else." The government team was drinking whiskey, but Mandela took only a few sips of sherry. "Why are you drinking that terrible stuff?" the notoriously abstemious Mandela asked the whiskey drinkers. "Somehow, in his mind, sherry was what one should drink."

Barnard was—and is—no liberal. In the days of the total onslaught, he was a committed supporter, and his fervent Afrikaner patriotism is never far from view. (I never spoke to him for longer than five minutes without his mentioning the Boer War.) But over the years I came to find his brand of pragmatic nationalism strangely appealing, to respect his shrewd and fiercely controlled intelligence, and to like him as a man. He has the courage of his convictions—a trait that Mandela, too, came to respect.

Barnard recalls the mutual suspicion that shrouded the start of the talks, stressing that the age gap between the young spy and the old prisoner—whose culture imposes a strict hierarchy of age—strained the atmosphere even further. Barnard knew that the political future of the Afrikaans nation he loves would depend substantially on his skill in conducting those talks. Even the impassive spy felt nervous at the thought. "It was quite a difficult task for a youngster—I was then thirty-six, thirty-seven—to go and talk to this man, knowing that it was the first step, and he would be released and would become the political leader of this country. It was a terrible responsibility."

Barnard recalls that Mandela helped him out by allowing him to speak in his native language. "I spoke almost every word to him in Afrikaans, and he spoke to me in English. The very first meeting I told him, 'I am representing a government, and I am not able to express myself in English as one is able to do in one's mother tongue,' . . . so the Old Man immediately said, 'Well, I can follow Afrikaans quite well. If I don't understand something, I will ask you.' In small talk I might speak in English, about cricket or rugby or something, but the moment we started talking business, I talked in Afrikaans."

But if Barnard displays an obvious fondness for Mandela, Fanie van der Merwe—then director general of prisons and the other strategic brain on the four-man government team—regards Mandela with something like awe. A genial man with a smooth bald pate tanned dark by the southern hemisphere sun, van der Merwe was the éminence grise behind the government team throughout the five-year negotiations. Though he spent his life as an apartheid bureaucrat, enforcing laws whose justness he never questioned, he became one of government's earliest and most passionate converts to majority rule.

Van der Merwe's story of the first meeting between the two men is a classic of the Mandela method. Always eager to establish a personal link with his interlocutor, however tenuous, Mandela claimed to remember appearing as a defense attorney opposite van der Merwe in the Johannesburg courts nearly thirty years before. Van der Merwe was not sure whether the legendary Mandela memory really stretched that far back, but he was flattered even so. He is almost speechless in Mandela's praise. "The measure of the man can never be . . . I don't think anybody would *ever* be able to record . . . I always lack words . . . to describe the measure of that man," he told me, soon after Mandela became president. Later, he found the words that had earlier escaped him; he said Mandela was his "chief." It is a word that evokes loyalty, dedication, subservience, the traditions of Africa. It is an extraordinary word for an Afrikaner to use about an African.

The vocabulary reflects the strong bonds of trust that grew between these two Afrikaners and the Old Man, Mandela, during the forty-seven long meetings they held between 1988 and 1990. That trust counted for far more than Mandela's policy position on any particular issue. Peace was made because Mandela was able to persuade such Afrikaners that he had the best of interests of the nation—their nation, his nation, the South African nation—at heart. They learned to trust him with their fate.

Mandela achieved that breakthrough partly by personality, and partly by skill. For in his case, it is sometimes hard to tell where the man ends and the politician begins. Though his interest in people is obviously genuine, it is also supremely politic. Every time he phones to convey birthday greetings to P. W. Botha or Harry Oppenheimer or other leading South Africans, he strikes a blow for reconciliation. Every time he remembers to ask after a wife or mother by name, or sends congratulations on the graduation of a child or the birth of a baby, he builds political capital for the ANC. Every time he remembers a kindness from the distant past, he builds another bridge to a non-racial future. He is not above manipulating human emotion, for a good cause.

That meant manipulating his own emotions, as much as any others.

Mandela, the supreme disciplinarian, banished bitterness because it would stand in the way of liberation. And he inspired millions of other South Africans to do the same. But it also meant manipulating men like Coetsee, van der Merwe, and Barnard. They entered the talks supremely confident about the outcome: Pretoria expected to be able to outsmart the ANC in negotiations, and intimidate them with the power of the Afrikaner state. The government's confidence was bolstered by the belief that it could split the ANC along the Nationalist/Communist divide, isolating the Communists it so feared, and striking a deal with the more moderate Nationalists.

Pretoria was even optimistic about electoral success, believing it could put together a moderate coalition with leaders like Chief Buthelezi of Inkatha, to outvote the ANC at the polls. At the very least, the National Party expected to emerge an equal partner with the ANC, after any election. Defeat, surrender, capitulation were not on the agenda.

Mandela had to manipulate this state of mind, for Botha and most of the Afrikaans hierarchy simply could not believe they were about to lose power. The habits of mind built over four long decades do not easily change. Mandela knew that nothing was to be gained by shocking them. So, the discussions were not about a handover of power; Pretoria was not offering that and Mandela was not demanding it. For endless hours, the Barnard team talked to Mandela about peace. Was he interested in a negotiated settlement? What were his views about communism? How would an ANC government treat minorities? The same old questions, the same reassuring answers—the same paralysis.

Mandela got more and more restless. He told Barnard, "You don't have the political power. I want to talk to the man with the power, and that is P. W. Botha. I want to talk to him." But many months would pass before the old president and the old prisoner would finally meet. In the meantime, Mandela's schedule was busier than ever.

For the first time, he was in close touch with both the exiled ANC and the UDF within the country. In 1988, Botha gave Mandela an open telephone line to Lusaka, to consult with Oliver Tambo. And at the end of that year, Coetsee took a dramatic step which allowed Mandela regular contact with the anti-apartheid movement inside the country—and the family that he had reluctantly sacrificed to the struggle.

Late in 1988, Coetsee told Mandela that he wanted to put him "in a situation halfway between confinement and freedom." By Christmas, Mandela was in his new home: a whitewashed warder's cottage in the grounds of Victor Verster Prison near Paarl in the Cape winelands, complete with swimming pool, three bedrooms, and his own key to the door. (Mandela liked the design of the house so well, and retains such pleasant memories of it, that he had a replica built at Qunu in the Transkei for his retirement.) Kobie Coetsee brought a case of wine as a house-warming present.

Mandela entertained regally there. Virtually anybody who was anybody in the internal anti-apartheid movement came for lunch, and a briefing, at this "office of the president-in-waiting." Mandela accused them of coming only for the excellent cooking of his chef, Warrant Officer Swart. He often tells the story of how he and Swart bickered over whether dry or sweet wines should be served with these meals.

Mandela sent the warder out to buy a cloying white, convinced his guests would prefer this. Swart, eager that his charge should not appear to be unaware of current wine fashions, returned with a dry white as well, and gave the guests a choice: they opted for dry, as he knew they would. Mandela retired defeated.

Barnard says the aim of the move was to "demystify the man and put him into a house where . . . he could live like a normal human being"—and where he could privately talk some sense into his radical young collegues from the UDF. They came in pilgrimage to their legendary leader, and he made each of them feel special. He knew the names of wives and children; had followed the career of each one with attention; he awed them with his grasp of the South African political situation. They left under the same spell of seduction as their enemies.

But the greatest seduction of all had yet to take place—the conquest of P. W. Botha. Toward that end, Mandela had spent months preparing a detailed memorandum on his view of the future, which he presented to Botha in March 1989. In it, Mandela defended without apology the ANC's policy of armed struggle and its decades-old alliance with the South African Communist Party. He offered a rather sentimental defense of Marxism, which must have reassured the UDF and worried the government, in equal measure. "We all accept the need for some form of socialism to enable our people to catch up with the advanced countries of the world and to overcome their legacy of poverty," he wrote.

The tone of the 1989 memorandum was magisterial. Democracy was the only solution to South Africa's problems; if it was good enough for whites (whose government was democratic, though it excluded blacks), then it was good enough for the whole country. There would be no peace until there was majority rule. On this, Mandela never compromised. But he recognized, crucially, that there were problems which simple democracy could not resolve. He outlined the central dilemma of South African political life in the years to come: How to reconcile the black demand for majority rule with white fears of black domination. Mandela made clear that this seemingly impossible task was his highest priority.

He outlined his terms for an honorable peace. The ANC would suspend violence, if the government would remove obstacles to negotiation, such as legalizing the ANC, releasing prisoners, ending the state of emergency, and withdrawing troops from townships. First, the two sides would talk about how to create the conditions for talks; then they would enter substantive negotiations.

This was the eventual deal in outline, though Mandela could not have known it at the time; for Botha had no intention of delivering that deal. But even he could recognize the memorandum for what it was—proof that Mandela was a man with whom he could do business, and probably the only man with whom profitable business could be done.

P. W. Botha poured the tea.

The old Boer president, symbol of all that was brutal in Afrikanerdom, steadied hands speckled and shaky with age to hold the teapot for Nelson Mandela, the Thembu herdboy who would one day be president. On July 5, 1989, the two men sat down to tea in the presidential office, the Cape Dutch mansion of Tuynhuys. There, in that eighteenth-century monument to white culture in Africa, surrounded by the antiques of Europe and the gardens of lushest Africa, the Afrikaner president poured out the tea. And Mandela was touched beyond words by the gesture. It was a simple sign of respect, which apartheid had made unthinkable.

Both men become strangely sentimental when recalling that meeting. I first heard Mandela talk it about over my chocolate mousse; I have since heard him mention the tea ritual in countless conversations. Only days after he himself moved into Botha's Tuynhuys office, Mandela raised the meeting in Parliament, to the interjected annoyance of his colleagues: "I came out feeling that I had met a creative, warm head of state who treated me with all the respect and dignity I could expect." As he notes in his memoirs, Botha was "unfailingly courteous, deferential and friendly. . . . "He completely disarmed me."

This was not at all what Mandela had expected from the "Great Crocodile." In fact, he went into the meeting prepared to walk out, if Botha proved too obstreperous. Mandela's minders were just as nervous. The commissioner of prisons took his blood type the previous day, and he had to be smuggled past Botha's own security police, to ensure that the meeting was kept top secret. The prison commander insisted on retying his tie, after Mandela—whose skills in this department had atrophied in prison—failed to produce a perfect Windsor knot. And the tall, dignified, intimidating figure of Niël Barnard stooped before Botha's door to retie the laces of Mandela's shoes, which the stiff, elderly gentleman could not easily do on his own. Everyone wanted Mandela to make a good impression on Botha.

The two old nationalists began with a civilized chat about South African history and culture, allowing Mandela to draw parallels between their rival nationalisms. The liberation struggle was, he said, not unlike the 1914 Afrikaner rebellion: the one pitted Afrikaans brother against brother; the other was a struggle "between brothers who happen to be different colours." It was a clever tack to take with Botha, whose mother was, ironically, related to the rebellion's leader, General de Wet. And though he could not condone what he saw as Mandela's revolutionary communism, Botha understood the nationalist motives for his struggle. He once told an opposition politician, *"Ek het begrip vir die ou man"* ("I can understand the old man"). Faced with the same circumstances, "I don't know what I would have done," he said. Few of his colleagues agreed. When the old president passed around a photo of the secret tea party at the next meeting of the State Security Council, the generals were furious.

Little of substance was discussed. Botha's memoirs record a general chat about politics. Mandela said he hoped the National Party would win the upcoming general election (preferring it to the ultra-right); Botha reminded him that the Afrikaner loved South Africa, which was his only home. And Mandela said he understood. Near the end of the half-hour meeting, Mandela asked for the unconditional release of all political prisoners and Botha replied that "he was afraid that he could not do that."

Mandela says he thinks South Africa reached a point of no return that day. To go further, he would need help—help which P. W. Botha would not have known how to give. For the two sides were only just ready to talk, far from ready to settle. The Afrikaner had still not faced the central truth of the negotiation decade: That he would have to give up power. Mandela had coaxed him part of the way down the path to capitulation. But it was a rough road ahead.

WE WERE SITTING ON *a high wall outside the tiny township bungalow, nursing a thermos of coffee. It was just after dawn, on a chilly Sunday morning in Soweto. The ceremonial goat was tethered nearby, ready for the slaughter. Together, we were waiting for history.*

Walter Sisulu, Nelson Mandela's seventy-seven-year-old best friend and fellow prisoner, had been delivered to the house by police van at 5.25 A.M., free after twenty-six years behind bars. We were waiting for a glimpse of the bespectacled, diminutive old gentleman who had so terrified the Afrikaner nation. Suddenly he was there, dwarfed by his corpulent wife, and ringed by his long-lost family. I craned my neck to see him, and fell unceremoniously from the wall into a rosebush at his feet. Walter Sisulu stopped, on the path to his first public appearance in twenty-six years, to express regret at my tumble. My notebook is my memorial: his momentous first words of freedom are obscured by the blood of fingertips torn by rose thorns.

I do not need my notes to remember the emotional tenor of that day, when every ANC leader apart from Mandela himself was simultaneously released from prison. The sight of seven elderly men, looking more than a little startled and bemused in the midst of so much unregimented emotion, would have been moving on its own. But their release meant so much more than an end to captivity; it was a sign from Pretoria. The ironclad cynicism which had for so long been my guide to South African politics began to slip that day. I began to dare to believe in the end of history.

6

Why the Boers Gave It All Away

F. W. DE KLERK stood up before the National Party caucus on the day he was elected leader of the party of apartheid, and said, *"Dit het tyd gekom vir 'n sprong"*—"Now is the time for a great leap forward." And the caucus replied, *"Spring, ons is langs jou!"*—"Leap, we are with you."

It was February 2, 1989, a unique moment in South Africa's history—the point at which politics and morality finally converged. Both political expediency and moral conviction demanded that de Klerk should make that leap: that he should legalize the ANC, release Nelson Mandela, and start talks to end white rule. But there is no iron law of history which says a politician will do what is either wise or moral. De Klerk could have fought on for apartheid for many years to come.

His relentless logic, the unfailing rationality of his mind, ruled out such willful blindness. For de Klerk was an aberration among ethnic nationalists, a man who put pragmatism at the service of ethnicity. Not so much a good man—though he was that, too—as a smart politician, a perfect hero for the reasonable revolution. Which is not to say that de Klerk masterminded that revolution. It was thrust upon him. South Africa's last white president did not set out to hand over power; he set out to preserve it—as much as possible, for as long as possible. He never intended to give it all away. But in the end, he did so, and happily. He traded power for influence, and gave his heart and soul to the democratic revolution which had so terrified his forebears. A man of less wit and boldness—or more fanaticism—could never have done the same.

De Klerk shut out the mad ideologies of the past and ushered in an era of heroic pragmatism. And he gave Mandela the chance to be a hero in his turn. For however shrewd or seductive, saintly or smart the old prisoner proved to be, he could not lead South Africa unless the Afrikaner willed it.

And there were objective reasons why F. W. de Klerk need not have willed it so. Though apartheid was in crisis when he became president, the state was not; the monolith was not about to crumble. And though the foreign loan embargo choked off economic growth, South Africa could have kept on getting slowly poorer for years to come.

De Klerk's options were frighteningly costly, but they were options nonetheless. He could have taken any number of small or large steps along the well-trodden path toward change. Instead, he left the road altogether, and leaped into the dark unknown, trusting only to God and his own political instincts to engineer a soft landing. He had been pushed to the edge of that cliff by the combined forces of history, economics, demography, and morality; by sanctions, and disinvestment, and sporting boycotts, and Nelson Mandela; by the process of decline which began the day apartheid was invented. But only a man who combined political skill with moral strength could have summoned the courage to leap. For only such a man would have realized that there was no alternative: that to win, the Boers had to give it all away.

F. W. de Klerk wept on the day he was inaugurated president of South Africa, but I did not. South African politics up to then—September 1989— had been a long and tedious tale of disappointments. The world expected perversity from the Boers, and they obligingly complied. Pretoria was so predictable.

All the signs were that F. W. de Klerk would be the most predictable of Afrikaner presidents. He was almost genetically predestined to defend white rule: child of an apartheid ideologue, nephew of a Nationalist prime minister, F.W. was nicknamed "Mr. National Party." Throughout his career, he had spoken with passionate and consistent commitment in defense of separate development. Never had he knowingly strayed from the party line.

My notebook captures my judgment of de Klerk on that day. I failed even to record his inaugural address, jotting down only a handful of bored phrases—"new South Africa,, blah blah blah," "free of domination, blah blah blah"—which demonstrated the depth of my skepticism. Rhetoric was valueless in the old South Africa; politicians used it only to disguise the nakedness of their will for power. Nothing F. W. de Klerk could have said would have impressed me. I did not then know about his promise to "leap." But even if I had, I would not have believed him.

When I first interviewed him in May 1989, four months before the inauguration, he said nothing to challenge my skepticism. To my eye, nothing marked him out for greatness: a small man with bad skin and worse taste in clothes, he dressed like all his political antecedents, in the shiny fabrics and dull gray tones that make Afrikaner leaders look like relics of a bygone age of fashion as well as politics. He spoke English badly, smoked heavily, and seemed, somehow, shifty. I did not warm to him as a person, or as a politician.

He drew from the same lexicon of reform as P. W. Botha. De Klerk outlined what sounded much like Botha's improved version of apartheid. The new South Africa would be governed through "power sharing" between racially defined groups; each group would be "master of its own destiny," through a form of ethnic self-determination not consistent with full democracy; he clung to a concept of "group rights," which would imply continued separation of the races—and, in many cases, continued domination by whites, who would retain what amounted to a veto. He was prepared to dilute power, share it, pass it around, and circumscribe it—but not give it away. Majority rule was out of the question.

The style was different. De Klerk managed an entire conversation without mentioning the Boer War, or indulging in physical displays of belligerence. Unlike P. W. Botha, his mother was never interned in a concentration camp, or threatened by a British soldier. That, in itself, was a major departure from past form. But I found the substance depressingly familiar.

Such cynicism was justified in part by the political track record of F. W. de Klerk, minister. For the man who sat in the cabinet of P. W. Botha was no closet liberal. In fact, he did such a convincing imitation of extreme conservatism that only a clairvoyant could have foreseen that he would ever act otherwise. But hindsight is clairvoyance after the fact, and with its assistance one can follow a single unbroken thread through the political metamorphosis of F. W. de Klerk, conservative revolutionary.

It is true—as P. W. Botha complained when I visited him at the Wilderness—that de Klerk threw up constant obstacles to reform within the Botha cabinet. In one of the most ironic such incidents, de Klerk objected strenuously when Foreign Minister Pik Botha suggested in 1986 that South Africa could one day have a black president. De Klerk insisted the foreign minister retract his statement. P. W. Botha says the future president was far more alarmed at the suggestion than he was himself.

De Klerk argued against the president's piecemeal reforms, within the special cabinet committee charged with constitutional development. At one of the committee's most important meetings, in January 1986, he objected to Constitutional Development Minister Chris Heunis's plan to bring blacks into the executive and the national legislature. Under the plan, he said, blacks would totally dominate Parliament. When Heunis noted that the position of president in a full democracy "could hardly be reserved for whites," de Klerk again objected, saying he favored a presidency that would rotate between groups (a view he clung to for years to come). He made clear that, though he envisaged the end of white hegemony, he could not yet contemplate the loss of white control.

At a public meeting in April 1987, he urged whites to report people of other races living in segregated white areas—even though government largely turned a blind eye to informal integration by then. He fought to keep blacks out of white universities. And he repeatedly stressed his commitment to "group rights"—the guiding principle of neo-apartheid. Such would hardly seem to be the footprints of the radical reformer.

The neatest way to explain this discrepancy is to suggest that de Klerk underwent a dramatic change of heart on the road to the new South Africa. De Klerk denies it; and though that does not necessarily make it untrue, the nature of his character makes it unlikely. The essence of that character is logic and pragmatism, not mysticism. God may have urged de Klerk to change, but his was hardly the only, or even the most persuasive, of the voices speaking in the presidential ear. De Klerk himself has offered another explanation of his early conservatism: that it was tactical. Colin Eglin, a leading liberal politician, remembers that when de Klerk was National Party leader in the most conservative of provinces, the right-wing Transvaal, he told him, "If you were leader of the National Party, with Andries Treurnicht [leader of the ultra-right Conservative Party] breathing down your neck, you might even sound like me." To cultivate a *verligte* or liberal image in de Klerk's province would have meant political suicide. It was smart to be *verkrampte* (narrow).

But if tactics provide a guide to de Klerk's conservatism, so do circumstances. De Klerk never ran a ministry involved directly with black affairs. His ministerial job was to champion the cause of whites, and conscientious man that he is, he did it with a devotion which was easily confused with bigotry. That is not to say that racial prejudice played no part in motivating his actions—for he was a man of his time, no better than most, and one who still firmly believed apartheid was right. But racism need not have been the primary wellspring of his actions. He was the loyal servant of a party, and a policy, whose aim was to separate the races.

It was something much more basic to his character which sealed de Klerk's reputation as a reactionary—his relentless pursuit of logic. This was the habit of mind which caused him to oppose P. W. Botha's piecemeal reforms—not because they were reforms, but because they were piecemeal. Stoffel van der Merwe° was a member of the enlightened wing of the Botha

---

° Stoffel van der Merwe and Fanie van der Merwe are not related. Afrikaners inherited only a handful of last names from their Huguenot, Dutch, and German forebears. Many Afrikaners share the same names.

government: "F.W. would say, 'Look, if you do this, that will inevitably lead to the next step, and then inevitably to the next step. Are you ready for that?' Where everyone else was saying, 'We do this little thing to counter this problem and we do that little thing to counter that problem,' he was saying, 'Think it through.' And when he spelled out the implications in that way, then everybody shrunk from their own proposals. And then, of course, he was seen as the spoiler."

De Klerk's colleagues were convinced he was a hard-liner. So when P. W. Botha announced that he was stepping down as party leader after suffering a stroke, the party caucus saw de Klerk as the conservative candidate to succeed him. Most of those who would later prove his closest political allies—men who would work with him to deliver the new South Africa—voted against him in that poll in February 1989. It is one of the rich ironies of history that de Klerk was elected party leader not by those who championed reform but by those who fought it.

De Klerk used his *verkrampte* power base brilliantly, to do from the right what no *verligte* minister could have achieved from the left: instantly unite the divided party behind one leader. *Verligte* candidate Barend du Plessis, who lost narrowly to de Klerk despite the backing of Botha, acknowledges this. "If I had won, I would have had to drag him and his whole *verkrampte* outfit screaming and clawing to the other side, and that would have taken years and we would have lost opportunities," he explains.

"But de Klerk could take this conservative bunch with him, in a very short period consolidate the caucus, and from that power base, he could move. And precisely because he had been a *verkrampte,* he could convince the electorate. He could say to people, 'I've been in the old system and it failed.'" Du Plessis concludes, "So he could justify a quantum leap to the populace much more easily."

That leap was among the best prepared in history. And the man who prepared it—in ways both positive and negative—was P. W. Botha, patriarch of the unintended revolution.

De Klerk is the first to acknowledge the debt. He has always insisted that he did no more than extend the reform policy pioneered by Botha. For it was Botha who, finally and completely, gave up the concept of a white nation; he who forced the right wing into the wilderness in 1982, when the Conservative Party split from the National Party; he who championed the cause of power sharing, in the 1983 Constitution and again in 1986, when it was extended to blacks; he who accepted the citizenship of all races in one undivided South Africa, abandoning the most basic tenet of apartheid, separate nationhood.

De Klerk has always said that the real "quantum leap" away from apartheid was taken by Botha at the August 1986 Federal Congress of the National Party. He insists he did no more than carry that Congress's resolutions—on one citizenship for all South Africans, on a universal franchise, and black participation in government—to their logical conclusion. Perhaps he is merely being modest. More likely, like the naturally conservative person that he is, he is trying to prove his links to the past. He wants to demonstrate that he is not—as so many right-wing Afrikaners have called him—a traitor to party and tribe.

Botha's greatest contribution, though, may not have been to prove what was possible for de Klerk, but to demonstrate what was impossible. For years he had tried to co-opt moderate blacks, and rule South Africa without the ANC. He succeeded only in showing that there was no alternative to a deal with Mandela. By the beginning of 1989, Botha had demonstrated conclusively that the slow boat to reform would never make it to port.

De Klerk was left with the stark, and ultimately simple, choice between war and compromise. Botha made that choice easier by doing nothing to advance reform for the last three years of his presidency, creating huge pent-up demand for change. So when fate intervened to afflict him with a stroke on January 18, 1989, the cabinet, the caucus, the party, and the nation were impatient for a new departure. He had launched the revolution, but then lost—in the words of Archbishop Desmond Tutu—"the convictions of his courage." It was up to F. W. de Klerk to discover both the convictions and the courage to finish what Botha had started.

I toured South Africa to seek the wellsprings of that courage and the roots of those convictions. I spoke to de Klerk, his closest friends, his nearest political allies, his teachers and classmates, his wife and brother, even his adversaries, to discover the mind of the man who destroyed the evil empire.

What I found was what I had known from the start: that human motivation is never one-dimensional; that it is a mixture of grand motives and base, an amalgam of selfless sacrifice and selfish ambition, of conscience and cynicism. Anything else would be superhuman, and everyone who knows him agrees that F. W. de Klerk was more human than superman.

My journey of discovery began with a trip to the Western Transvaal town of Potchefstroom, where all that is best and worst about Afrikaans society clusters round the single Puritanical spire of the local church. Here, de Klerk attended the appropriately named Potchefstroom University for Christian Higher Education, an oasis of greenery and white Afrikaner values in the scorched African veld. Here, in this university dominated by the conservative Dopper strand of Calvinism to which the de Klerk family belonged,* the cautious early prophets of the Afrikaner enlightenment taught the future president.

I turned to F.W.'s former Potch classmate, law partner, and close friend Professor Ig (Ignatius) Vorster, dean of the university law faculty, for the definitive answer to the obvious question, Why did F.W. do it?

We spent the whole of a hot summer morning discussing this question in the refreshing gloom of the Potchefstroom law faculty, where generations of Afrikaners learned their perversely conscientious attitude to the law. Unlike other dominant peoples, who merely ignore the law when it gets in the way of their repression, the Afrikaner nation took the opposite approach. Afrikaner leaders insisted on obtaining legal authority for their abuses, where possible; and where this was not possible, they often, surprisingly, desisted from them. Universities like Potchefstroom taught them both to reverence the law and to exploit it for their own ends. No one was better at this feat of double-think than F. W. de Klerk.

Yet thirty years later, it was de Klerk—whom Vorster describes in his university days as "an ordinary, typical, Potch white Nationalist, Dopper student like most of us"—who restored the integrity of the law so devalued by his forefathers. We were discussing this extraordinary transformation when Vorster broke off to phone home. With the spontaneous hospitality which is the hallmark of his people just as surely as any of their abuses, he had invited me to lunch. Then I saw a qualm of doubt cross his face. Would the luncheon fare be adequate for the honored foreigner? Better check the menu—spaghetti? Hmmm. Was there any meat? No? His carnivorous soul rebelled at this—the guest must have meat. So a teen-aged son was sent scurrying off to buy some, and we sat down shortly thereafter to a delicious meal of spaghetti with meat sauce and chilled Cape wine.

Vorster recalled the evening when he summoned the courage to ask his friend, why did you do it? "He was sitting there in that armchair," Vorster gestures at an overstuffed chair drawn up by the fire. Screwing up his courage, he asked the president: "F.W., what happened in your mind? Did you go for a walk at the seaside in Cape Town, did you sit on a rock watching the breakers and say to yourself, 'What is my purpose?'

"And you know what he said?" Vorster goes on. "He said, 'There are certain crevasses in my mind which even my friends do not have the right to probe.' And I felt ashamed of myself. I shouldn't have asked."

De Klerk must have had to answer the same question thousands of times since that day. But he probably never gave a more honest reply, one

---

* The "Dopper" or Gereformeerde Kerk (Reformed Church) is the smallest of the three Afrikaans churches. The culture of the church is strict and sober-minded, with heavy reliance on dogma and a rejection of religious fanaticism.

that suggests the true complexity of the issue, the confusion of motives which are as difficult to discern clearly for him as they are for anyone else.

The nobler motives are quickly enumerated. They are ones which, not surprisingly, de Klerk himself stresses publicly. As he said in November 1994 at the Center for Strategic and International Studies in Washington, D.C.: "It was a matter of conscience. We went through a period of deep self-analysis and came to the conclusion that we had dismally failed in bringing justice to all South Africans through the establishment of nation states, and that, instead of achieving justice and full political rights of equality for all South Africans, it had just resulted in racial discrimination and minority domination. And it was a matter of conscience to say we were wrong. It didn't work out, we admit it was wrong, it led to injustice, we are sorry about the injustice, let us make a 180-degree turn on this."

But I find Ig Vorster's more basic explanation also more persuasive: "If he didn't do it, if he persisted in the old ways, he would have gone down for sure. It was a dead cert." Vorster adds, almost as an afterthought, "And it was right to do it." The order of his phrase probably mirrors the order of de Klerk's motivation. Both morality and politics prompted him to act—but politics came first. Which is not to say that de Klerk's morality is spurious; it is not. Indeed, it is central to his character. But in the mind of F. W. de Klerk, conscience follows only where pragmatism leads. Strategic considerations first pushed him to change; then he provided, ex post facto, the morality to go with the politics.

This conjunction of politics and morality was central to his actions. De Klerk is a religious man, a moral man, a Calvinist and a Dopper; if he had not believed what he was doing was right, he would not have done it. And even more importantly, his actions would not have captured the imagination of the international community, for the world loves nothing better than a morality tale in which the hero acts for the best in the best of all possible worlds. Foreigners did not want to see pragmatism defeat ideology in South Africa; they wanted to see good triumph over evil. Nothing else would have kept their attention—and kept international pressure focused on South Africa—quite so well.

Ironically, de Klerk himself often obscured the moral content of his actions by refusing to apologize for apartheid. He always insisted that though apartheid was wrong, it was not conceived in evil. He could not bring himself to issue an apology until years after he had accepted the impracticality of apartheid; when he did say sorry, in April 1993, it was too late to do him much good among blacks.

Even religion, for de Klerk, is something of a practical matter. He bridles at the idea—popular among those who seek a mystical explanation for his conversion—that he was called by God to save South Africa. "I'm not a mystic who goes into a trance and says, I've got a message from God, or anything like that. I think all of us who believe in God need to ask ourselves constantly, what does his word tell me? But it's not that I've been called by God Almighty as His special emissary to achieve certain things, no. It is more my work ethic."

Morality, religion, ideology—in the end, they all bow to pragmatism. For de Klerk, apartheid's greatest sin was that it failed the reality test. "If one believes a policy is unworkable, it become immoral to advocate it . . . [apartheid] is wrong *because* it is unworkable," he once told a television interviewer. His logic, as always, was impeccable: Apartheid had failed, therefore it became immoral; because it was immoral, it must be replaced; to replace it, government must talk to the ANC; but the ANC could not negotiate without its leader, so he must be released from jail; and he could not be released to lead an illegal organization, so the ANC must be un-banned. Simple, really.

But it is a rare breed of ideologue who would let logic carry him so far from original principles. De Klerk was just such a man—he calls himself a "pragmatic idealist"—and luckily for South Africa, so were most of his compatriots, from both sides of the political divide. Both he and his opponents responded to reason in a way that true fanaticism would never have allowed. De Klerk, for his part, was fanatical about only one thing—resolving the dilemma of the Afrikaner in Africa. That, he once told Mof Terreblanche, one of his closest friends, was his only philosophy of life: To find a solution. For he is the perfect embodiment of the popular Afrikaans saying, " *'n Boer maak 'n plan"*: when his back is to the wall, the Afrikaner will look for a way out. He is a survivor.

Survival meant, not emancipating blacks (though that was a byproduct) but liberating the Afrikaner himself from the prison of racist nationalism. Faced with the threatened demise of Afrikaans culture, language, freedoms, of the very nation itself, de Klerk calculated the odds and decided they favored a deal with the ANC. He set out to get it, on the best possible terms. Logic, which led him to conservatism in the 1980s, now told him there was no alternative to radicalism. South Africa could have a fast or a slow revolution, but it would have its revolution either way. As one of his former colleagues, Leon Wessels, puts it, "F. W. de Klerk is like a well-programmed computer. Give him the right set of facts, and he will always come up with the answer."

When he became party leader in February 1989, de Klerk set out to review those facts. Politically, matters had reached a crude sort of balance.

All the main pillars of the Afrikaner establishment—the Church, the press, the universities, the business community, the Broederbond—had withdrawn their support for apartheid. But its rival ideology—communism—was in even more trouble. Only weeks after de Klerk became president, the Berlin Wall fell. Deprived of their cherished ideologies, both sides were more amenable to reason.

In the townships, government and the ANC had reached checkmate: Pretoria could not govern, but neither could the ANC. Most township residents had ceased to pay rent and service charges; hundreds of thousands of children were not attending school; government employees in the townships—police and local councilors—were assassinated with regularity; government assets in the townships were destroyed. But the ANC's attempts to govern black areas on its own had been crushed. Both sides were tired of fighting.

It was in the area of economics however that the stalemate was most telling. The economy had not been destroyed by the forces ranged against it, from trade sanctions to disinvestment to the foreign lending ban to the township revolt; but neither could it grow. By early 1989, that fact had begun to worry both sides. The wisest heads began to recognize the threat of a scorched-earth outcome to their conflict—a result that would prevent either side from delivering the economic fruits of victory to their supporters. For economic prosperity was by then a major concern of both sides. Afrikaners were rapidly outgrowing their ethnic paranoia, and worried as much about their swimming pools as about their language; and Africans wanted development even more than they wanted democracy. Neither would be able to enjoy the good things of life if South Africa was left a wasteland. Both sides were coming round to the view that the price of victory was simply too high.

These were the same signs visible to P. W. Botha. But de Klerk read them differently. He discerned a basic reality which forever eluded Botha: that economics and politics were inextricably linked. De Klerk, already a master of one discipline, set out to conquer the other. During his apprenticeship to the presidency, between February and September 1989, men like Wim de Villiers, former chairman of the giant Gencor mining group and a leading free marketeer, gave him weekend courses in economics. The future president learned that the South African economy was in trouble, not crippled but hobbled by a range of factors, internal and external.

Many of those factors were structural, and had nothing to do with the international campaign of financial and trade sanctions against Pretoria. Growth constraints did not suddenly emerge with the advent of serious sanctions; growth had declined by 1 percent in 1985, even before sanctions took effect. Economic activity had been minimal since the 1970s; from 1980 to 1985, it averaged only 1.2 percent per year.

Growth was depressed by apartheid itself; by a number of economic shocks, including the severest drought of the century, and fluctuations in the gold price; by the uncontrolled spending of homeland governments and the huge triplicated bureaucracies introduced under the tricameral constitution; and by the rising costs of internal unrest (man-days lost to strikes, most of them political, rose nearly 1,000 percent between 1983 and 1986, and the government lost hundreds of millions of Rands a year in township rent and service payment boycotts). Sanctions exacerbated the situation, but they were not its primary cause.

South African exporters were proving well equal to the task of circumventing trade sanctions, albeit at a cost. After dipping initially, while exporters looked for new markets—and clandestine ways to penetrate existing ones closed by sanctions—export volumes rose by 26 percent from 1985 to 1989. Disinvestment also appeared to have had little direct effect on economic growth. Many disinvesting companies simply sold their assets cheaply to local white businessmen, but maintained non-equity links such as franchise, licensing, and technology agreements that permitted them to keep operating.

But if these politically inspired sanctions had only limited effect, the same could not be said of the restrictions imposed by the international financial markets, where decisions were determined more by risk than by politics. By the time de Klerk became president, South Africa had lost some R30 billion in capital outflows (a hemorrhage of R6 billion per year, or $2 billion at the prevailing exchange rate), both in debt repayments necessitated by the foreign loan moratorium and in illegal capital flight. Foreign reserves had shrunk to a level where they could cover only just over five weeks' imports, a perilous situation for any country.

South Africa, which needed to import capital to grow, was forced to export it to repay old debts. The government was in an impossible bind. To make repayments in foreign currency, it needed a trade surplus. That meant boosting exports and depressing imports; but suppressing imports, in this import-dependent economy, meant choking off growth; and without growth, it was impossible either to buy off the township revolt or to keep white constituents in the style to which apartheid had accustomed them.

Quite apart from capital exported to pay debt, large amounts were spent at home to develop strategic industries that would circumvent the international oil and arms embargoes. South Africa spent many billions building a sophisticated arms industry as well as an oil-from-coal industry to supply its energy requirements. The cost of only one of these energy projects—the Mossgas oil-from-gas plant—was R11 billion, equivalent to the national budget for ten years' worth of new housing construction.

Government officials of the day, never eager to admit they acted under pressure, always insisted that sanctions—and the broader campaign of international isolation, which included sporting and academic boycotts, and travel bans—were counterproductive. In the case of P. W. Botha, that was probably true. But they had a major impact on the national psyche—and prepared the ground well for de Klerk's radical departure. Businessmen, whose international links gave them glimpses into the global economic village closed to them by sanctions, began seriously to pressure government for change. Henri de Villiers of Standard Bank Investment Corporation, investment arm of one of the country's leading banks, spoke for many when he said in 1988, "In this day and age, there is no such thing as economic self-sufficiency, and we delude ourselves if we think we are different. South Africa needs the world. It needs markets, it needs skills, it needs technology, and above all it needs capital." Increasingly, the business community made clear that Fortress South Africa was not an option.

The white elite, which had ruled unchallenged as polecat of the world for decades already, was tiring of that dubious distinction. They cherished their cultural and sporting links with the Western world. Now they were shut out of international cricket and rugby; their academics were shunned; their planes could not land in the United States or overfly the continent of Africa; and they were the object of universal moral disgust. Nobody likes to be disliked—least of all Afrikaners, who yearn for understanding and approval like insecure children. They live 10,000 kilometers from Europe, but they hate to feel left out.

De Klerk could read all these smoke signals. He could see that Fortress South Africa, by definition, could not grow; he could feel the tide of history flowing strongly against him. He could detect no easy way out of the vicious cycle in which his people were trapped. Sanctions were only part of that trap, which was psychological as much as economic, social as much as political. They did not inflict enough pain to force change on their own, though they intensified the general state of malaise. But as de Klerk himself says, sanctions "made people realise that we were in a dead-end street." And F. W. de Klerk, problem solver extraordinaire, was not about to abandon his nation in such a cul-de-sac.

De Klerk toured the globe looking for a way out of the impasse. He was determined not the make the same mistake as the old president, who was crippled by schizophrenia in his relations with foreigners. In public, Botha denounced the West's campaign against apartheid as "one of the most extreme forms of political fraud of the twentieth century"; in private, he yearned for Western approval, tailoring his reform policies to please Washington and London rather than Soweto and Lusaka, and succeeded in pleasing no one.

De Klerk, though still suspicious of foreigners, with their morality-tale approach to South African complexities, had left the paranoia of Botha far behind. He was a modern politician, able (when he liked) to project an image of confidence, charm, and sincerity which made a welcome change from the belligerent irrationality of the Groot Krokodil. Most of all, he listened; everyone who met him before he became president (foreign leaders, businessmen, anti-apartheid activists) remembers that. So he went overseas, to listen.

Again and again, he heard the same mantra: Unban the ANC, release the prisoners, start talks. Logic told him that no deal which excluded the ANC would be accepted by the West, and that a deal rejected by the West would be worse than no deal at all. He set out to find out just how far he would have to go to satisfy outsiders. Yet he also gained reassurance from these visits; his confidence grew, as he tested his wits against the likes of British Prime Minister Margaret Thatcher and West German Chancellor Helmut Kohl; so did his desire to be accepted in such circles, and to secure a place in history as a great modern leader. But he also began to see the West as guarantors of a deal that would protect the white minority as well as satisfying blacks. Western leaders made clear they would insist on a negotiated deal, not just a handover of power to the ANC. They indicated they would back him in demanding protection for minorities, so long as these were consistent with democracy. He returned to South Africa reassured, and more committed than ever to radical change.

There was more than de Klerk's innate good sense, and concern about the economy, to make him receptive to foreign urgings. Only weeks before he became party leader, South Africa had signed a deal—brokered by the United States and the USSR—to give independence to Southwest Africa (Namibia), which had been run illegally as a colony of Pretoria since World War I. In return, South Africa secured the withdrawal of Cuban troops from neighboring Angola, where most of the Namibian independence war was fought. The Cubans went to Angola to fight, on behalf of communism, against the apartheid occupation of Namibia. Their departure—inspired by the Soviet Union's loss of interest in regional conflicts—substantially eased Pretoria's concern about a Communist takeover.

The deal to end the war was concluded by P. W. Botha, but F. W. de Klerk reaped the benefits. Defense spending could be substantially cut; and white morale improved once white conscripts stopped coming home in body bags. The deal also boosted Pretoria's confidence: the Western world had been demanding Namibia's independence for over a decade; by agreeing to it, South Africa gained both credibility and welcome plaudits from the international community. Even more importantly, the deal proved to South Africans themselves that there was profit to be gained from talk. Their world did not end simply because they decided to negotiate rather than fight.

The settlement in Namibia also marked a development that would prove far more important to de Klerk, the terminal decline of the Soviet Union. Fear of communism had motivated Afrikaner governments for decades. It inspired the total onslaught against neighboring countries, including (Marxist) Angola and Mozambique; and it explained Botha's fierce and uncompromising opposition to the ANC.

Understandably, communism terrified the Afrikaner, for in South Africa, where race and class were synonymous, Communist class warfare would mean race warfare. And there was no way whites, representing only 12 percent of the population, could win such a battle; they saw communism as an invitation to race suicide. Afrikaners objected to it on economic, and political, but also religious grounds; many believed that an ANC Communist government would not only confiscate their homes and farms but abolish churches altogether.

The demise of that ideology made it possible for Pretoria to make peace in Namibia, but it also made South Africa safe for black rule in the eyes of Afrikaners. It removed the last remaining obstacle to talks with the African National Congress, whose commitment to socialism had never been complete in any case but was now seriously eroded by the demise of its ideological mentor.

The ANC's second thoughts on communism profoundly influenced the thinking of de Klerk. In January 1990, Joe Slovo, then chairman of the South African Communist Party, published a paper entitled *Has Socialism Failed?* Though he concluded that it had not, stressing his "complete faith that socialism represents the most rational, just and democratic way for human beings to relate to one another," he made clear that this utopia remained only a distant goal. For his lifetime, and even that of his children, what was needed were free elections and multi-party democracy—not one-party rule and the nationalization of swimming pools. As he told me, sitting by the side of my own Lusaka swimming pool in early 1990, South Africans must bake bread, not slogans. De Klerk could not have hoped for a more positive message.

But it was the fall of the Berlin Wall in November 1989 which had the most impact. That event was possibly the most important factor—certainly the most important external factor—that motivated de Klerk to act. "It was as if God had taken a hand—a new turn in world history," de Klerk told his brother Wimpie soon afterward. "We had to seize the opportunity. The risk that the ANC was being used as a Trojan horse by a superpower had drastically diminished."

The demise of communism gave de Klerk what he most required to be able to act—the sense that he was operating from a position of strength; the chance to play the game against the ANC without the certainty of losing. Without Soviet support, the African National Congress could not intensify the war against Pretoria. ANC secretary general Alfred Nzo acknowledged this candidly in January 1990—in a speech meant for a closed meeting of the ANC executive, but delivered by the hapless Nzo in error to a public gathering. "We must admit that we do not have the capacity within our country to intensify the armed struggle in any meaningful way," he said. And de Klerk was listening. He had to acknowledge that if the ANC could not escalate the struggle, neither could he continue to suppress it indefinitely. The perfect condition of stalemate had at last been achieved.

De Klerk's reasoning was persuasive, but his timing was inspired. He recognized that South Africa was on the brink of a racial conflagration that would destroy all hope of future reconciliation; so he forced white South Africans to make peace with their black compatriots while they still had the chance. He looked to neighboring Zimbabwe, which fought a liberation war in which twenty thousand people (a grimly high proportion of the 6 million population) died, and he turned away. No South African government led by him would make the same mistake.

But I did not then know that de Klerk was susceptible to such attacks of rationality. So I was amazed when, in January 1990, I found a small quote tucked away on an inside page of my morning newspaper. De Klerk, it seems, had told a meeting of senior police officers that more fighting would lead not to victory but to racial conflagration. "For if this Armaggedon takes place—and blood flows ankle deep in our streets and 4 or 5 million people lie dead—the problem will remain exactly the same as it was before the shooting started," he told the startled policemen. Optimism was beginning to get the better of my cynicism.

De Klerk can claim that I ought to have known better. For on February 8, 1989—almost exactly a year before he unbanned the African National Congress and released Mandela—he delivered his maiden address as National Party leader, foreshadowing all that was to follow.

"Our goal is a new South Africa, a totally changed South Africa, a South Africa which has rid itself of the antagonism of the past, a South Africa free of domination and oppression in whatever form," he told Parliament. Later, I heard him make a similar emotional appeal to the white voters of his Vereeniging constituency. "Give me your hearts, and I promise, as never before, to try to break through. I'll give all I have for this goal of a new, strong, just South Africa, the most wonderful fatherland in the world," he told them. I could not help being moved—until he brought me back to earth with a bump. Asked whether a black man could be president of this mystical fatherland, he resorted to plain speaking, asserting, "That question is not on the agenda." So I concluded that skepticism remained the best tool for translating the utterances of F. W. de Klerk. Rhetoric alone would make no cheap convert of me.

But soon I would have more than rhetoric to go on. On September 13, 1989, de Klerk took the first irreversible step toward the new South Africa. He gave permission for the first legal African National Congress march in thirty years, allowing tens of thousands of anti-apartheid protesters to throng the streets of Cape Town. In fact, if not yet in law, he had unbanned the African National Congress. South Africa would never be the same again.

Mof Terreblanche well remembers the scene at the de Klerk home in Cape Town, as the president and his friends watched television news reports on the night of that march. The streets of white Cape Town had never seen such a sight, for in the old South Africa, protest was confined firmly to the townships. "The ladies were shocked. But F.W., he was calm," Terreblanche marvels. "He said to me, 'How can we stop them?' "

Not only ladies were shocked. Johan Heyns, the top Afrikaans cleric of the day, helped mediate the agreement to legalize the march between de Klerk and anti-apartheid churchman Desmond Tutu. Speaking days before he was assassinated for his role in supporting the new South Africa, Heyns recalled his amazement at de Klerk's decision: "A march, in this country! That happens only in foreign countries, not in South Africa. And surely not with the consent of the National Party government. It's impossible!"

De Klerk's chief adviser of the day, Gerrit Viljoen, says the decision to allow the march was a more fearful leap into the dark than any the president made later—including the release of Mandela. De Klerk's mind's eye was filled with images of the recent massive demonstrations which had brought down East European governments. Cape Town could have been the same. His own security services thought he was mad to risk it. But de Klerk's logic was undeniable. He told Viljoen, "We cannot have a democracy without protest marches." So democracy went ahead.

It was pragmatism taken to heroic lengths to allow the protest to proceed. If an Eastern European–sized crowd had demonstrated against de Klerk's rule, he could not have continued to govern. But the new president knew he had to take that risk. It made neither good sense nor good politics to continue banning ANC gatherings. "We realized that if we didn't allow such marches, then we might have seen half a million people marching on

Parliament, and not thirty thousand," de Klerk remembers. "There was the possibility of a tremendous revolutionary upsurge—it was the "in" thing then, it happened across the world."

De Klerk knew that repression intensified these revolutionary pressures, and he could only gamble that, once the lid was removed, they would dissipate rather than explode. He was right: The Cape Town crowd never exceeded the thirty thousand which de Klerk considered manageable. He began to believe—and this was crucial to his future plans—that he could manage not only protest marches but the entire process of change.

The march was the first major test of the new leader's bona fides, but it was also the first time in recent memory that an Afrikaner leader had reacted, positively and rationally, to pressure. That pressure was considerable. At the head of the procession marched not only Archbishop Tutu, an anti-apartheid figure of international renown and winner of the 1984 Nobel Peace Prize, but also the managing director of Shell South Africa (one of Cape Town's largest companies), as well as the town's white mayor. Even more persuasive was the pressure from the Afrikaner establishment and the foreign diplomatic community. Johan Heyns, then moderator of the National Party's religious wing, the Dutch Reformed Church, rushed to Cape Town hours before the planned march, filled with dread at the news that de Klerk's police meant to prevent it.

Heyns persuaded de Klerk to wait in his office, on standby for a meeting with Tutu. That fact alone signaled an extraordinary reversal of South African realities—whites did not wait for blacks in the old South Africa, and white presidents waited for no one. De Klerk accepted not only the symbolic indignity but an outright rebuff from Tutu, who refused to meet him. The archbishop gave Heyns assurances that the march would be peaceful. Heyns believed him, and persuaded de Klerk to take the risk. Then he went home, to pray that he was right.

Simultaneously, Sir Robin Renwick, Margaret Thatcher's Machiavellian ambassador to Cape Town, was running a one-man mediation service between Tutu and Foreign Minister Pik Botha. De Klerk knew he could not afford to alienate, simultaneously, the West, the Church, the business community, thirty thousand black Capetonians—and the redoubtable Mrs. Thatcher.

I remember the march as a series of impossible snapshots: the image of a black man (Archbishop Tutu) speaking from the balcony of the ornate Victorian city hall, symbol of white power and European architecture; the sight of the black, green, and gold flag of the banned ANC flown for the first time with pride in this whitest of all South African cities; the image of white police lurking down side streets and around corners, hiding from marchers they would previously have provoked. These were snapshots I had never thought to take, signs of a new beginning.

Over the weeks that followed, the signals kept getting stronger: de Klerk was ready for another great leap forward. He made it at the dawn hour of that silent Sunday morning in Soweto, as I sat waiting on Mr. Sisulu's wall. On October 15, 1989, de Klerk released from prison every ANC leader apart from Mandela himself, a step which, more than any other, was truly irreversible. But if that meant de Klerk could not go back, his path forward looked to me equally impossible. Inevitably, he must release Nelson Mandela, who, just as inevitably, must become president of the new South Africa. Yet even the most fertile imagination, the most flexible intellect, could not then grasp this truth as imminent reality. De Klerk had set out to end the world as he knew it—as his people had known it, as I had known it, as it had always been. That fact would take time to sink in.

"WE WANT TO MAKE PEACE *with our black people, while we still have the chance!" Con Botha, mouthpiece of the National Party, was waging such a struggle to control the timbre of his voice that I could not doubt his sincerity.*

The language echoed the old South Africa—"our black people"—but the urgency was something all new. Mr. Botha had glimpsed the chance of a permanent solution to the age-old problem of the white man in Africa, and he was ready to rush at it. F. W. de Klerk had "liberated" him, he said, smiling at the irony that a man like himself—the Afrikaner tribe's chief propagandist—should ever be moved to use such a word. He was speaking on the eve of Nelson Mandela's release from prison. Within hours, the ANC leader would be free. "We all feel a great weight lifted from our shoulders," Con Botha exclaimed, putting words to the collective sigh of relief already audible throughout the corridors of power.

Con Botha told me that day that South Africa was headed for majority rule—and that whites, in the end, would accept and embrace it. It was a remarkable prediction at the time, and one that F. W. de Klerk would not have shared. But as I came to know well in later years, Con Botha was a man of Africa prepared to think even more flexibly than de Klerk about the Afrikaner's future. I left his office, in a parliamentary office building in Cape Town, and was overcome in Parliament Street by excited tears, and by a sudden hope that there might, indeed, still be time for the Afrikaner to make his peace with Africa. As Mr. Botha had said, the weight was now on Mandela's shoulders. So much would depend on him.

7

The Great Leap

"THE PROHIBITION OF the African National Congress, the Pan Africanist Congress, the South African Communist Party and a number of subsidiary organisations is being rescinded . . . the Government has taken a firm decision to release Mr. Nelson Mandela unconditionally."

A gasp of disbelief ran through the corridors of power—this really was the end of history. F. W. de Klerk had stepped to the podium in the ornate chamber which housed the three-color Parliament to announce the end of 350 years of white rule in Africa. On February 2, 1990—exactly one year to the day after he promised the caucus a "great leap forward"—de Klerk had jumped. For the next five years, South Africa would be in freefall.

His speech came as a shock to almost all who heard it; only the tightest inner circle had known what he intended to say. The caucus had not been informed, and even Marike de Klerk, the president's wife, was kept in the dark. Surprise was of the essence.

"It was the best-kept secret ever." Roelf Meyer is a boyish Afrikaner, a member of the younger generation of National Party politicians who immediately jumped on F. W. de Klerk's bandwagon to the new South Africa. They knew they would have no future as politicians until some kind of deal was done with the ANC. For them, the conjunction of morality and ambition was particularly potent.

Meyer, who would later emerge as de Klerk's chief dealmaker with the ANC, delights at the memory of how his boss deluded the press, the diplomats, and even his own supporters to maintain the crucial element of stealth. On December 3 and 4, 1989, de Klerk had taken Meyer, his cabinet, and a large group of advisers to a bush retreat called D'Nyala, near the northwestern Transvaal town of Ellisras. It was to be their strategic hideaway throughout the years to follow. There, amongst the giraffes and the reactionary whites who populate this arid province, de Klerk and his cabinet took the decisions announced two months later in Parliament.

There, in an oasis of European luxury in the wild African bush, de Klerk set out his plan to preserve the life the Afrikaner had built for himself in Africa. He told his colleagues the stark truth of their plight: "We could have clung to power for another five to ten years, I could have remained president of South Africa until the end of my political career. But that was a path towards destruction." Instead, he outlined a new path to power.

De Klerk says he had decided to unban the African National Congress already by the time of the Cape Town march in September 1989, which would have served as its de facto legalization in any case. But he needed to bring the core of his party with him, and crucially, he needed to persuade them to unban the ANC's ally, the South African Communist Party (SACP). That, he achieved at the D'Nyala summit. There was fierce argument over unbanning the Communists. But in the end, the decision was taken in principle to release Mandela and to legalize the two organizations. It was Big Bang, at last.

De Klerk knew that anything less would have been universally dismissed as more Boer posturing. It would also have been impractical. The African National Congress and the South African Communist Party were symbiotically linked at leadership level: many of the most influential leaders belonged to both organizations. It would be a nonsense to legalize one without the other. De Klerk understood this, but even more he understood the tactical advantages of radical action. He aimed to cut the ground from beneath the ANC's feet, by removing all rationale for the armed struggle; had the SACP remained illegal, the ANC would have had an impeccable reason to fight on.

No detailed plan was agreed at the D'Nyala *bosberaad,* or bush summit. But everyone knew where F.W. was headed. He would do whatever was necessary—including unbanning the SACP and the ANC's military wing, *Umkhonto we Sizwe*—to seize the moral high ground from his opponents. As Kobie Coetsee told his colleagues that day in the bush, "Fasten your seatbelts, we are going places!"

Veteran cold warriors like Defense Minister Magnus Malan—relic of the total onslaught and confidant of P. W. Botha—argued, until the very last moment, that the African National Congress should be legalized but the South African Communist Party should remain banned. Their approach was tactically the opposite of de Klerk's. He thought the best way to defuse the "red menace" was to legalize it, and deprive it of its romantic appeal; Malan and the other total onslaughters remained determined to crush it. De Klerk was not tempted by their arguments. He could not risk falling between two stools of reform; it was time to take the gap.

He left D'Nyala determined to unban everything and release everyone—and then set out to persuade Western diplomats, journalists, and even his own information chief, Con Botha, that he would do just the opposite. For de Klerk was the first Afrikaner leader to understand the modern art of politics as packaging. He knew that he must not only do the right thing but be *seen* to do it—preferably on network television. And the only way to capture network headlines would be to shock the news editors.

At its first meeting of the new year, in January 1990, cabinet discussed the speech. But the main focus was on form, not substance. De Klerk was obsessed with getting the presentation of the speech exactly right: he and the cabinet spent hours second-guessing reaction to it. In the end, the cabinet members felt they were making progress toward a speech worthy of the Great Communicator. "I trust all of you," de Klerk said to close the meeting, "but remember, no one outside this room must know what I am going to say."

Just to make sure that they did not, de Klerk sent Foreign Minister Pik Botha—the man whose advance sales of the Rubicon speech had caused such a public relations disaster—to dampen expectations. Everyone knew the new president was due to deliver an address at the opening of the first session of Parliament under his presidency, on February 2. In the days before the speech, local and foreign journalists were contacted and told to expect a major reform statement, but explicitly *not* the unbanning of the ANC.

"To this day, I'm thankful that on that occasion there wasn't a leak," de Klerk says blandly—as though he had not orchestrated a major disinformation campaign to ensure the element of surprise. His deviousness was a stroke of genius. He had created the perfect conditions in which to drop a public relations bombshell.

Niël Barnard was one of the privileged few involved in the preparation of the speech, right up until the final hours. And he was instrumental in persuading de Klerk and cabinet to accept its most important element: the unbanning of the Communist Party.

But in the early days of the de Klerk presidency, Barnard was not willing to trust his powers of persuasion. So he decided to do what he could to force the president's hand. On the night before the Cape Town march—as protesters were painting their placards and Johan Heyns was saying his prayers in Pretoria—a clandestine meeting was taking place in Europe that would bounce de Klerk into the kind of action he eventually took on February 2.

Unbeknownst to de Klerk, the National Intelligence Service was holding a secret meeting with their rival intelligence men from the ANC. Barnard had had his conduit to the ANC—Willie Esterhuyse—for a couple of years already. But NIS says its own officials had never, up to then, met with the

ANC directly. Esterhuyse was asked to set up such a meeting. With a mixture of nostalgia and sheepishness, he recalls the cloak-and-dagger antics that followed. He met Thabo Mbeki to discuss the meeting, ironically, on Republic Day, 1989. "We met at the offices of BAT [British American Tobacco] in London, and I was talking all sorts of nonsense to Thabo, because I was worried that the room was bugged. So I wrote him a note and said, 'I want to talk to you, meet me in a pub,' the Albert, which was close to BAT."

They met in the Albert, and Esterhuyse told Mbeki that the National Intelligence Service wanted to meet with him. "He was very very nervous, but I gave him a sort of personal guarantee that if I pick up anything, if I think it's going to be a trap, I'll let him know," Esterhuyse recalls. The two sides met secretly in Switzerland, on September 12, 1989, at the Palace Hotel in Lucerne, in an atmosphere of tension and suspicion which both sides recall now with amusement. The heads of the two delegations—Mike Louw and Thabo Mbeki—were terrified that something would go wrong. According to Mbeki in the BBC documentary *Death of Apartheid,* the NIS was afraid that "even when we walked up the stairs if one of us sprained an ankle we might say that this was a trick of the Boers."

Both sides tell a very plausible story about the trepidation they felt at that first meeting. Jacob Zuma, head of ANC intelligence, who was also present, recalls that Mbeki spoke to him in Zulu to say, "sitting here with the enemy I feel my stomach moving."

What is strange about this story is that so many senior figures, from both the Botha cabinet and ANC national executive, believe it to be untrue. They are convinced that contact began much earlier than the September 1989 meeting—which took place less than five months before the ANC was unbanned. Most say clandestine talks were taking place between NIS officials and the ANC from about the time that the Barnard team started to meet with Mandela in prison, in mid-1988. They may be wrong—none claims to have been present himself—but it seems unlikely. And one of those who did participate initially acknowledged the earlier meetings, then developed a convenient amnesia about dates when pressed.

Certainly, Western intelligence agencies believe direct contacts began before September 1989. British intelligence picked up evidence of meetings in London, and U.S. diplomats and Zambian officials say they believe contact was also made in Lusaka, where Barnard journeyed often, sometimes in disguise. But as Jacob Zuma once told me, intelligence people make concealment a habit of life. "I doubt you will get clarity on this one," he said, adding, "there are circumstances and there are circumstances."

Some of those circumstances almost certainly permitted NIS officials to meet the ANC well before either side is prepared to admit. The reason for their reticence could be Mandela, who opposed direct contact between NIS and his exiled colleagues, fearing that the NIS would try to split the movement. Barnard says that he tried for months to get Mandela to drop this objection, but he would not; so (Barnard claims), the NIS did not proceed.

Louw explains the thinking at the time: "We were getting worried that [Mandela] was losing the confidence of those outside, so we had to do something to get the other side on board. But we were afraid that it could backfire on the Mandela talks. . . . He could have turned around afterwards and said, you have gone behind my back, I don't even want to speak to you."

The NIS never did get Mandela's permission for those talks. The September 1989 meeting took place without Mandela's knowledge, and he was not pleased. But he was not the only one to be antagonized by this evidence that NIS had its own separate agenda of contact with the ANC. F. W. de Klerk was equally outraged when he learned of the meeting. When Louw reported on it to the new president after his return from Switzerland, de Klerk demanded to know who had given him permission to negotiate with the ANC.

Louw was able to point to a resolution of the State Security Council, passed in August 1989 (after de Klerk was sworn in as acting president, at a meeting over which he presided) calling on the NIS to obtain "more information . . . concerning the ANC, the aims, alliances and potential approachability of its different leaders and groupings." This should be procured, the resolution said, through "special additional direct action" by the intelligence service.

Clearly, de Klerk did not realize that this careful wording implied a meeting between Louw and Mbeki. Intelligence sources say that was exactly the intention—to keep de Klerk in the dark. For by then, NIS officials were absolutely convinced that dramatic action had to be taken to normalize South African politics. They could not yet be sure that the new president would agree, so they decided to present him with a fait accompli that would force his hand. De Klerk might well have moved quickly, with or without their intervention. But the fact that the intelligence service—the top strategic brains in the government—was behind him pushing must have accelerated progress.

By the beginning of December 1989, the pace of change had picked up to the point where de Klerk was ready for Big Bang. But at that point—a fact which makes his courage all the more extraordinary—de Klerk had never even met the man to whom he had consigned his nation's future, Nelson Mandela. The new president had never come under the spell of the great seducer. He took his decisions largely without benefit of the sweet reason of Mandela, without his personal reassurances, and certainly without succumbing to his charm.

De Klerk knew that his colleague and close ally, Justice Minister Kobie Coetsee, considered Nelson Mandela a reasonable man; and he knew, at third hand, that Mandela had been making conciliatory noises in his talks with the Barnard team. But de Klerk was not part of the inner circle kept informed of those talks. Like the rest of the cabinet, he did not even know they were taking place until shortly before he became party leader in early 1989.

The two men did not click. When president and prisoner met for the first time, on December 13, 1989, the relationship that would define the future of South Africa got off to an indifferent start.

Mandela, true to form, dredged up a tenuous personal link with de Klerk from the distant past: a black legal colleague of Mandela's had appeared in court opposing the young attorney de Klerk; he had given a good report of his Afrikaans opposite number. Mandela, who greatly valued such personal judgments, took it as a sign of de Klerk's bona fides. But Mandela also made clear that he respected the new president—a man of a different generation, nearly twenty years his junior—because of his political pedigree. He valued the bloodline of de Klerk, perversely, in almost the same way as that of any African chief. De Klerk was a leader, descended of leaders, as he was himself. Each must respect that.

De Klerk, for his part, was not impressed by this approach. Close aides who spoke to him soon after the first meeting say he appeared strangely unmoved at the encounter. Perhaps it was inevitable that two such different men—the one a politician to his bootstraps, a heavy drinker and smoker, a shrewd operator, not a grand soul; the other strict, abstemious, and self-sacrificing—would not be best friends. Maybe the generation gap had something to do with it. Mandela expected deference from younger men, as is the African way; de Klerk, filled with the potency of office, did not easily defer. Perhaps Mandela detected some caginess about de Klerk, or even some condescension. Maybe it was just that de Klerk did not pour the tea. But everyone who knows both men says that there was never any magic between them, and that their relationship only deteriorated as time went on. The great seducer did not disarm de Klerk, whose mental computer was not programmed for seduction.

But if the two men did not bond souls at their first meeting, they at least decided they could work together. Nelson Mandela recalls in his memoirs that he was impressed both by the style of the new president and by the substance of their discussion—"from the first, I noticed that Mr. de Klerk listened to what I had to say. This was a novel experience." So the prisoner gave his captor a bit of free political advice, counseling him to abandon the concept of group rights. "I told him it was not in his interest to retain this concept, for it gave the impression that he wanted to modernise apartheid without abandoning it . . . and the ANC had not struggled against apartheid for 75 years only to yield to a disguised form of it."

De Klerk listened and did not argue. "You know," he said, "my aim is no different from yours. Your memo to P. W. Botha said the ANC and the government should work together to deal with white fears of black domination, and the idea of group rights is how we propose to deal with it." Mandela said he was impressed by this response, but argued that the idea of group rights did more to increase black fears than allay white ones. So de Klerk, ever the man of compromise, replied, "We will have to change it then."

Mandela wrote immediately to Lusaka to tell the exiled ANC leadership that, "echoing Mrs. Thatcher's famous description of Mr. Gorbachev," de Klerk was "a man we could do business with." Theirs would be a marriage of convenience, not of love; but it would be a marriage nonetheless.

"If you decide to cut off a dog's tail, you don't cut it piecemeal, you cut it off and get it done with," says Mrs. Marike de Klerk, the president's wife. The former first lady's habit of plain speaking, especially on racial questions where her image is extremely conservative, has often embarrassed her husband and his party. But in this characteristically graphic phrase, she seems to have captured the no-nonsense mood of F. W. de Klerk, husband and president, on February 2, 1990.

Those who know de Klerk well marvel at his confidence in the weeks and months leading up to the speech. Con Botha, who as National Party propaganda chief was one of the president's closest aides, shudders as he recalls the unnatural calm with which de Klerk contemplated steps that might well have meant ethnic suicide. "He never gave the thing one second thought," Botha says, shaking his head in disbelief even now. Marike de Klerk remembers, not a troubled husband but almost a mischievous one. "I had no idea what my husband was going to say, nothing, not an inkling, and I didn't ask," says the dutiful wife. "But we had invited some of our friends to the opening of Parliament, and these friends kept nagging at him, 'You know you've got to have something up your sleeve.' And he said with a twinkle in his eye, 'I do think I have something up my sleeve.' And that morning as we drove to Parliament, I said, 'Are you sure it is worthwhile what you have up your sleeve?' and he said, 'I'm sure.' "

De Klerk attended the sixtieth birthday party of a friend on the eve of the speech, but left early to complete his text. The cold warrior faction in cabinet was fighting a rearguard action against unbanning the Communist Party. But de Klerk remained adamant. During the long night that followed the birthday party, de Klerk labored over the section of the speech dealing with Mandela's release, which was announced in principle but without a firm date set. That the release would take place was not in doubt; but de Klerk did not want news of it to overshadow the unbannings. He wanted to package his plan for maximum public relations impact.

At 1:30 A.M., he set the speech aside, went to bed—and slept. As de Klerk told me in 1994, "I believed in what I was doing. And I didn't lie awake worrying about whether I had taken the right decision."

On February 2, 1990—almost thirty years to the day after British Prime Minister Harold Macmillan delivered his "wind of change" speech to the same Parliament, presaging revolution in black Africa—de Klerk spoke the words that would change South Africa forever. When he reached the part of the speech unbanning the Communist Party, there was an audible gasp in the chamber. In the sandwich bars and shops around Parliament, where coloured staff clustered around radios and TVs, a stunned silence was followed by shrieks and whoops of excitement. With those words, F. W. de Klerk destroyed the world as whites knew it, and opened up a whole new universe to everyone else.

But if there was no going back to the land of apartheid, it was just as hard to discern the shape of the new landscape ahead. Only one thing was certain: de Klerk was not promising to give it all away. He was not—as many outsiders assumed—recognizing the historical inevitability of black majority rule; he does not recognize that to this day. As de Klerk said often in the months to follow, whites were not prepared to "bow out apologetically from the stage of history," and he was not about to push them. His plan, on February 2, was to share power with blacks, subject to an effective white veto, not to hand it over.

Roelf Meyer believes the opposite: that de Klerk knew that black rule was inevitable. He recalls a conversation in December 1989, when he stood with the new president on the veranda of the appropriately named Botha House on the Indian Ocean coast in Natal Province, and de Klerk pondered what he was about to do. "We were standing alone on the stoep, and F.W. said to me, 'We are the liquidators of this firm,' knowing that, as we are both lawyers, I would understand what he meant," Meyer says now. But the weight of evidence suggests that de Klerk meant to liquidate exclusive white rule, not white power. For from the beginning, he and Meyer always had a different goal in mind. Meyer—young, ambitious, modern—thought it was a waste of time to fight majority rule. F.W. did not; he fought it to the very last days of his presidency.

In his autobiography, Nelson Mandela is extremely scathing about his rival's intentions, pointing out that

despite his seemingly progressive action, Mr. de Klerk was by no means the great emancipator. He was a gradualist, a careful pragmatist. He did not make any of his reforms with the intention of putting himself out of power. He made them for precisely the opposite reason: to ensure power for the Afrikaner in a new dispensation. . . .

His goal was to create a system of power sharing based on group rights, which would preserve a modified form of minority power in South Africa. He was decidedly opposed to majority rule, or "simple majoritarianism," as he sometimes called it, because that would end white domination in a single stroke . . . although he was prepared to allow the black majority to vote and create legislation, he wanted to retain a minority veto.

I would dispute none of Mr. Mandela's judgments; but I cannot share his condemnation. He censures de Klerk for being a politician and not a saint. But if South Africa had had to await a holy man for its liberation, it would be languishing still in apartheid captivity. Ethnic self-interest motivated de Klerk to act, more powerfully and reliably than morality alone could have done. And the sense of doing right—on its own—could never have sustained de Klerk through the difficult years to follow. He had to believe his side could win.

De Klerk joined the battle because he thought he had a fighting chance to outsmart and outmaneuver the ANC in negotiations; just possibly even to outvote them, by forming a coalition with moderate black leaders like Chief Buthelezi, or at the least to deny them an overwhelming majority; and if all else failed, to overrule them in a new power-sharing government.

Race was still his guiding principle then, as he admitted to me himself in 1994. Minorities would have special rights, and whites special powers, in a political system constructed—as in the days of apartheid—from separate racial groups. De Klerk believed the presidency should rotate between white and non-white leaders, with matters of importance decided collectively by all of them—an arrangement that would have given whites a veto over the majority. He wanted this form of power sharing enshrined in the Constitution, forever.

In February 1990, in the earliest days of the new South Africa, most Afrikaners still found black rule unimaginable. The vast majority found it hard enough to accept universal suffrage. At a pinch, they could envisage majority rule—but only after a ten- to twenty-year transition. They could not foresee the speed with which political power actually moved from white hands to black. Perhaps whites were tricked by their own centuries-old illusion about blacks—that Africans were born to serve. Whether from the front or from the back, whites thought they could continue to lead. The nature of this leadership, of course, would have to change. White domination, white hegemony, white rule were out; but white power was not. De Klerk knew a revolution in power relations was inevitable; but he thought he could manage the revolution.

De Klerk wanted to limit democracy because he still saw it as the enemy of the white man in Africa. It would take a revolution in his thinking—one as radical as any that had gone before—before F. W. de Klerk was ready to surrender, heart and soul, to democracy as savior.

On February 2, 1990, that transformation was invisible on the horizon. As he took the parliamentary podium, de Klerk radiated confidence. Master of an undefeated monolith, he was ready to take the political offensive. He beamed with the pride and the absolute certainty of believing what he did was right, and was suffused with the potency that gave him. He looked—well—liberated.

Archbishop Desmond Tutu, speaking for those who had most cause to doubt de Klerk, captured the excitement of that day when he told a hastily convened press conference, "What he said has taken my breath away. It's incredible!" And he added: "Give him credit, give him credit, man; I do."

If de Klerk had left the good cleric breathless, he had seriously deflated the ANC's sails. As he told his brother Wimpie, the plan had been to seize the initiative from the ANC, and it appeared to have been spectacularly successful. The ANC could no longer mobilize the fight against apartheid if de Klerk was promising to abolish it. "I remember sitting with Thabo [Mbeki] the day after de Klerk's speech, and so far as Thabo can go white, he was white," says Frederik van Zyl Slabbert, a liberal Afrikaner who helped mediate between the two sides. " 'What do we do now?' he said. 'What do we do now? We can't say, put Mandela back in' ! "

De Klerk had upstaged the ANC on its own cherished turf, overseas. He had cleverly exploited the gap between the international perception of South Africa and the reality—the perception that nothing had changed and the reality that much had already been done to dismantle apartheid. He had leaped, but not nearly as far as international reviewers thought he had done: not from apartheid to majority rule, but from Botha-style power sharing to a new, more marketable version.

The public relations impact of his move was enormous. It was eagerly welcomed overseas (though no country except the United Kingdom relaxed sanctions as a result, and the British sanctions had been minimal). Domestically, de Klerk was fêted as a hero among non-whites, giving him delusions of grandeur about the size of the gratitude vote he might expect from the newly liberated. But de Klerk knew beforehand that he could count on support from his opponents; his concern was for his own constituency. They were presented with a fait accompli of shocking proportions. Yet no voice was raised in opposition.

Obedient as always to the figure of authority, Afrikaners fell into step behind their president. Within hours of de Klerk's speech, I interviewed working-class Afrikaners—those with the most to lose from his revolution— as they went about their normal Saturday errands at a shopping center in Cape Town. Without exception, they displayed the herd mentality which de Klerk was to find so useful in the years to come. "If the president decides, it's all right by me," I was told by one young Afrikaner, with a bored shrug of the shoulders. That might have been the motto of de Klerk's caucus as well; where the president led, they would follow.

De Klerk's colleagues were not merely displaying an Afrikaans habit of mind. They were reacting to the qualities of their new leader: an earnest, affable style; an absolute conviction that his was the only way to save the Afrikaner nation; and, underlying it all, personal political ambitions they could readily understand. For if de Klerk, then fifty-three, wanted to secure his place in history as a statesman, he wanted at least as much to ensure his immediate political future. He managed to persuade his party that a deal with the African National Congress could be had on terms which would guarantee them continued political influence. They trusted him, because his future was on the line just as much as theirs.

De Klerk was asked later, in 1995, whether he knew when he took office in 1989 that he would be the last white president of South Africa. "No," he replied, "and I don't believe it today either." It was that confidence which permitted de Klerk to keep the caucus together throughout the difficult years to follow. Several ministers had nervous breakdowns, or retired from the cabinet in financial or political disgrace; others quietly faded from the scene. But no major faction broke away to form a rival political force. If it had done, the new South Africa might have been born in civil war.

The earth moved the day F. W. de Klerk opened South Africa's last white Parliament; and before the aftershocks had subsided, he was back in action. Seven days after the February 2 speech, de Klerk invited Nelson Mandela to Tuynhuys, the presidential mansion, to tell him he would be released from prison the following day—and to toast the freedom of the man who would take his job from him forever.

The two men spent the evening before the release squabbling over whether it should take place at all. Mandela wanted a week's notice, to prepare his followers; de Klerk wanted to get it all over with. The power struggle between the two men—forced into a partnership that neither found truly congenial—began that night at Tuynhuys. Mandela was intensely annoyed at de Klerk's decision to free him without warning and without consultation. The president had told the foreign press corps of the release before Mandela himself was informed. He had drawn up a release plan without even asking the prisoner's views.

Mandela had sharp words to say to de Klerk about the bad old authoritarian habits which made him think he could dictate to the leader of the ANC. De Klerk told Mandela he would be released in Johannesburg, despite his desire to walk free from the gates of his prison near Cape Town. "I told him that I strongly objected to that," Mandela records in his autobiography. "I would make my way back to Johannesburg, but when I chose to, not when the government wanted me to. 'Once I am free,' I said, 'I will look after myself.' "

De Klerk was taken aback by all this. He was not used to taking orders from black men, much less from prisoners, and he must have found it cruelly ironic. Mandela's captivity had, more than anything else, ruined South Africa's reputation worldwide. Now de Klerk was ready to put that right—and Mandela was denying him the chance.

In the end, as they would do so often in the years to come, the two men found their way to a reasonable compromise. Mandela knew that de Klerk's international image would suffer irreparable harm if he failed to release his prisoner as announced; and he cared enough about that to accept his captor's timetable. De Klerk agreed that the ANC leader could be released in Cape Town, and make his own way to Johannesburg—even though this would make it much harder to control the circumstances of the release and ensure public order.

They sealed their pact over twin tumblers of whiskey—though the abstemious Mandela only feigned to drink his, confiding coyly in his autobiography that "such spirits are too strong for me." Then, for the first time ever, the new South Africa had its portrait taken: A government photographer snapped Mandela and de Klerk standing stiffly side by side—not smiling, not touching—in the presidential office. That was the picture South Africans awoke to the next morning, splashed across their Sunday newspapers, on the day Mandela would be free.

> "Don't you understand, for the first time in my life I'm a free man!"
> —The words of a tearful F. W. de Klerk on the release of Nelson Mandela

MY HOSTS WERE AMAZED, *the children gawped, the neighbors came in to watch. The white lady was doing the dishes. It really was a new South Africa.*

The Mafolo family of house number 1152, Molapo, Soweto, did not readily associate white "madams" with dishtowels, or toilet brushes, or ironing boards. Such domestic instruments were wielded by large black ladies from Zululand, not small blond women from Detroit.

But I had to find some way to thank the Mafolo family for their extraordinary hospitality. I was spending the weekend with them, in their Soweto "matchbox" home—four tiny rooms; no toilet, no bath, no running water; only a cold tap in the yard. Two Mafolo children had given up their bed so that I could sleep in it. But that only aggravated an already desperate bedding crisis. Even when I was not there, two teen-aged sons slept every night under the kitchen table. It was the only spare bit of floor available.

I was displayed to the neighborhood as a prized artefact of another civilization. My least bodily function was a subject of fascination. Whenever I needed to use the outdoor facilities, toilet paper was produced as a sign of honor. Water was boiled and tipped in a basin for me to wash—while elder Mafolo ladies shooed away the children, who desperately wanted to watch. In the concrete backyard, a sheep was executed for my benefit. Soon a mess of steaming intestines—a Soweto delicacy—was put before me on a ceremonial platter.

When I expressed a preference for a nice chop, or maybe a bit of shank, there was stunned incomprehension. To like tripe was more or less the definition of being human. I tried to explain that not all whites were so perverse; the French, for example, seemed quite to like offal. But I think my hosts just accepted the fact that tripe was a racial gap they could not bridge.

I had gone to Soweto, under the auspices of a local church group, because the Mafolos and their neighbors wanted to show their willingness to close such gaps. It was their answer to F. W. de

Klerk's gesture in Parliament: the hand of Soweto, held out to white South Africa.

Relations between the races are never as simple as that, of course. Black South Africa's attitude toward whites is a cocktail of mixed and contradictory emotions—envy, awe, fear, condescension, and a desperate desire to be accepted by whites. Sometimes I think black South Africans pity me for living my soulless white life. Sometimes they seem to shrink before the power of my skin.

But that weekend, all Soweto wanted to do was show off. White visitors are exceptionally rare—perhaps as many as 90 percent of whites have never been inside a township—and black South Africa was proud to be hosting visitors on its own turf. I scarcely passed anyone in the street who did not welcome me. Grandmothers in housecoats called across full clotheslines to greet me, and stern-faced young comrades loitering on bits of waste ground reached out to shake my hand. One man stopped his taxi to tell me "thank you for your support." Everyone had to know if I was enjoying Soweto; and everyone was delighted to find that I was.

That weekend was a small epiphany for a girl from Detroit. And it was powerful therapy for a cynic.

8

Siamese Twins

T HE SCENE WAS TOTAL MAYHEM: Gunfire, the sound of breaking glass, the shouts and cries of the wounded. Paramedics scurrying from one prone body to the next. Fear of suffocation in the vast and manic crowd. And then having to hit the deck again to avoid stray birdshot. It was a sorry start to the greatest day in black South Africa's history.

My psychological snapshots of Nelson Mandela's release are not happy ones. Everything went wrong from the start. Mandela, who is himself obsessively punctual, arrived five hours late to greet tens of thousands of impatient supporters massed on Cape Town's Grand Parade. The delay was not his fault: his wife Winnie had arrived grievously late at the prison to collect him. His motorcade was swamped by well-wishers who impeded its progress; and the ANC, which had insisted on handling crowd control, proved unequal to the task. Mandela could get nowhere near the balcony from which he was to deliver his speech; when he tried, his car was nearly crushed by the adoring crowd, which kept him imprisoned in it for over an hour. The delay proved tragic—frustrated, overexcited youngsters turned to looting. Police responded with live ammunition. Several were killed, and scores wounded.

This was the very scenario Mandela had feared when he insisted on an extra week in prison to allow the ANC to prepare. But de Klerk could not afford delay, so at 4:16 P.M. on February 11, 1990, Mandela walked from prison into chaos.

He stepped from the gates of his prison, clutching the hand of his beloved Winnie—and blinked like a rabbit caught in hostile headlights. She, a seasoned political performer, shot her left arm up proudly in the black-power salute. Her startled husband followed suit, but almost as an afterthought. She beamed; he just looked bewildered.

Mandela can be forgiven for his dismay. When he went to prison in 1963, he was only a minor celebrity. He did not fully realize that the twenty-seven intervening years had made him one of the most prominent figures of the late twentieth century. He walked into a media circus of unprecedented proportions, largely unprepared. But the media was not his only problem: the ecstatic Grand Parade mob had petrified his driver, who sped away in panic. Mandela took him to a colleague's home to calm him down, but the delay further exacerbated the rioting in the city.

Only with the onset of dusk did Mandela finally step onto the ornate balcony of the city hall. Then he found he had no spectacles—having left his behind in prison—and was forced to borrow an ill-fitting pair from his wife. Unfortunately, he seemed to borrow her radical, uncompromising views along with her eyeglasses. For the speech he read out that day, the most important of his life as a free man, was not his own. It was written by committee—a committee which he clearly declined to lead. Radical UDF leaders, profoundly suspicious of de Klerk, had penned a speech from hell, a speech without warmth, vision, or humanity; a speech for the warpath.

Mandela delivered that speech, pitifully punctuated by gunfire, to the largest audience he would ever reach, totaling many millions worldwide. It was a missed opportunity of epic proportions. One short sentence gave sole cause for comfort, to those who hoped to find in Mandela the great conciliator. "Mr. de Klerk is a man of integrity," Mandela said. But it was lost in a flood of militancy. The message of the speech was clear. "Now is the time to intensify the struggle." That was fine for the leader of black South Africa; but from the putative father of the rainbow nation, it fell short of what was needed. The truth could not be denied: Mandela was a disappointment.

The next morning, he set out to correct those first impressions. Mandela the peacemaker made his first public appearance, on a perfect Cape Town morning, in the manicured garden of Archbishop Desmond Tutu. The elderly Mandela stiffly descended the steps of Tutu's elegant Bishopscourt home, and apologized to our motley collection of hard-bitten journalists for his failure to address us, as promised, on the day of his release. He begged our pardon as though we were honored guests, not the wild dogs of the world's media. We were not used to such deference.

Then Mandela used us to broadcast his message of reconciliation, loud and clear. "The ANC is very much concerned to address the question of the concerns of whites," he told us—the first time that he had voiced such sentiments publicly. "They insist on structural guarantees to ensure that . . . majority rule does not result in the domination of whites by blacks. We understand that fear. The whites are our fellow South Africans. We want them to feel safe."

Mandela's moderation and generosity were well known to the small band of Afrikaner officials who had been his interlocutors in prison. Hints of his reconciliatory message had even leaked out in the left-wing press. But until he spoke to the world's media on the Bishopscourt lawn that morning, few had dared believe rumors of his flexibility. For the first time, the realistic prospect of a deal between African and Afrikaner opened up before our eyes.

Mandela did all he could to further that prospect. He pinned the label "man of integrity" to F. W. de Klerk's breast—this time with fanfare—simultaneously signaling to 28 million black South Africans that it was safe to trust the white leader, and easing the fears of whites that his release would provoke a violent backlash. Though he spoke in favor of nationalizing South Africa's mines, a long-standing policy of the ANC, he also stated, in no uncertain terms, that he was not a Communist—an assurance which did much to calm white property owners.

But the image Mandela projected that day owed as much to his manner as to his words—he wooed millions of viewers worldwide with his warmth and charm, and impressed them by his dignity and bearing. He fielded questions with confidence, and answered them with spontaneity and wit. It was the performance of a world-class politician, all the more striking for his long isolation. Mandela had proved himself a leader to rival de Klerk. History had thrown up not one but two skillful politicians to plot a path to the future.

Before these two leaders could start their long courtship in earnest—before they could begin "talks about talks" on a new constitution—their officials would need to hold "talks about talks about talks," discussions on removing the obstacles which kept the two sides away from the negotiating table.

That task, as always, fell to the intelligence community: NIS for the government, and from the ANC, Jacob Zuma, head of intelligence. At the end of March 1990, NIS smuggled Zuma and ANC lawyer Penuell Maduna into South Africa from exile, to make arrangements for the return of the ANC's guerrillas and diplomats. For though the ANC was now legal, individual ANC leaders were still branded criminals under South African law. They risked arrest for past acts of terrorism. Before talks could begin, the two sides had to agree on an amnesty.

This proved a difficult business, in the atmosphere of distrust that reigned during the early days after Mandela's release. But true to form, the two sides quickly found a way to lighten the atmosphere. Zuma (whose gentle wit soon made him a favorite among government leaders) gets a twinkle in his eye when he recalls one such visit to the land of the Boers. As soon as he descended the steps of the plane that had brought him secretly from Lusaka, he was plonked down in the back seat of a government vehicle next to Lieutenant General Basie Smit, then head of the brutal security police. (Smit resigned in 1994 after he was accused of helping arm Chief Buthelezi's Inkatha Freedom Party to fight Zuma and the ANC.)

"Basie Smit was very keen to sit next to me," Zuma recalls, with his characteristic throaty chuckle, remarking on the cordiality with which the two sides shared the South African sacraments of grilled meat and strong drink that same evening. Smit and his colleagues even laid on a tour of Pretoria, geographical symbol of apartheid. Under cover of darkness, they took their ANC visitors to see the Voortrekker Monument, the squat sandstone shrine built to celebrate the triumph of a few hundred Afrikaners over thousands of Zulu warriors at the Battle of Blood River in 1838.

Zuma recalls with greatest mirth the following day, when the state radio reported that police had issued a warrant for his arrest. He guffaws at the thought that while the security police mounted a manhunt to find him, he was sitting comfortably with their chief, General Smit, who refused even to tell his own men that he was breaking bread with terrorists.

Smit and Zuma were not just playing at secrecy. The incident reveals the deadly serious process by which leaders on both sides had to distance themselves from their own constituents, in order to approach the middle ground. In those early days of contact, the rank and file of the opposing sides were radically polarized; only the elites were beginning to edge along the tightrope toward a meeting in the middle.

Problems arose immediately over the composition of the ANC delegation to preliminary talks. F. W. de Klerk was horrified when he learned that Joe Slovo, the Communist leader, would be part of the ANC team. De Klerk's constituents had taken the news of the unbannings quietly. But for their president to entertain the "red menace" to tea might be a step too far. De Klerk insisted Slovo be removed.

He nearly got his way. De Klerk's prohibition caused consternation in ANC ranks. "Some of our people thought that it was not politic to include the general secretary of the Communist Party as part of the delegation," Slovo once told me with a chuckle. "But Mandela put his foot down." The ANC leader was nothing if not loyal: White communists were virtually the only whites who had supported the liberation struggle from the beginning; an alliance built on such foundations could not be sundered for the pleasure of de Klerk. Mandela could not afford, in any case, to leave the Communists out. Many of the best brains in the ANC and UDF—Slovo, Maharaj, guerrilla leader Chris Hani, National Union of Mineworkers leader Cyril Ramaphosa—were Communists.

Urged on by Niël Barnard, de Klerk dropped his objection. Within weeks, the irrepressible Slovo—who, ironically, would become one of the

greatest advocates of moderation within the ANC apart from Mandela himself—was showing off his trademark red socks at Cape Town Airport.

Slovo and his fellow exiles had come home to attend the first ever round
of formal negotiations between white and black South Africa, to be held at
the magnificent Groote Schuur estate, for three days in early May 1990.

Putting the two sides together proved a major operation. Mandela
forced the postponement of the first round of talks, scheduled for April 11,
after police shot eleven demonstrators dead in the township of Sebokeng
near Johannesburg. And he did not spare de Klerk from blame. "If Mr. de
Klerk continues to sit down with his arms folded while police shoot our
people," he said flatly, "then negotiations have no future whatsoever."

Pretoria feared that either right- or left-wing radicals might make the
talks a target. So officials prepared three alternative venues. Groote Schuur—
a gracious Cape Dutch stately home whose entrance door is decorated,
appropriately, with a frieze depicting Jan van Riebeeck, the first European
settler at the Cape, negotiating with the local natives—was their first choice.
If that became untenable, the whole group would evacuate to a nearby
airbase, or else to Simonstown naval station at the tip of the Cape Peninsula.
To make matters worse, ANC officials refused to reveal details of their
movements to the security police charged with protecting them. Motorcades
would zoom in and out of the Lord Charles Hotel in Somerset West, where
the ANC delegation was housed, while frantic securitymen tried to find out
where they were headed.

"But the *moment* they met at Groote Schuur, *yullll,*" says Fanie van der
Merwe, a member of the government delegation, rolling fondly off his
tongue this term of Afrikaans amazement. "Suddenly they felt, but this chap,
I *like* this chap." Van der Merwe laughs. "And it went off *famously.*"

To many in the government team—whose interaction with blacks had
been limited to illiterate laborers, poorly educated homeland officials, and a
handful of academics—the sophisticates of the ANC were a revelation. "We
were quite impressed by the quality of their intelligence, their logic, and
their ability to interact informally," says Gerrit Viljoen, who was then de
Klerk's chief constitutional guru. Guerrilla commander Joe Modise—"the
guy who was in charge of all the killing"—proved intelligent, reasonable,
practical, pragmatic. And *Umkhonto we Sizwe* chief of staff Chris Hani was
even more of a revelation. Viljoen, a respected South African classicist,
debated the classics with Hani, who studied Latin at South Africa's Rhodes
University, and with Pallo Jordan, ANC director of information, an impres-
sively erudite historian. Such evidence of a common cultural background
and shared values derived from ancient civilization were immensely im-

portant to a man like Viljoen. No natural politician, he was less concerned
with power than with the survival of Western Christian culture in Africa; at
least he knew the ANC were not ignorant of its attractions.

Humor was also a great binding force, with jokes made about the most
unlikely subjects. Former prisoners chuckled with their captors over the
circumstances of their arrest; terrorists showed off their prominent ribs, and
joked that they had grown thin evading the security police; captor and captive reminisced about mutual acquaintances. Thabo Mbeki summed up the
mood. "Within minutes everybody understood that nobody in the room had
horns."

But if cordiality was the norm at tea breaks and mealtimes, tough words
were exchanged at the negotiating table. De Klerk defended Verwoerd,
Vorster, and Botha. And though Mandela impressed the government delegation by delivering, partly in Afrikaans, his patented treatise on the history of
Afrikaner nationalism (with a subsection thrown in on Afrikaner socialism),
he stunned them as well with his vigorous defense of the ANC's historical
commitment to violent struggle.

Some members of the National Party delegation were horrified. "Short
of them having horns, all our worst expectations were met," one participant
recalls. And some of the jokes cut a bit close to the bone. When Mbeki,
the ANC's equivalent of a shadow foreign minister, suggested that serving
Foreign Minister Pik Botha could be his deputy in an ANC government,
Botha was not amused. As far as the government was concerned, the talks
were not about creating a new government in which white men would serve
black men.

Solving such contentious issues as the balance of power was not, in any
case, the business of Groote Schuur. Its brief was simply to clear obstacles
to constitutional negotiation. Reading between the lines of the so-called
Groote Schuur Minute, the agreement signed at the end of the talks, these
are obvious. Pretoria must lift the state of emergency; the ANC must recon-
sider the armed struggle; and the two sides must agree on a definition of
political crimes before they could bring up to forty thousand political exiles
back home and get the remaining political prisoners out of jail. Then, constitutional negotiations could begin.

In reality, Groote Schuur was about bonding, and being seen to bond,
in the eyes of the nation and the world. Nothing substantive was agreed
there—except to keep on talking. But the images of Groote Schuur will
remain, like postcards, in the national memory.

At the end of the meeting, Mandela and de Klerk did an extraordinary
double act, to camera. Their words were striking on their own. Mandela
spoke of the talks as the "realization of a dream," and promised—to the

amazement of many of his colleagues—to look "very hard and earnestly into the whole question of armed struggle," a promise which delighted de Klerk. The ANC leader went far out on a dangerous limb to endorse de Klerk, once again. "I have not the slightest doubt that the State President means what he says," Mandela insisted, adding later that he had "no doubt whatever" about the government's integrity.

The two men disagreed over whether sanctions should be lifted, and over another matter that would prove even more difficult to resolve, the issue of "minority rights," National Party code for special constitutional protection for whites. But the real message of Groote Schuur was in the body language: in the bald head of de Klerk, inclined in exaggerated deference to Mandela; in the beam of Mandela's smile, and the easy jesting of the white leader; in the assiduous courtesy with which each man helped the other with the most difficult questions. (De Klerk went so far as to reprimand one questioner, who pressed Mandela on the delicate issue of the armed struggle, interjecting irritably, "But you've dealt with that already," and moving the conference on to less sensitive subjects.)

With the first words of his freedom—"Mr. de Klerk is a man of integrity"—Mandela had bound himself to the white president by the strongest possible bond, not affection or affinity, but mutual need. The body language of Groote Schuur reaffirmed that bond. Both men emerged from the talks thinking they could cut a deal between themselves—a sort of power fix between African and Afrikaner—in which there would be no losers. The nation's mental timetable was drastically revised, to take account of their unexpected optimism. The idea was to present South Africa with a fait accompli before radicals from both sides could mobilize against it.

Within weeks, the new optimism had foundered. Mandela and de Klerk had formed their de facto alliance too quickly. It easily fell prey to extremists. The first threat to the partnership came from radicals within the ANC who— without Mandela's knowledge—were running their own private insurance policy in case negotiations failed. Worried that the ANC would appear too weak at the negotiating table, the insurrectionist wing of the movement had kept "Operation Vula" (the underground operation spearheaded by Mac Maharaj in the late 1980s) alive. Vula had never flourished, and by July 1990, it existed far more powerfully in the mind of Maharaj than in fact. Still, when Pretoria uncovered the operation and arrested Maharaj and other Vula leaders, Mandela was furious—not at de Klerk but at his own people. The ANC could not afford to create the impression that it had a secret agenda to overthrow the state.

Pretoria, too, misplayed its hand. In an attempt to drive a wedge between the ANC and the Communists, the government used Vula documents to try to incriminate Joe Slovo and secure his ouster from the ANC negotiating team. But the "Joe" of the documents turned out to be a codename—not Slovo. Pretoria was forced to back down and accept him as a negotiator, once and for all.

The incident highlighted divisions within the African National Congress that would bedevil negotiations for years to come, between those who wanted to talk and fight, and those who saw the two as mutually exclusive. The two groups—the strugglers and the diplomats—had been battling for control of the ANC for years already. The organization had only publicly committed itself to negotiation a scant six months before Mandela left prison (by which time Mbeki and Mandela had already been carrying on talks for several years). In August 1989, it published the document known as the Harare Declaration, which set out a host of preconditions to negotiation: Legalize the ANC, release all political prisoners, end the state of emergency, remove all troops from townships. And even then, the document sparked fierce debate within the movement.

Then ANC and UDF leaders got wind of Mandela's memorandum to P. W. Botha, in which he made his startling offer of special constitutional protections for whites. Instructions went out, through parts of the fractured leadership chain of the UDF, to shun Mandela, and refuse invitations, then being sent out, to visit him in prison. "The word was, Madiba [Mandela's clan name] was wearing a three-piece suit, drinking wine, you name it, he was a sellout," Mac Maharaj recalls.

When Mandela emerged from prison, and for years to come, the ANC would remain divided between those who cherished two competing paradigms for the future: seizure of power or negotiated transition. In May 1990, when the Groote Schuur talks took place, the lobby in favor of compromise was frighteningly small. Most ANC members thought talks should focus on one issue only—the transfer of power.

The organization had little in the way of a negotiating strategy, scant organizational competence, and few ideas about the new South Africa, or how to achieve it. As Joe Slovo told me at the time, "We've had to devote the bulk of our energies to getting here—not to what we're going to do when we arrive."

When they did arrive, it took months to set up the most basic infrastructure. Phones rang maddeningly off the hook at ANC headquarters at 54 Sauer Street in downtown Johannesburg; officials made appointments but seldom kept them; administration was in chaos. Meanwhile three separate, autonomous groups of leaders fought for control: the released prisoners, many of them elderly, who had run the ANC before it was banned; returned exiles, a close-knit group who had little direct experience of South Africa of the 1990s; and internal acitivists from the UDF, many of them from the unions, who had borne the brunt of struggle during the 1980s and had been chastened by the experience. Even Mandela's leadership was not secure. I remember being told by senior UDF leaders just before he emerged from prison that Mandela was just "an ordinary ANC member like any other." It would take time for him to consolidate his power base.

The divisions were never clearcut, even so. Mindful of the prevailing wind, ANC insurrectionists were careful not to oppose negotiations in principle. They simply argued that the movement should not negotiate from weakness. Vula was defended, not as an alternative to talks but as an accompaniment to them. Maharaj claims that, far from opposing the negotiations, he was carrying a draft of the agreement to suspend the armed struggle, a major negotiated concession, when he was arrested. He believed there must be no easing up in the townships, just because the leadership was at Groote Schuur.

But Operation Vula revealed that, though Mandela had chosen to trust de Klerk, his colleagues remained suspicious. As Ronnie Kasrils, another Vula leader, said at the time, "Mr. Mandela thinks there's integrity and honesty. I think there is an element of that, but there's something else too. We cannot be sure of the real intentions of F.W. We've got to put in place an insurance policy."

"Just because Comrade Mandela is free doesn't mean apartheid is finished," said the fierce child terrorist, sipping a chaste Coke as she sat on the sofa of my old Lusaka cottage. I had gone to Zamiba, only days after Mandela left prison, to see how well the ANC was adjusting to freedom. I had brought whiskey from South Africa as a treat for this group of young guerrillas. But these were military puritans; they drank Coke.

"As long as any kind of special privilege exists—whether political or economic—we will not abandon the struggle," said the young girl, who chose anonymity. She was one of the ten thousand-odd child soldiers the ANC had left behind in dismal camps in Zambia and Tanzania. After spending all her young life dreaming of the Battle of Pretoria, she found it hard to alter her mental landscape to see negotiation as victory. She had been raised on the promise of revolution, which was just about all the ANC could provide for her subsistence, apart from the most basic rations of food and clothing. For all her other needs, she was given K14 a month—about 30 cents.

The *Umkhonto we Sizwe* political education machine was working overtime on these fierce children, in the wake of Mandela's conciliatory gestures toward "the regime." The young terrorist, who wore a fetching black beret, seemed to be having particular trouble with Mandela's conduct. She had battled hard to accept the non-racial philosophy of the ANC: "When I left South Africa in 1985, all I wanted to do was *kill*. If I'd been given a weapon then, I would have killed the first white person I saw. I had to learn that it is the system we're fighting, and not individual whites." But the idea of de Klerk as a man of integrity, and the notion of ending the armed struggle, were still abhorrent to her.

She was not alone in arguing that the struggle should not end until South Africa entered a state of non-racial, Communist nirvana, which might be visible in the mind's eye of a child bred on myths of insurrection, but which seemed to adults only a dream. It was hard to see how Mandela could hope to satisfy her.

Over time, Mandela would be able to redraw that young girl's sketch of a new South Africa along more realistic lines. But in the middle of 1990, he did not feel he had that time—so he simply overruled her. He trusted he would soon have impressive results from Pretoria to show for his moderation.

In August 1990, Mandela decided to do what the ANC had always insisted was impossible: unilaterally suspend the armed struggle against apartheid, in exchange for very little except a piece of the moral high ground. He hoped the concession would boost the progress of negotiations, bogged down since Groote Schuur had ended three months earlier.

He was advised to make this extraordinary concession by no less a figure than Joe Slovo, whose immaculate radical credentials made him the perfect advocate of moderation. In July 1990, in the midst of the Vula crisis, Slovo went to Mandela to propose a unilateral suspension. Mandela's first reaction was negative. But he soon realized it was time to seize the initiative from de Klerk, who had wrongfooted the ANC by unbanning it and kept the movement constantly running to catch up ever since. Slovo would propose the measure within the ANC national executive, and Mandela would support him. It was a dream ticket. After strong initial reservations, the ANC executive agreed.

In the early hours of August 7, 1990, Mandela emerged from fifteen hours of exhausting talks with the government at the Union Buildings in Pretoria to announce that the African National Congress was suspending the armed struggle launched nearly thirty years before. The government was delighted: from its point of view, the ANC had cleared the last remaining obstacle to constitutional negotiations.

ANC publicists struggled to explain to their own constituents what seemed an unnecessary concession. For with the cease-fire, the ANC had publicly renounced the strategy of seizure of power, so dear to the soldiers of MK, to the township street fighters, and to virtually every ANC supporter except a small handful at the very top. It was the most important shift in ANC strategy in thirty years—and it had been made, crucially, without preparing the ANC grass roots. Slovo admitted to me afterward that 90 percent of ANC supporters thought the decision was a sellout.

The movement placed full-page advertisements in the local press to try to present the cease-fire as noble compromise, not capitulation. Pallo Jordan, the ANC's intensely bright director of information, took his defense of the agreement to suspend armed struggle, known as the Pretoria Minute, to the press. He sketched a relationship between two men—and two organizations—which can only be called symbiotic. De Klerk "felt very much over a barrel on the question of a cease-fire," Jordan explained. The ANC had long insisted it would only suspend the armed struggle once government agreed to do the same (withdrawing troops from the townships and ceasing hostilities against the ANC). But that would have meant Pretoria recognizing the ANC as a legitimate belligerent, and as Jordan more than reasonably explained, de Klerk could not afford to do that. The white president had a problem with his constituents to the right; so the ANC decided to solve it for him, on the grounds that they could not gain by weakening the reformist president. De Klerk had jumped. As irony would have it, only Mandela could hold the net.

"The National Party *must* remain on board. Should it pull out, there is no *knowing* what the future will be," Jordan told us, his already high nasal voice rising even higher to stress the risk of an anti–de Klerk backlash. The ANC needed him as much as he needed them. Both desperately needed a deal.

Those would remain the central facts of South African politics, from beginning to end of the negotiated revolution. But in the difficult years to follow, they were destined to be obscured, again and again, by anger and ambition, and above all, by violence.

The marriage of convenience between Mandela and de Klerk, which seemed to proceed so smoothly in the early months of the ANC leader's freedom, rapidly became a union of acrimony. As violence emerged to blight black lives—violence which the ANC blamed on de Klerk—Mandela came under heavy criticism for his spontaneous impulse to trust the white president. Within days of the signing of the Pretoria Minute, South Africa descended into an orgy of violence unprecedented even by its own woeful standards. Leaders on all sides bickered over responsibility for the carnage, but did nothing to stop it. They would carry South Africa to the brink of destruction.

SHE WAS WEARING *a tattered pink bathrobe, and her feet were bare. If only death were not so terribly mundane.*

I never discovered the identity of the body which lay, with one cheek pillowed in the mud, across a steep footpath in Natal. The anonymous limbs were arranged at angles impossible in life, but otherwise, the corpse was entirely plausible. A middle-aged, poor, rural Zulu woman, with a scarcely perceptible bullet wound in the back of the head. A slippery trickle of blood through the mud.

I stood there beside the still-warm body, trying to summon up some appropriate emotion: pity, outrage, horror, revulsion. But the voyeur in me (masquerading as a journalist) merely felt a kind of morbid fascination, a frisson of guilty excitement at being involved, vicariously, in murder. To me, to the colleagues around me, to the nervous policeman dressed in jeans and submachine gun at my side, she was just a body. Not a dead human being. A body. Detritus of civil war.

To those who killed her—the ragged band of Zulu warriors who had disappeared minutes before over the crest of a distant hill—she was equally anonymous. They would not have known her name, or needed to know it; they would not have cared about her politics. They killed her because of where she lived. In Natal, geography is a life-and-death issue.

9

The Third Man . . . and the Third Force

THE BATHROBE LADY lived at Henley, the kind of village one can find in any steep green valley in Natal—an untidy sprawl of mud-walled shacks, a few desultory vegetables, and the peculiar stillness born of poverty.

Like every other such village, Henley had chosen sides. It supported the "comrades," the United Democratic Front, formed in 1983 as a legal front for the banned African National Congress. The killers came from Inkatha, the traditionalist Zulu political organization headed by Chief Mangosuthu Buthelezi. It might have been, and often was, the other way around; for in the area melodramatically nicknamed Natal's "valley of death," the two were at war. This lady was roughly the three thousandth victim.

Had she survived, she would no doubt have described herself as a "comrade"—a ludicrously inappropriate term for a matronly lady in a bathrobe, but a bit of shorthand she would have found indispensable. Certainly, all her neighbors—including the grandmother who hid in the bushes beside the path and watched her execution—used that implausible label. They explained that, when the fighting started in 1987, "people had to choose sides." So Henley chose to be comrades.

Why comrades?

"We had to do what our children wanted." And the children of Natal overwhelmingly supported the urban-based UDF, which opposed what it considered Inkatha's "backward" tribalism. They condemned Chief Buthelezi as a "collaborator" with the white government, for though he had refused "independence" for his KwaZulu black homeland under apartheid, he accepted a salary from Pretoria to run it. He paid traditional chiefs from the homeland coffers, and so controlled them. That gave his Inkatha movement an iron grip over rural Zululand, which the "comrades" fought with their lives.

The radical UDF, on the other hand, was run largely by Communist trade unionists in the province. It promised equality, industrial power, and socialist redistribution of wealth. Employed, educated, urban, youthful Zulus inclined to the UDF; the rural poor, squatters, older traditionalists, and migrant workers preferred Inkatha. In crowded, underdeveloped, underemployed Natal, these were the perfect conditions for civil war.

The rivals began to stake out their turf. And once a hard core of UDF activists—or a small group of Inkatha traditionalists—had claimed a village as their own, every man, woman, and child in the area took on the victor's label. Then, each area was "politically cleansed" of rival supporters, and those who could not, or would not move, were forced to fall in line. Their political choices were made for them by the deadly geography of Natal; their lives, from then on, depended on it.

There is a hill in Natal—a place of many, many hills—which is known as Patheni, or "the place of goodness." The poignant beauty of the name is like a bitter joke played on those who live in the two rival villages separated by its blue-green ridge—including Samuel and Joseph Njilo, childhood playmates, brothers in war.

For the geography of Natal divided not just villages but families as well. Samuel and Joseph Njilo (whites would call them "cousins," though they prefer the looser African term, "brothers") grew up in the same household, on the slopes of Patheni Hill. They went through the same rites of passage to Zulu manhood, observed the same festivals, and grew together in unenviable poverty. Until politics—and the hill—came along to divide them.

I went to them, to try to understand the genesis of this Zulu tragedy, the causes of the bestial violence which began slowly in Natal in the 1980s, exploded in earnest after Mandela's release, and soon became an almost insuperable obstacle to the birth of the new South Africa.

How did they end up, forty years after a shared childhood, on opposite sides of the political divide? Why did Joseph (who lives at Ndaleni village) join the ANC, and Samuel (of Patheni village) join Inkatha? "Because one lives at Patheni and the other at Ndaleni," Joseph explained, his face betraying surprise at the stupidity of the question. For Joseph, geography was the only reality.

In 1990, Ndaleni village held a meeting, and decided unanimously to join the ANC. The decision had to be unanimous, Joseph explained; Ndaleni had no room for opposing viewpoints. "If I didn't join the ANC"—the course urged by his children—"I would have had to move to Patheni."

At Patheni, a few arduous kilometers away, Samuel Njilo did not try to pretend things were any different. "Even here, people *say* they are Inkatha when really they are ANC, because they've got houses here and they know it's too expensive to build another house." Faced with that overwhelming economic imperative, it would be a rare man who would vote with his conscience and not with his neighbors.

Politics had nothing to do with the first fighting between the two villages, which began in the early 1980s. These were traditional "faction fights" between rival clans, the normal stuff of social life in Zululand since the days of Shaka, their nineteenth-century warrior-king, great founder of the Zulu nation.

After Mandela left prison, fighting escalated, leaving several hundred dead. And that battle was generational: the youth of Patheni began to ridicule the local chief—Nkosi Dhlamini, hereditary chief of the area (who sat by, uncomprehending, as I interviewed Samuel Njilo in English). They ignored his authority and insisted he sever ties with the KwaZulu homeland, which paid his salary. They denigrated the trappings of his office—which, in this pathetic village, are scarcely ostentatious, a bracelet of goat's hair and a slightly larger hut—and refused his authority. And when they did that, according to Samuel Njilo, they ceased to be Zulus.

To be a Zulu, in Inkatha's book, meant youth must obey age, and everyone must obey the chief and his headmen. They control access to land, housing, health care, education, water, and other services, and are empowered by the KwaZulu government to decide all but the most serious criminal cases.

Tradition was at the crux of the dispute, as Samuel explained. And he punctuated his angry comments by jumping up to demonstrate the proper walk for a Zulu man wearing the traditional *beshu,* or skin skirt. "Raise yourself. Everyone must see. This is a *man.* Look at his culture," he roared, with that combination of machismo and bluster which makes such traditional Zulus objects of fun to more sophisticated urban Africans. But the dispute was deadly serious. The youth of Ndaleni tried to "necklace" the local chief, who fled. Ndaleni became ANC, and the youth of Patheni—who had similarly confronted their chief—moved to the other side of the hill. Marauding parties from both villages came over the ridge at night. Many died.

They were fighting, ostensibly, about politics. But few people in either village could have identified the policies of their adopted parties if their lives depended on it (which they did not). Joseph was ANC; but he confidently assured me that "Zululand is for Zulus and Transkei is for Xhosas," apparently unaware of his party's devotion to the idea of a South Africa where such tribal labels are shunned. Samuel could recite Inkatha policies; but his affiliation appeared to be based on his position as a paid Inkatha official rather than true commitment. They were fighting about power, not policy.

And that fight began, not when Nelson Mandela emerged from prison, but many years before.

The ANC likes to claim that Chief Mangosuthu Buthelezi, as leader of a tribal black homeland, was a creation of apartheid. It would be closer to the truth to say he was a creation of the ANC.

Buthelezi is a descendant of the Zulu king Cetshwayo, one of the kings who succeeded the childless Shaka. (Cetshwayo is famous for defeating the British at the 1879 Battle of Isandlwana, the biggest military debacle of the British imperial era.) Buthelezi cut his political teeth in the ANC Youth League. Mandela, who headed the youth league at the time, says he saw the Zulu chief as a rising young leader for the ANC. So when Buthelezi decided, in 1975, to form a "cultural movement" known as Inkatha, to mobilize support in the KwaZulu homeland which he headed as chief minister, ANC President Oliver Tambo encouraged him. Inkatha was to have been the ANC's Trojan Horse in South Africa. It was even referred to as the "internal wing of the ANC."

"Forming Inkatha was the ANC's idea—to have a political organization to undermine apartheid from within." Or so Jacob Zuma—the only senior Zulu in the top ANC leadership—once explained the matter to me. And for decades, Buthelezi did just that, refusing to accept independence for KwaZulu (which remained a so-called self-governing territory of South Africa), and campaigning locally and internationally for Mandela's release. National Party leaders took Buthelezi's opposition very seriously; without him, their policy of "separate development" could not succeed. He led the largest tribal group in South Africa (the Zulus, variously estimated at 7 to 9 million, are the country's largest ethnic group). Unless he accepted independence, separate development would fail.

By the mid-1970s, with the ANC's leaders all jailed or exiled, Buthelezi had become the dominant black political personality in South Africa. Whites liked his moderate views—he defended free enterprise, opposed sanctions, and nominally espoused democracy—and blacks saw that he had real power. P. W. Botha tried hard to entice Buthelezi to join his National Council, a vehicle for limited power sharing with blacks. Buthelezi refused. Botha's whole reform strategy was aimed at co-opting moderate blacks like Buthelezi into government; when the Zulu leader made this impossible, Botha's reforms had no future.

But if the white president found Buthelezi uncooperative, the ANC found him totally intransigent. Naively, ANC leaders had expected the proud and astute Zulu politician simply to act as their surrogate in South Africa. They were enraged when he took an independent line, criticizing their policies of armed struggle and sanctions. Differences came to a head in 1979, after a meeting between Buthelezi and Oliver Tambo in London. Each side tells its own inflamed tale of this famous falling out, involving accusations of breach of confidence. But the bottom line is that the rupture was terminal.

Zuma, who does not share the visceral hatred of Buthelezi common among most ANC leaders, acknowledges that the ANC mishandled the Zulu leader. They encouraged him to use the KwaZulu homeland, created by Pretoria, as a foothold for the fight against apartheid, but then allowed their youthful supporters to demonize him as a "stooge of Pretoria" for so doing. Buthelezi was vilified in exactly the terms most hateful to a proud Zulu. The legitimacy of his birth was questioned; he was described as a "snake," to be hit on the head by the ANC; he was depicted, in ANC posters, as an oversized baby in diapers. ANC officials in Lusaka, during my residence there in the mid-1980s, made no secret of the fact that they would like to kill him.

It often struck me that the ANC seemed to hate Buthelezi more than P. W. Botha himself—on the principle, no doubt, that the traitor in one's own camp is more dangerous than the enemy. And though the ANC moderated its position on many issues—negotiations, communism, armed struggle—it remained uncompromisingly opposed to Buthelezi. Gavin Relly, who headed the Anglo American delegation to Lusaka in 1985, recalls that Buthelezi was the only issue on which the ANC and the businessmen violently disagreed. When Relly suggested that the ANC and Inkatha should cooperate to achieve liberation, "it was like lighting a firecracker. Tambo just went off the handle."

Once the UDF gained strength in Natal, from the mid-1980s, the ANC began to believe it could neutralize Buthelezi. To most ANC leaders, it was incomprehensible that anyone would support a politician with such obvious megalomaniac tendencies, an ethnic dictator whose government oppressed and exploited them, and worst of all, used money from Pretoria to help him do so. ANC leaders began to regard Buthelezi as an evil but ultimately impotent menace.

But these leaders—Western-educated, detribalized Africans—failed to reckon with the power of ethnicity, which Buthelezi exploited to his enormous advantage. "Shenge," as he is popularly known, was revered in rural Natal as the Zulu's champion. Rural Zulus did not care what methods he used to defend their nation. Zulu culture is violent by nature, and strength, even brutal strength, is respected rather than condemned. To these Zulus, the ANC is foreign: they say it is dominated by the Xhosa tribe, which provides much of the top leadership; they resent the smugness with which its leaders condemn their cultural customs; and in general, they distrust men from other tribes who wear suits and ties. Buthelezi appears to them unashamedly dressed in leopard skin. He is their kind of leader.

The ANC finds such overt ethnic nationalism abhorrent, and for very good reason. Pretoria shamelessly exploited ethnicity to divide and rule South Africa; apartheid was based on the premise that only rigid ethnic separation could maintain peace. But the Afrikaners did not invent ethnicity, even so. Tribalism is a reality throughout Africa, ignored only at one's peril. The rapid urbanization of South Africa has reduced this impulse in developed areas, but in rural districts it is as real as ever.

Buthelezi always knew that, and he used it to build his power. For there is nothing artificial about the Zulus' sense of ethnic identity, fed by a powerful historical memory of a glorious military past under King Shaka. Buthelezi worked hard to rebuild the sense of a Zulu nation, so strong in the days of Shaka, but undermined by the emasculation of Zulu chiefs under British rule after the turn of the century. He spent years coaxing the embers of Zulu nationalism into full flame; and he used Shaka to do it.

To the squeamish foreigner, it can be hard to understand the appeal of Shaka, who remains a hero to almost all Zulus, modern or traditional, urban or rural, educated or illiterate. Historians dispute the details of the atrocities he committed in his campaign to unite two hundred-odd clans in a new Zulu nation, but none deny that many died in often arbitrary slaughter. Shaka was a visionary, an illegitimate son of the then insignificant Zulu clan, who inherited a territory of 100 square miles, and multiplied it to 200,000. Almost single-handedly, he created a culture of discipline, obedience, and total submission to authority.

His methods were ruthless and his genius sometimes lunatic. His royal kraal was called *KwaBulawayo,* "the place of killing"—and with reason. The explorer and medic Henry Francis Fynn, among the first whites to meet Shaka, describes in his diary how perfunctory executions were carried out to impress visitors. Offenders had their necks broken in full view of the guests, or were impaled on stakes and left to die a slow death. Shaka's brutality reached new heights on the death of his mother, Nandi. He decreed that no cultivation should be allowed in the year following her death, no milk was to be drunk (tantamount to a sentence of starvation, as milk curds were the Zulus' staple food); pregnant women were to be executed, along with their husbands. No proof exists of any of this, and the many generations which have intervened since Shaka's death in 1828 have no doubt left their mark on the story. But the fact remains that Zulu culture is at once authoritarian, violent, and militaristic. And that contributed in no small way to the outbreak of a low-level civil war in Natal, the country's most populous province, in the mid-1980s.

At that time, Inkatha embarked on a major recruitment campaign, forcing virtually every teacher, nurse, policeman, and public servant in Kwa-Zulu to join the movement by withholding employment if they did not. Villagers were also intimidated into joining, and Inkatha chiefs demanded money from them which they could ill afford. With its control of the Kwa-Zulu police, and the financial backing of Pretoria, Inkatha had the upper hand. But the UDF also made major advances, with its own campaign of coercive recruitment. By the time Mandela emerged from prison, more than three thousand people had died.

The ANC leader had high hopes of being able to settle the conflict with Buthelezi. "He kept saying that it was the ANC's failing that blacks had resorted to violence," recalls a member of the Commonwealth Eminent Persons Group, one of the few outsiders to see Mandela in prison. "And he said he was sure that once he was out, he could bring Buthelezi around." Mandela hoped to exploit their ancient friendship, and the intangible understanding that exists between two men of royal blood. With his tribal background, Mandela respected Buthelezi in a way his colleagues did not; and as a brilliant student of human nature, he also had a better intuitive understanding of how to deal with him.

Dealing with Buthelezi has never been easy, for anyone. Certainly not for journalists (including myself) whom the Zulu leader insults and abuses in a manner that has gained him an understandably hostile press. Buthelezi harbors a powerful resentment at the center of his soul, an insecurity and sensitivity that borders on paranoia. One need not try to antagonize him in order to succeed.

Mandela traces Buthelezi's immensely difficult persona back to his childhood when (the ANC leader claims) he was treated as an outsider at the royal court. "He was deprived of parental love and care, so he grew up with this insecurity," Mandela explained in a *New York Times* interview. "Once you understand that, Buthelezi is a very fine person. When we are together, he is very, very courteous. But when he is away from you, he behaves totally differently, because he does not know if he is still your friend."

Mandela seems to have based his early approach to Buthelezi on this pop psychoanalysis of his character. He always understood that the way around the Zulu leader was to "stroke" him, to give him the love and approval he craved from the world—and especially from Mandela himself. Mandela kept in touch with him from prison, writing respectful letters to the ANC's worst enemy. When he left jail, Buthelezi was one of the first people he phoned, to thank the Zulu leader for his long campaign to secure his release. Within days of his freedom, Mandela proposed that the two men should meet; but the ANC national executive was vehemently opposed. Mandela says he thought they would "throttle him" for suggesting it.

Convinced that contact must nonetheless be established immediately, Mandela urged Walter Sisulu to take up an invitation to visit the Zulu king, Goodwill Zwelithini, who was Buthelezi's nephew, and totally subservient to him politically. But the two sides could not agree on a venue. King Goodwill had invited Sisulu to visit him at the KwaZulu capital, Ulundi, and this caused problems for the ANC. "Mandela believed that we needed Buthelezi, we needed the king, we needed the Zulus," Sisulu recalls. "But I did not want to meet him at Ulundi"—because that would have meant recognizing the KwaZulu homeland, which the ANC opposed. "So I offered to meet him at his *kraal* [seat] at Nongoma." The ANC strongly endorsed this position; but Sisulu admits now that it was probably a mistake to refuse to go to Ulundi.

Certainly, it had unfortunate repercussions (among them the death of the lady in the bathrobe, who died as part of the fighting which broke out when Zulus thought their king had been snubbed). Subsequent efforts to arrange a meeting were also aborted, again over venue disputes. In the end, Mandela and Buthelezi did not meet until the ANC leader had been a free man for almost a year. By then, another 1,600 people had died in Natal, and a further 2,000 nationwide.

Violence had transcended politics and become a way of life. Criminals exploited it to their advantage; clans used it as an excuse to settle old scores; and revenge multiplied its effects manifold. (I remember being told by an old Zulu man that his culture did not recognize the equivalence of "an eye for an eye"; that for every member of one family who dies, at least two must die on the other side.) Politics had started the conflict, but by January 1991, politics alone could not end it.

Jacob Zuma does not defend Buthelezi, but he sees the root of the deathly battles of the last few years in the ANC's early failure to let Mandela meet the Zulu leader and work his psychological magic on him. "It was important for Buthelezi to feel welcomed, embraced, and part of the process," Zuma says. If Mandela had embraced him, and called him brother, right at the beginning, "you could have had absolutely the end of the problem, that is my feeling." Mandela was ready to do so, says Zuma, but the local leadership of the ANC in Natal prevented him from acting.

Zuma's is very much a minority view within the ANC, which accepts little responsibility for the carnage. Sisulu, for his part, blames Buthelezi for being concerned with "personal power"—as though this tendency were rare among politicians—and for failing to understand that he had to sacrifice Inkatha for the sake of African unity. "Buthelezi, in his heart of hearts, must accept that there is no other way except our way," the gentle Sisulu once told me, oblivious to the chilling import of his words. Little wonder that the goal of peaceful multi-party competition has proved so elusive.

Enter the third man.

Throughout the first half of 1990, one would have been forgiven for thinking there were only two political leaders in South Africa, F. W. de Klerk and Nelson Mandela. Nelson and F.W., shaking hands at Tuynhuys, cozy at Groote Schuur, celebrating the Pretoria peace. This was as it should be: if Mandela and de Klerk were not reconciled, nothing else would matter. The first priority was a black-white deal.

Buthelezi looked on as the other two cemented their de facto alliance—and went quietly mad with rage. Clearly, he surmised, they planned to carve up South African power without reference to the Zulus (or to him). De Klerk counted on Buthelezi as a kind of silent partner in a moderate multi-racial alliance, which the white president would lead. Mandela wanted the Zulu chief on his side, but was not prepared to defy his colleagues to ensure his cooperation. Neither envisaged an independent role for Buthelezi himself.

The ANC soon launched a nationwide campaign to emasculate him. Anti-Buthelezi protests were held in July 1990, calling for the dissolution of the KwaZulu police and the abolition of the KwaZulu government. ANC leaders told me at the time—referring to the chief by a nickname which he hates—that their plan was to "cut Gathsa down to size, and *then* to deal with him." In Natal, Cosatu (the ANC trade union federation) organized some 3 million people to stay away from work in anti-Buthelezi protest.

The Zulu leader fought back—as the ANC ought to have known he would. For the first time, he mobilized seriously in the crowded townships around Johannesburg, where many of the 2 million Zulus who live outside Zululand reside in migrant workers' hostels. These hostels—desolate, barrackslike buildings with few access points and long exterior walls—were perfect bases for Inkatha. A majority of the residents were highly traditional Zulus, who went to Johannesburg to work but kept their roots in rural Natal. And within the hostel communities, strict, quasi-militaristic authority structures already existed. Zulu *indunas,* or headmen, governed every aspect of hostel life, just as they would in a village in rural Natal. Their men were easily organized into fighting units.

Social conditions in the hostels also predisposed residents to belligerence. Hostels, like homelands, were part of the grand design of apartheid. The Stallard Commission of 1922 had set out the theory: "the native should only be allowed to enter the urban areas . . . to administer to the needs of the white man and should depart therefrom when he ceases so to minister."

Single men were allowed to live temporarily in hostels, but wives and families were excluded. As the Soweto civic leader Nthatho Motlana explained to me in September 1990, "You have a captive audience living a deprived life, away from the civilizing influence of women and children. That is asking for trouble." Local ANC activists put the problem even more simply: "They attack our grandmothers and our children, because they know that if we attack the hostel, their grannies are not there, their children are not there, they are safe in Natal." With so few ties to the surrounding community, it was easy to mobilize these men against their neighbors—especially with the help of the ANC, and its provocative campaign against Buthelezi.

To them, the anti-KwaZulu campaign was a serious ethnic affront, an insult to their nation. And like their thin-skinned leader Buthelezi, hostel Zulus do not take insults lightly. So, though they had lived in peace with their township neighbors for decades, they were soon ready for war. Tired of the superior attitude of local ANC youth—who often looked down on the illiterate, tribalistic migrants, stuck at the bottom of the township social heap—their pride was fighting back.

Few disguised the fact that they looked forward to battle. As elderly Zulu ladies were constantly reminding me, "The Zulus like to fight." Their culture values physical strength and military skill, with cultural events like weddings marked by ritual battles between young men wielding sticks (and drawing blood). Traditional Zulus defend their right to carry "cultural weapons" to any public gathering, as a sign of their manhood. But there was nothing "cultural" about the use to which nineteenth-century weapons like the assegai (spear) and knobkerrie (club) were put; they were to prove efficient twentieth-century instruments of death.

The first large outbreak of fighting took place on July 22, in the black township of Sebokeng, south of Johannesburg, where Inkatha staged a big show of force. The ANC found out that Inkatha planned to bus in supporters from hostels around the city, and feared the consequences. Mandela pleaded with police and Minister of Law and Order Adriaan Vlok to forbid the rally, or at least to prevent it leading to violence. He was ignored. Some thirty people died, most of them from the ANC.

Mandela was furious—not (at least not publicly) with Buthelezi, but with F. W. de Klerk. As he recounted afterward in his memoirs, Mandela demanded a meeting with de Klerk and accused him of responsibility for the Sebokeng massacre: "You were warned in advance, and yet you did nothing. Why is that? Why is it that there have been no arrests?" De Klerk had not even had the decency to make a statement of condolence to the relatives; in what other country would that happen? Mandela demanded. He got no satisfactory reply.

Still, scarcely a fortnight later, he handed de Klerk the biggest political gift of his presidency, by agreeing to suspend the armed struggle. The two sides declared the agreement, in a joint statement, "a milestone on the road to peace." How wrong they were.

Two weeks after the signing of the Pretoria Minute, which boded so well for a black and white peace, I went to spend the night in Soweto, the giant black township outside Johannesburg.

Five hundred people had died since the Pretoria peace, many of them in Soweto. Naively, I thought that if I slept with the violence, I might begin to understand it. I persuaded Mrs. Sheila Bodibe, of house number 1187, Mapetla, Soweto, to allow me to spend the night on the concrete floor of the shebeen, or illegal beer hall, in her backyard. She thought I was mad. For house number 1187, Mapetla, was on the front line of the conflict which had engulfed Soweto and other black townships virtually from the moment the Pretoria Minute was signed. The shebeen's one high window faced the Merafe migrant workers' hostel, from which warrior bands of Zulus known as *impis* had attacked local residents. The night before, they had murdered a seventy-two-year-old grandmother in the house next door.

Mrs. Bodibe went fatalistically to bed, in her four-roomed "matchbox" house, along with her seven children. And I spent a sleepless night, comforted by the whiskey I had brought along for emergencies, imagining a petrol bomb crashing through the shebeen window, and listening to the gunfire. Ungratefully, I was not comforted by the fact that the Mapetla "self-defense unit" was patrolling the streets outside. This group of ANC-supporting youth had banded together to protect Mapetla's surviving grandmothers from a power struggle they neither willed nor understood.

Earlier in the evening, the "comrades"—a group of soft-spoken young men armed with plastic revolvers and kitchen knives—had assured me of their protection. They had parked my car where its tank could not be drained to fuel petrol bombs; all night long, they assured me, they would be keeping watch. The setting for their vigil was vintage Soweto: a stuffy, low room packed with furniture, lurid in the light of a red bulb overhead. Outside, this city of between 2 and 3 million people had virtually disappeared in a pall of the smoke from coal fires, used to keep the winter night at bay. Powerful cars roared up and down the street, driven by plain-clothed white policemen armed with submachine guns.

The comrades struggled to understand what had happened. The facts were clear. The week before, Zulu residents of Merafe hostel—a grim prison reeking of urine, home to hundreds of unfortunate migrants—had attacked the surrounding suburb, Mapetla. But why? The two sides had never had much contact; in Soweto, like everywhere else on earth, there is a strict hierarchy among the poor. Mapetla was definitely destitute, with its tiny crowded houses, its outdoor taps and toilets. But Merafe was worse: cooking fires blackened the interior walls of rooms that held eight pitiful beds each; ablution blocks were open to the bitter southern hemisphere winter; no water ran from the outdoor faucets.

Until August 1990, they had never let competition turn to battle. Occasionally, a local husband had fought back, when a resident of the single-sex hostel poached his wife; and there were other petty disputes. But pitched battles were unknown—until the Pretoria peace. Suddenly, submerged hostilities came to the surface, including tribal tensions virtually unknown in Soweto for years. Although Pretoria had decreed that different tribes must live separately, even within Soweto (its name, though it sounds African, is actually drawn from the acronym So-uth We-stern To-wnship), tribal barriers were soon destroyed by intermarriage, the physical proximity of urban life, and the rise of trade unionism. Mapetla is a Sotho area, and Sheila Bodibe's husband is Sotho. But she herself—like those in the hostels—is a Zulu. Many of those who died in the fighting, on both sides, were Zulus.

So the tribal element of the problem was not simple, not just a question of Inkatha Zulus versus ANC Xhosas. But it was real, nonetheless. For despite the ANC's denials that ethnicity was a factor, local people always articulated their worries in tribal terms. When Mapetla got wind of an attack from the hostel, the cry went up, "The Zulus are coming"—not Inkatha is coming. And at Merafe hostel, residents complained that they were not welcome in Mapetla "because we're Zulus." They made no secret of the fact that they did not want an ANC government "because we don't want to be ruled by Xhosas."

The Mapetla comrades did not help matters by suggesting that Merafe hostel should be razed to the ground. This was official ANC policy at the time, and it was not entirely cynical. The ANC saw the hostels as symbols of apartheid degradation, and wanted them upgraded and converted to family housing. But this virtuous intent was lost on Merafe residents. They thought the ANC merely wanted to eliminate them (which was, of course, not wholly absent from ANC calculations).

They explained to me—as hostel residents had done throughout Soweto—that they did not *want* to bring their families to Johannesburg. Their traditional beliefs required them to retain land in Natal, where the souls of their ancestors could rest in peace and where cultural rites could be performed. Unless their families remained in Natal, they would lose the right to ancestral land. (They did not find it necessary to point out to the nice white lady that they also enjoyed a wider pool of sexual partners in Johannesburg.)

After my night in Soweto, I understood the position of each side quite clearly. The comrades wanted the hostel Zulus sent back to Natal; and the hostel wanted Nelson Mandela put back in prison. Mapetla put paid to my dreams of a rapid transition to the rainbow nation. One comrade said it for me: "I don't think we're ready for a new South Africa. There is a war coming."

He was to prove a prophet. The carnage which began in Sebokeng in July 1990 migrated around the country, visiting Soweto, lingering tragically in the East Rand triple township of Katlehong-Thokoza-Vosloorus, and then settling firmly in Natal, where it all began.

No one could predict where the whirlwind of violence would touch down next. But there was one constant in the chaos: the certainty that, wherever murders were committed and for whatever reason, police would be blamed. Seldom did they actually pull the trigger; whereas police were openly responsible for hundreds of deaths of activists in the 1980s, from 1990 onward the figures dropped dramatically. But I do not remember visiting a single site of massacre in South Africa—and there were scores of them—where police were not alleged to have been involved. Eyewitnesses veered wildly between obvious fiction and possible fact, and many seemed unable to distinguish between third-hand hearsay and firsthand observation. Certainly, all of them believed police had been involved; far fewer actually had any evidence of it.

But even if only a fraction of the stories were true—tales of white police blackening their faces and attacking alongside Inkatha *impis;* stories of police armored cars disgorging armed Zulus in ANC areas; sightings of policemen delivering arms to Inkatha hostels—then police bias was a serious problem. And I had seen enough, myself, to believe this was so. Police were guilty of sins of omission far more often than commission. But they were guilty even so.

Neither I, nor any journalist I know, ever saw policemen fighting alongside Inkatha Party members. But it was never hard to tell which side they were on. On the fateful day when the bathrobe lady fell dead in the mud in Natal, Major Piet Kitching, the local police spokesman, offered me this helpful analysis of the problem. "The solution is not with the police. If you keep two bulldogs separated, as soon as you let them go, they are back at each other's throats. If people want to fight, they'll fight." At the very least, the police were guilty of exactly that—failing to try hard enough to keep the bulldogs apart. Not to mention answering distress calls selectively, or very tardily, or not at all. Disarming one side and not the other. Keeping well out of the way when they knew a clash was imminent.

Their lack of zeal in preventing violence was exceeded only by their evident disinterest in prosecuting perpetrators. This fact was made painfully plain to me when one of the *Financial Times'* employees, Anna Maleka, fell victim to the fighting. Anna, a jovial, rotund Zulu lady who collected and delivered our mail, was stabbed in the back and shot during an Inkatha attack on a Soweto commuter train. She was left gravely injured; twenty-six people died. As the first and worst such attack, it attracted considerable publicity. Police and prosecutors ought to have pursued the case with a vengeance, to prove their impartiality. But that was not their way.

Such cases are notoriously difficult to prosecute. Witnesses fear for their lives if they testify. When the investigation starts, they disappear. But in this case, Mrs. Maleka and a brave band of her fellow commuters were willing to risk their lives for justice. Anna was terrified of what might happen, but she was adamant that the lives of her two companions, slaughtered beside her—middle-aged, God-fearing ladies who joined her in singing gospel songs to pass the journey—should not go unavenged. When she was summoned to attend an identity parade of suspects, more than a year after the crime (itself an unpardonable delay), she went. I went along, trying to use my white skin as a barrier against her fear.

Obviously, anonymity was crucial. So police provided one-way glass to protect witnesses—one of the first times such a system had been used in Soweto. This order had clearly come from the top; but if there was concern for witness protection in Pretoria, the same was not true in Soweto. The policeman operating the parade carelessly ushered Mrs. Maleka through the wrong door after she had made her identification—straight into the presence of the suspects. After that incident, her fellow witnesses vowed to attend no further parades. Despite numerous positive IDs from the victims, government did not pursue the case. No one was ever convicted. No one paid the price for what was done.

About a year later—a year during which top police had tried hard to combat bias and improve their relations with local (ANC) communities—I spent a night on patrol with the police Internal Stability Division, the riot unit, in one of the worst sites of violence, Thokoza township on the East Rand. During eight hours of nighttime patrol, not surprisingly, I saw no evidence of the atrocities which the local community firmly believed were committed nightly. Nonetheless, I left with a new understanding of the community's resentment and suspicion of police.

For part of the night, we sat outside the moonlit shacks of the Phola Park squatter camp, an ANC stronghold, while Police Sergeant Jakes Bleeker and the other young constables taunted the residents in Afrikaans, over the loudhailer of their "Nyala" armored personnel carrier. "If we sit here long enough, they always shoot at us," he explained confidentially, while his colleagues called out, "Come, shoot at us," not even trying to conceal their lust for action. If the Phola Park residents had obliged, it was not hard to imagine the police response.

The real problem was not the actions of the young policemen but their attitude. When we stopped to collect a dead body, they laughed and joked in the presence of the bereaved husband. When they dumped the body on a stretcher, they did not notice that the movement had left the woman's skirt indecently above her waist. They looked for no witnesses, asked no questions, and merely collected spent cartridges from the scene of death. They assured me that "these people" no longer noticed death—they might have added, "and we no longer try to stop it."

That attitude, from young men who had seen too much of death and violence, was perhaps comprehensible. The policemen were badly trained, appallingly paid, poorly motivated—and in the case of black police (a majority of the force), targeted by ANC youth for assassination. With the best will in the world, they could not hope to stop the fighting; there were too many guns, too much hatred, too many scores to settle—and too little commitment from the politicians to make peace.

The ANC was not accusing the police and other security forces of having a bad attitude. It was accusing them of causing the violence itself. The ANC believed that a "third force" of dissident security force members used violence to try to prevent the transfer of power. That they planned and executed the attacks on commuter trains which became so terrifyingly common; that they used black operatives to carry out political assassinations which disrupted negotiations; that they masterminded the drive-by shootings which claimed so many lives; that they supplied arms to hostel dwellers, and trained them for murder. In short, that they conspired to abort the birth of the new South Africa, and preserve white power.

Within days of the signing of the Pretoria Minute, Nelson Mandela complained privately to F. W. de Klerk about the existence of a third force, and soon he was publicly blaming the third force for every significant act of violence. He made clear that he thought de Klerk knew about the third force, and was either unwilling, or at the very least unable, to stop it.

Evidence of violent political destabilization by the Botha government was not hard to come by. In October 1989, a black policeman, under sentence of death, earned a stay of execution by revealing details of the 1981 "death squad" murder of Durban lawyer Griffiths Mxenge. A government commission of inquiry investigated another death squad operation, a South African Defence Force unit known as the Civil Cooperation Bureau, and concluded that its actions had "contaminated the whole security arm of the state." De Klerk ordered the unit closed down.

But this was ancient history. What mattered was whether the third force was continuing to operate in post-Botha South Africa—and crucially, who knew about it. The body charged with examining third-force allegations under de Klerk's government—the Goldstone Commission, headed by a liberal, Judge Richard Goldstone—initially struggled to find direct evidence of a third force. Then, in November 1992, Goldstone's investigation unit raided a Pretoria office building and found evidence of a secret military intelligence unit which ran a dirty tricks campaign against the ANC. The inquiry found that the unit used "prostitutes, homosexuals, shebeen owners and drug dealers" to "compromise" ANC guerrilla leaders by involving them in crime. The existence of the unit, run by the army's top intelligence officer, provided the most damning evidence to date of a deliberate strategy at senior government levels to destabilize the ANC. The cautious Goldstone said it provided "some evidence" of a third force.

Six weeks before the 1994 elections, Goldstone dropped a second bombshell: He released a report alleging that top police officers had supplied illegal weapons, arms, and ammunition to Inkatha in the run-up to the poll. A subsequent report from Goldstone, never published but leaked to the Johannesburg weekly, *The Mail and Guardian,* said that the security branch of the police "has been involved for many years in the most serious criminal conduct including murder, fraud, blackmail, and a huge operation of dishonest political disinformation," adding that "the whole illegal, criminal and oppressive system is still in place and its architects are in control of the South African Police." Goldstone recommended that Police Commissioner Johan van der Merwe be removed from office immediately. This was not done.

The allegations made by Goldstone against figures such as police second in command Lieutenant General Basie Smit (the man who took Jacob Zuma touring the night spots of Pretoria), and the chief of police counterintelligence, Major General Krappies Engelbrecht, have not been proved in court. But they constituted a damaging prima facie case for the existence of a third force. According to Goldstone, a special unit channeled weapons to Inkatha leaders active in Johannesburg hostel violence, and in Natal. Its operatives were used in commuter train attacks. Its commander, Colonel Eugene de Kock, was convicted of murder in a Pretoria court in 1996.

Since the election, there has been no shortage of former operatives eager to tell their nefarious tales to the newspapers, or to South African courts, to get on the right side of the new government. They have told of murdering ANC activists, fomenting violence, training Inkatha hit squads;

and their testimony has been backed up by some very gruesome evidence, including the decomposed bodies of hit squad victims unearthed on a Transvaal farm.

The retiring commissioner of the KwaZulu police, General Roy During—who certainly ought to have known what he was talking about—also gave credence to such stories. Just after the election, he told a local newspaper that he believed "hit squads" had almost certainly operated within the KwaZulu police, and alleged that the killings had been ordered from "a high level," implying direct involvement by Buthelezi.

The full picture, if it ever becomes clear, will do so only after the recently appointed Truth and Reconciliation Commission has heard testimony from all those involved. But there seems little doubt even now that at least some right-wing members of the security forces did constitute a third force—though the original conspiracy theory, which blamed all political violence on the third force, has failed to hold water. And there appear to have been several third forces, not just one grand force of evil.

What does seem clear is that some individuals in government tried to prevent the South African transition. The pattern of violence suggests this; whenever negotiations picked up momentum—as with the Pretoria Minute—violence intervened to stop them dead. The confessions of operatives suggest this. And the evidence of Goldstone and the Truth Commission suggests it.

Perhaps these men acted out of ideological commitment; perhaps they wanted to preserve the immense personal power apartheid had given them; perhaps they simply had trouble shifting mental gears as rapidly as politics required. Certainly, the psychological adjustment was huge, as one former "footsoldier of the cause" explained in an eloquent letter, published in a local newspaper:

We were brought up to detest communism . . . we were taught that "our blacks" were the spear point of the communist thrust into our society and that only through apartheid could we keep the communist threat from our doors. We believed that our "cause" was just, and we believed in our leaders. . . . We believed in our leaders when they ordered us, either directly or by suggestion, to rid them of their enemies, and provided us with the means to do so.

Where are those leaders now? where are the cabinet ministers and politicians and senior security force officers whom we believed in? . . . Have our leaders all run for cover? Is their cry, "we didn't know," to be believed, and is this not in itself an indictment of gross ineptitude?

These questions may never conclusively be answered. F. W. de Klerk, for his part, has repeatedly insisted that his conscience is clear: he says he did not know about, and certainly did not direct, the third force and its activities.

The closest he has come to accepting responsibility for third-force violence is to say that, if he had known "certain facts" earlier, he would have "taken certain decisions differently." "But in so few cases could we gain evidence," he told me in our 1994 interview. "What more could I have done?"

De Klerk poses the most important question himself: What more could he or should he have done to save black lives? Was he directing the carnage? To suggest that he was strains belief, not because such murders would offend de Klerk's morality, but because they would violate the first principle of his politics, self-interest. De Klerk had gambled all—his political career, his place in history, the survival of his people—on a negotiated settlement. Why would he deliberately jeopardize the chance of a deal by engaging in activities which, time and again, sabotaged agreement? Why would he court civil war and economic ruin, when the whole point of unbanning the ANC and suing for peace had been to avert just such an outcome?

Certainly, de Klerk wished to weaken his adversary; he would not be a politician if he did not. So a campaign of dirty tricks against the ANC is entirely plausible. In the early stages of the violence, de Klerk probably calculated that the African National Congress paid more dearly for it than the National Party. Certainly, ANC leaders felt that the early violence favored de Klerk: their supporters blamed the ANC for failing to protect them. And as Pallo Jordan, ANC information chief, told me at the time, the violence tended to reinforce black fears of what life would be like without apartheid. "People have always had drummed into their heads that there are primordial conflicting interests between ethnic groups, that's why we need apartheid; now they're beginning to think, maybe those people were right." Maybe such factors tempted de Klerk to do nothing to stop the violence.

In July 1991, however, that calculus changed dramatically. The left-wing *Johannesburg Weekly Mail* uncovered a security police operation to fund Inkatha rallies, and an Inkatha trade union, Uwusa, to rival the ANC and its union, Cosatu. De Klerk was forced to admit his government's guilt in the so-called Inkathagate scandal. His image of integrity, at home and abroad, was irreparably damaged. From then on, the benefit of the doubt in cases of alleged third-force involvement always went against de Klerk. Whites blamed him for failing to keep the country under control, and in the black community it became an article of faith that the president was behind the violence. Thenceforth, de Klerk had everything to lose from supporting the third force.

But if logic suggests that de Klerk was not masterminding violence, it cannot fully explain why he did so little to stop it. Stamping out the third force would have gained him enormous kudos, from black South Africans and foreign governments alike. Failing to do so hurt him politically, until the very day of the election. So why did he not act against those who jeopardized his image as a world statesman, and his chances at the polls? The answer seems to lie less in evil duplicity than in human weakness.

De Klerk came to preside over the security establishment in 1989 as a total outsider; he had never held a security portfolio; he did not share the friendship and confidence of Botha's securocrats; his friends say he was temperamentally disinclined to believe that members of his cabinet would lie to him. But lie to him they did, and regularly. As one member of cabinet recalls, "Every time we would discuss it, they would try to convince us that there was no third force. I was present several times when de Klerk challenged first [Adriaan] Vlok [his first police minister] and Hernus Kriel [Vlok's successor]. He said to them, 'But how do you explain this?' He really got into them. But they always had very convincing answers. I think it was a question of trusting the people who advised him."

Probably, de Klerk thought he could not afford to distrust them. He needed the support of the army and police—even their incomplete support—to pull off the transition. He felt he could not jeopardize that support by prosecuting generals. (Mandela seemed implicitly to endorse this judgment when he thanked Police Commissioner Johan van der Merwe—a man branded by Goldstone as "depraved"—for having helped manage the transition. Upon becoming president, Mandela did not fire van der Merwe; he allowed him to retire several months later.)

Still, de Klerk's concern for stability was a convenient excuse for doing nothing. He seems to have chosen to remain in a state of negligent ignorance rather than face the impossible choices with which knowledge would confront him. And for that, history will fault him. For even if his morality did not fail him, his judgment did. Senior military officers confirm that, although the third force posed a grave danger to a negotiated settlement, it never threatened the government itself. Negotiations were "like a very elegant performance on a crossbar; all you need to do is just tap, and the person will come tumbling down." Even a small group within the security forces could have caused such a tumble. But they could not overthrow the state. And by 1993, at least, they would not even have wanted to do so; the military was already making its separate peace with those who would soon be their bosses. De Klerk ought, by then, to have stopped fearing a coup and acted more strongly against them.

The truth of de Klerk's calculations may never be known, since he refuses to reveal them. Perhaps he thought he could garner more right-wing votes by failing to quash the third force; maybe he feared he was not strong enough to act against the generals; quite likely, he thought that to do so would cause more harm than good. So he acted only when he had no alternative, demoting Police Minister Vlok and sacking Defense Minister Magnus Malan in 1991 only when the Inkathagate scandal had left him little option. And even when he purged twenty-three senior South African Defence Force officers in December 1992, he managed to leave the topmost levels of military authority untouched. None of the twenty-three was prosecuted, raising the suspicion that the public relations value of their removal was designed to be greater than its practical impact. The move certainly sent a signal—at least to the international community—that de Klerk would not tolerate dirty tricks. But military insiders say he was far more concerned to be seen to act against the third force than really to hobble it.

De Klerk paid dearly for that failure, which hurt his reputation at home and abroad. But the worst casualty of all—from de Klerk's point of view—was his relationship with Nelson Mandela. The ANC leader never forgave de Klerk for what he saw as an unpardonable sin: a callous indifference to the loss of black life, coupled with a willingness to play politics with death. What de Klerk did or did not know ended up being less important than what Mandela thought he knew.

The ANC leader records in his memoirs how, within weeks of the Pretoria peace, he began to doubt the motives of de Klerk, and the wisdom of abandoning armed struggle: "Many in the government, including Mr. de Klerk, chose to look the other way or ignore what they knew was going on under their noses. We had no doubts that men at the highest levels of the police and the security forces were aiding the third force . . . any understanding that had been achieved with the government seemed lost."

Mandela soon dropped this almost reluctant tone of reproach in favor of far more bitter invective. Those close to both men recall countless occasions on which Mandela accused de Klerk of sacrificing black lives on the altar of his politics, a charge that infuriated the Afrikaner leader. Mandela sealed the breach by withdrawing the badge of approval that had done so much to cement their early partnership—he publicly questioned de Klerk's integrity. His criticisms became more and more virulent as time went on. In 1991, he was still willing to grant that de Klerk's inability to stop the violence stemmed from his "problems with his own constituency." A year later, he insisted that de Klerk's involvement in violence included "both commission and omission." By 1993, he had abandoned restraint altogether, saying, "it is impossible to defend him . . . he doesn't even take the simplest precautions to curb violence. In his view their [black] lives are cheap. When it comes to blacks, he is absolutely insensitive."

In the end, Mandela even reached the point of suggesting de Klerk was a racist. In a BBC documentary on the third force, he labeled de Klerk "an ordinary white man"—and left no doubt what he meant by it. He leveled the same charge in cabinet. In January 1995, the two men had a furious row in a cabinet meeting, which ended with the new president accusing de Klerk of acting "like a white man talking to a black man."

"Mandela could never understand how a head of state, who had all the apparatus of governance, could not do something openly and meaningfully to stop the violence," chief ANC negotiator Cyril Ramaphosa recalls. He thought that "F.W. was still essentially playing politics at a great price, at a great cost to the lives of our people. And he lost respect for F.W. because of it."

De Klerk was mortally wounded by Mandela's anger. He told me, in 1994, how horrified he was by Mandela's accusations "that I have blood on my hands and that I'm a murderer," charges repeated even shortly before the two men jointly received the Nobel Prize for Peace.

"I felt at times that he was not sufficiently understanding of the complexity of the situation, that he did not give significant recognition of the numerous steps I have taken to ensure that the security forces should not be involved in any way whatsoever, that he was unreasonable in requiring action on the basis of unsubstantiated evidence," de Klerk told me, adding, "That really was the most important cause of friction between us."

The violence which emerged almost before the Pretoria ink was dry was to transform the South African political landscape totally. It destroyed the cozy relationship between Mandela and de Klerk, and with it any hope of an early settlement; it introduced the third man, Buthelezi, to the political equation, making a solution that much more difficult. Further, it did serious damage to the fabric of South African society, fostering the growth of a culture of violence, crime, revenge, and brutality that became the inheritance of the new South Africa.

For the cost of the violence should be calculated not just in terms of lives lost, injuries sustained, and economic dislocation, but in terms of damage to the national psyche. I met many people in South Africa—especially young people—who were permanently damaged by violence; some committed violent acts, and some suffered them, but they all paid the price. That could yet prove one of the most enduring and tragic legacies of the South African transition.

DINA CRONJE INVITED ME IN *for tea before she even knew who I was or what I wanted. She called to me, over the double-dutch door of her rough, stone-walled kitchen, and invited me to sit down while she withdrew to put on a dress in honor of the visitor.*

Mrs. Cronje does not think apartheid was wrong. She thinks it was "an unfortunate choice of words." Apartheid, she says, exists in England and America. It is just not called "apart-hate." Our conversation took in AIDS—"God has sent us AIDS to lessen the number of blacks"—and other platteland classics: blacks are lazy, shifty, and childlike.

Dina Cronje lives in a rough, African-style round cottage in the low dry hills of the Northern Transvaal. Apartheid made her life just about comfortable; her husband worked on the railways, that preserve of Afrikaner employment, and she worked for the Post Office. Now they have retired to this bit of ultra-right-wing territory near Nylstroom (Nile-Stream), the town built when nineteenth-century Afrikaner pioneers thought they had found the source of the Nile.

I did not think it was worth asking what Mrs. Cronje thought of the new South Africa. But she told me anyway. "Somebody should have done what F. W. de Klerk has done, twenty years ago. Mandela should have been released twenty years ago. Then we would have a much healthier situation in the country." I did not want to interrupt. So Mrs. Cronje went on. She did not mind if nice, middle-class blacks came to live on the farm next door. There were plenty, she told me, who were educated and earning good salaries. "We can all live together in peace."

She told me she quite liked F.W., but said her neighbors despised the bald-headed president. "They say, 'Eierkop gee alles vir die kaffirs' " ("Egghead is giving everything away to blacks"). Never mind the neighbors, she said. "They just talk, and do nothing."

Might they be right about "Egghead" giving it all away? Dina Cronje was not worried. "We're not really going to be ruled by blacks," she told me confidentially. "Not to start off with." The ANC might become the government, "but they won't really be in power." After all, God would not allow anyone to hurt the Afrikaner, who had done nothing intentional to harm the black man. "God won't punish us for committing a sin unknowingly," she explained. "The Lord won't allow them to walk all over us."

10

Rollercoaster Revolution

AT A FEW MINUTES BEFORE 7:00 P.M. on December 20, 1991—just in time for the prime-time nightly news—Nelson Mandela did what no black South African had ever done before. He publicly assassinated the character of a white president, and got away with it.

Never had South Africa heard a black man speak to a white man that way—with the disgust and loathing, the scorn and venom of centuries. Mandela, the master of self-discipline, lost all restraint that day, when he spoke to the first session of the constitutional conference, Codesa (Convention for a Democratic South Africa). Codesa's task was to share out power in the new South Africa. Mandela treated the delegates to an early foretaste of post-apartheid power relations.

As de Klerk sat listening, Mandela put the white president in his place and then pinned him to the spot, with insult after insult. De Klerk was "the head of an illegitimate, discredited, minority regime," a man who could not even be trusted to live up to its low moral standards. He was guilty of duplicity, trickery, and lying, a man with "very little idea what democracy means." The kindest thing that could be said of him was that he was "a product of apartheid," and even that was no excuse. He was "not fit to be a head of a government"—and if Mandela had his way, would not long remain in that post.

De Klerk, caught offguard by Mandela's vituperation, began by taking notes. Then he put down his pen, scowled, stroked his bald pate, and surrendered to apoplexy. By the time he rose to answer the tirade, he was hyperventilating with rage. De Klerk, his party, his nation, and his race, had been humiliated by a black man on national television. The aura of power which had cloaked Afrikaner leaders for the best part of fifty years began to dissipate that day. The balance of power, which had weighed so heavily in his favor since February 1990, began subtly to shift.

In fact, the dispute arose from a misunderstanding. For nearly eighteen months—since the signing of the Pretoria Minute in August 1990—the

African National Congress and the National Party had done little except bicker about the details of ending armed struggle. De Klerk demanded that the ANC disband its guerrilla army and put its arms caches under joint control; Mandela refused, arguing that in the atmosphere of violence, this would be tantamount to committing suicide. Delegations from the two sides fought over the issue until late on the eve of the first meeting of Codesa, when they gave up in deadlock. Kobie Coetsee, the National Party's negotiator, told the ANC delegation that de Klerk would raise the issue again the next day. This message never reached Mandela.

So, when de Klerk rose to deliver his speech the next day, Mandela was amazed to hear him attack the ANC on the arms issue. He went rigid. How could de Klerk suggest that the ANC could not be trusted to negotiate peace, just because they refused to disband *Umkhonto we Sizwe*? How could he use such a tone of voice, "like a schoolmaster, admonishing a naughty child"? The fiery Mandela temper, held in check through twenty-seven years of prison indignities, exploded with the full force of long suppression.

Mandela's rage was fueled by the fact that he believed de Klerk had tricked him. The white president had asked for the right to deliver the last of Codesa's opening speeches; the ANC leadership strongly resisted giving de Klerk the last word, but Mandela persuaded them to grant him that favor. When de Klerk used that privileged position to attack the ANC, Mandela felt he had been duped. He rose and went to the podium, out of turn, to deliver the attack that dominated the nightly news.

Once his temper had cooled, Mandela went out of his way to make peace with his rival, crossing the floor to shake de Klerk's hand—and making sure that the gesture was captured by the same TV cameras which recorded his earlier tirade. But their relationship would never recover from the beating it took at the first meeting of Codesa. Mandela felt he now had incontrovertible proof of what he had begun to suspect over the issue of the third force: that de Klerk was dishonest.

So, Codesa opened on a note of spectacular misunderstanding. But it soon became clear that Mandela had misunderstood not only de Klerk's reason for asking to speak last but the very principles that motivated him as a leader. Mandela and the ANC seemed to have read the wrong smoke signals from de Klerk's speech on February 2, 1990. They thought he was acknowledging the inevitability of black rule, and setting out to deliver it. They soon found out how wrong they were.

Mandela thought de Klerk was "playing politics" with his Codesa speech. He was right; the white president's main aim was to reassure whites that he was tough on the ANC and violence. De Klerk saw nothing wrong in that; he saw the process of negotiating a settlement as a political battle between opposing interests, not an exercise in national catharsis. He had leveled the political playing field so he could fight Mandela on that field. But when he tried to do so, the ANC leader accused him of "playing politics," as though that were an unpardonable sin. Mandela seemed to think of de Klerk as a kind of handmaiden to help him deliver the new South Africa. Only later did he realize—to his evident disgust—that he was facing a rival in politics.

By the end of Codesa I—as the convention's first meeting later became known—it was clear that the misunderstanding at the center of South African politics went deeper even that that. Codesa I revealed fundamental discord over the largest question of all: Who would wield power in the new South Africa?

The National Party remained convinced that it would win what amounted to a veto in the new structure of power—a little bit of extra help to give the white minority, a scant 12 percent of the population, a real chance in the political battle. For though de Klerk paid lip service to democracy, he did not yet believe it could be the white man's saviour. He wanted to pick and choose between the various attributes of a democratic state, to find those that would best protect the power of his minority constituency. So he wanted a bill of rights to protect the civil and property rights of the individual; an independent judiciary as a check on state power; and separation of powers between legislature and executive, and between central government and the provinces.

But he did not want the majority to rule, the most central tenet of democracy, for that would consign his people to permanent, hopeless, impotent opposition. Whites and other minorities could not hope to outvote the black majority. The politics of blood and tribe and race were simply too strong to permit such a thing. As long as that was so, democracy—on its own—would not satisfy de Klerk.

So he sought artificially to balance power between vastly unequal ethnic groups, with a constitution that enforced multi-party coalition government. That would mean cabinet posts shared out according to each party's proportion of the vote; extra representation for minorities in an upper house of Parliament, coupled with special high majorities for passage of some legislation in the lower house; a presidency that would revolve between the leaders of rival parties, rather than residing in one man; the requirement that cabinet decisions be taken by consensus, a system that would give each party an effective veto over the others. In short, a system in which each group had more or less equal power.

The effect of this would be to allow minorities to veto the will of the majority—which was not what the ANC had fought for decades to achieve. Mandela dismissed de Klerk's blueprint, calling it a "loser-takes-all" system.

He would accept nothing less than majority rule. But de Klerk dubbed Mandela's proposal "winner takes all" because it would allow 51 percent of voters to dominate 100 percent of the nation. The disagreement was fundamental.

Codesa also revealed a third rift in the terrain of negotiation, one that was ignored at the time, but later reemerged to stymie progress for months. The issue was federalism. The ANC wanted a highly centralized state, a fact that enraged Chief Buthelezi, who manufactured a reason not to attend Codesa. Buthelezi was fighting for maximum devolution of power, the only constitutional formula which would give regionally based leaders like himself any power at all.

Buthelezi's Inkatha Party, which attended the talks in his absence, refused to sign the "declaration of intent" that was Codesa's sole concrete achievement. Inkatha said the declaration ruled out a federal state, because it called for the creation of an "undivided" South Africa. The disagreement would fester for years to come, nearly preventing the holding of peaceful elections. And it would remain a sore at the heart of the new South Africa well after the new government took power.

Codesa I demonstrated fundamental discord over the nature of the new South African state, with the three paradigms of majority rule, minority power, and federal devolution competing for predominance. Yet it also revealed a new and unexpected willingness on the part of the National Party— without whom no deal could be done—to bridge that gap. It was scarcely noted at the time, but de Klerk's much-maligned Codesa I speech included not only an attack on the ANC but a major concession to the opposite side. He offered that day to clear away the biggest obstacle to a deal, when he agreed for the first time that the new South African Constitution should be written by elected representatives of the people.

Up to then, the National Party had insisted that appointed delegates must do that job. De Klerk reasoned it thus: If delegates were elected, they would come mostly from the majority population, Africans; such delegates would inevitably write a majority-rule constitution. If, on the other hand, the Constitution was written by all the nineteen parties present at Codesa— homeland parties, ethnic parties, parties with massive support, and those with no support at all—then a power-sharing constitution would emerge. Those nineteen parties would all want their cut of the action, and so they would vote for power sharing.

De Klerk had always argued that to say that the majority should draw up the Constitution was tantamount to saying that it should rule. He was looking for a way to avoid that. So he proposed a compromise: the nineteen Codesa parties would write an "interim" constitution. That document would provide the ground rules for the first all-race elections, which would choose a constituent assembly and an interim government to rule for at least ten years. The elected constitutent assembly would then give South Africa its final Constitution. But it would not have a free hand. It would be bound by firm principles agreed to at Codesa, including, if de Klerk had his way, permanently entrenched power sharing, devolution of power, protection for minorities, and other checks and balances. The old would not give way to the new overnight, as the ANC demanded, but would fade imperceptibly away. Whites would have something like ten years to get used to the idea of losing power.

The compromise proposal suggested by de Klerk—that Codesa should write an interim constitution, and elected representatives should write the final document—had already been made by Mandela nearly a year earlier. But the key was for de Klerk to accept it. He seems to have been motivated to do so by a combination of foreign pressure, the desire to get the ANC quickly locked into an interim government (which whites would still dominate), and to help him over a legitimacy problem that was making it ever harder to govern. De Klerk was eager to get to the first elections; he was convinced that delay could only hurt the National Party's electoral chances.

De Klerk's Codesa I speech was to prove a major turning point; with the offer to allow elections to a constituent assembly, he put South Africa irrevocably on the path to majority rule. But that was not at all his intention. He thought he could prevent the constituent assembly from choosing what he called "simple majoritarianism" by binding it—in many different ways and with many different chains—to the principle of perpetual power sharing.

He thought he could achieve that because, at Codesa I, the balance of power in South Africa still heavily favored him. De Klerk held unchallenged control of the state—the police, the military, the administration. The business community, frightened by the ANC's confused socialism, adored him. The international community applauded him continually, and flattered him with its welcome when he traveled overseas. At home, opinion polls showed that the ANC had less than half of the popular vote, giving de Klerk the idea that he could capture a large share of it himself by leading a moderate anti-ANC coalition. Indeed, some of his ministers even thought he might win, with the support of minority coloured, Indian, and black homeland parties. By the end of 1991, de Klerk was inclined to serious delusions of grandeur.

The ANC, straining to adjust to the world of freedom, had scarcely proved a formidable adversary up to then. De Klerk had found it easy to outmaneuver them. His early strategy had been based on seizing the initiative—he told a visiting newspaper editor, "Speed is my only weapon." He planned to get the international community behind him, keep his opponents permanently offguard, and make a dash for a deal. Within six months of Mandela's release, de Klerk had deprived the ANC of two of its most important tactical weapons: armed struggle had been abandoned with the Pretoria Minute; and the international sanctions campaign was rendered all but moribund when de Klerk unbanned the ANC and released its leaders. "The initiative is in our hands. We have the means to ensure that the process develops peacefully and in an orderly way," de Klerk explained. And with the arrogance bred of too long in power, he thought that would remain so, forever.

Exploding the myth of Mandela was also part of de Klerk's plan. The ANC leader complains in his memoirs that de Klerk wanted him to "fall on my face and show that the former prisoner hailed as a saviour was a highly fallible man who had lost touch with the present situation." And initially, that was more or less what he did.

Mandela developed a disconcerting habit of contradicting himself—and his colleagues—in public, giving the impression that the ANC had no clear vision of the future. When townships exploded in violence, he insisted that de Klerk use the full force of the law to quell the unrest; but when the white leader did so, sending in extra troops and police, Mandela condemned him. Contradictory pronouncements on economic issues were even more frequent: one day he would defend nationalization, and the next day seem to question its wisdom. Local newspapers began to ask, "Will the real Mandela please stand up?"

He seemed to find it hard to do so. For Mandela had set himself a near-impossible task: To try to satisfy the whole broad range of what he defined as his constituency, from rich white businessmen to unemployed black squatters, from conservative Afrikaners to militant black youth. Leading the ANC was like riding several horses at once; leading South Africa was even more difficult. Keeping all the horses moving in the same direction seemed, for a time, impossible. Even among his core constituency, the mass of black South Africans, Mandela was in trouble. ANC supporters blamed him for giving up armed struggle, and leaving them at the mercy of the third force. They wanted guns from Mandela, and all they got was negotiation.

Violence was not the only disappointment of life in the Mandela era. De Klerk had removed most of the props from apartheid's house of cards, but it was still refusing to fall. Segregation persisted in health (where it was illegal), in schools (where it had not yet been abolished), in libraries and swimming pools. The Transvaal town of Bethal filled its pool with sand rather than let blacks use it; libraries in conservative white towns claimed that their membership lists were "full," or charged an exorbitant R500 fee for "non-residents"—inhabitants of the townships. In Johannesburg, which had previously had separate hospitals for each population group, there were now separate wards in integrated hospitals. In one Transvaal town, black women in labor were forced to lie on the floor while well-equipped maternity wards in the hospital's white section remained relatively empty. And per capita spending on black education, though it had increased rapidly, was still only about a fifth of the white level.

By the time the ANC met in July 1991 for its first conference inside South Africa for thirty-three years, the situation was desperate. Outgoing ANC secretary general Alfred Nzo provided an anatomy of the crisis. "We lack enterprise, creativity and initiative," he wrote in a confidential report to delegates. "We appear very happy to remain pigeon-holed within the confines of populist rhetoric and cliché." Mass action—the ANC's only remaining strategic weapon against the government—was in trouble. Attendance at recent rallies had been embarrassingly low (Nzo gave figures). Rallies were poorly prepared, badly advertised and organized, and likely to start hours after the appointed time. Membership recruitment was also a problem: in its first year of legality, the ANC managed to sign up only 200,000 members. Disillusioned activists quipped that it was easier to join the movement when it was banned than when it was legal.

"Clearly we have not utilised our full potential to mobilise millions of our people into effective action," Nzo concluded, warning that the ANC was in danger of being "removed from the leadership pedestal it now occupies." F. W. de Klerk could not have said it better himself. The ANC had given him every reason to feel invincible.

The same conference which bemoaned the ANC's malaise also took the first steps to cure it. The movement elected a dynamic new secretary general, Cyril Ramaphosa, head of the National Union of Mineworkers, who had spent a decade honing his skills as a negotiator. While most of his ANC colleagues were locked in the romantic politics of struggle, Ramaphosa was learning the hard facts of how to compromise with the capitalist world, and win. His brand of tough pragmatism was perfect for the task ahead: putting the ANC on the offensive.

At the July 1991 conference, the ANC committed itself to a new policy, as well as a new leadership. For most of the previous year, it had acted on the principle that negotiations on a new constitution could not start until violence stopped; so every time there was a new massacre, the ANC pulled out of talks. From the moment Mandela was freed in February 1990, until nearly two years later, at Codesa I, negotiation yielded only one significant agreement—the Pretoria Minute. Violence, and the fight over responsibility for it, prevented all other progress.

Under the influence of the pragmatic Ramaphosa, the ANC reversed that strategy: Those who favored violence would no longer be given a veto over the new South Africa. In future, the ANC would use violent incidents to force the pace of change, not stop it. Both sides were now ready to move beyond phase one of negotiations—the details of ending armed hostilities—to the real business of the negotiated revolution, carving up power.

"I believe in the will of God, but it's hard. We can try to live together, but I don't think it will ever be good or pleasant. They are so *different* from us." That was Tannie (Auntie) Lettie Swart's view of the new South Africa—a frightening place, a dark and alien place, a foreign country.

F. W. de Klerk had just announced that he was putting his more optimistic vision of the future to a vote: he had called a snap referendum of white voters to take place on March 17, 1992. They would be asked to endorse or reject the new South Africa. De Klerk was gambling his political career on the hope that Tannie Lettie would find it in her heart to vote yes—or if she did not, that others would, and in sufficient numbers to give him a clear mandate for change. He had shocked his colleagues, and the nation, by calling the unexpected referendum, after the right-wing Conservative Party defeated the National Party decisively in an important by-election in de Klerk's old university town of Potchefstroom. When he was elected president in September 1989, voters had given him an ambiguous and unenthusiastic mandate for reform. Now he hoped to stun opponents into silence, and consolidate his power base, by securing a large referendum majority for change.

In the Northern Transvaal, where Tannie Lettie makes her home, this was not going to be easy. It was and is an ultra-conservative, highly traditional area. When I turned up to visit Tannie Lettie—the title, "Tannie," is an Afrikaans honorific used to address any woman past girlhood—she was baking rusks in an old wood-burning stove, just like her grandmother before her. Immediately, that grandmother cropped up in conversation. She and her two daughters had been interned in a British concentration camp during the Anglo-Boer War, and the earlier farmhouse on the site reduced to rubble.

Resentment against the British still festered in Tannie Lettie's heart, but a newer resentment of Africans was far stronger: "The white people worked so hard, since Jan van Riebeeck's time. Nothing was done by the blacks. In the past four centuries, the whites are responsible for all the growth. Now the blacks want to take it from us." Tannie Lettie had caught the mood of the platteland, where the prejudice of centuries was making its last stand. One of her neighbors was Buks Viljoen, the man with the color-conscious dog.

De Klerk was asking these people to do what, for many of them, was impossible: he was asking them to face the inevitable. It looked as though they might well turn him down. Eve-of-poll opinion surveys showed the "yes" vote at only 55 percent and falling, raising fears that the "no"s might prevail. Fear of a "no" vote so terrified the pro-reform lobby that the business community spent heavily campaigning for a "yes." And though the ANC abhorred the notion of an all-white poll, it swallowed its objections to call loudly for a "yes" vote.

As it turned out, South Africans voted massively for change—by a majority of 68.7 percent on a turnout of 86 percent of the white electorate (only the northern Transvaal voted against). The result demonstrated what de Klerk had always suspected, that most Afrikaners had outgrown apart-heid. Tannie Lettie and Buks Viljoen still felt they needed it. But their middle-class counterparts—their confidence bolstered by the education, jobs, and business opportunities provided by a government dedicated to lifting them out of poverty—were happy to take their chances. They were embarrassed by apartheid, and terrified that their newfound prosperity would be ruined unless they rejected it. The right-wing Conservative Party, which campaigned for a "no" vote, asked them to make a choice between "the survival of the Afrikaner volk and two cars in the garage." Nearly 70 percent of them chose a future of happy motoring.

What they did not choose was the future eventually delivered to them by F. W. de Klerk. For the most explicit promise he made in the referendum was to prevent majority rule—the National Party advertising campaign ex-horted voters to "vote yes, if you're scared of majority rule," and de Klerk's public appearances were devoted to this theme. These were the kind of promises which had won over Dina Cronje, in her Northern Transvaal kitchen. They were to prove a monumental deception.

A number of voters probably disbelieved them in any case. Many were fatalistic: they simply did not think majority rule could be held off for long. They were far further down the road to peace than anyone had imagined—and less likely to resist than anyone had feared. De Klerk said the referen-dum marked a fundamental turning point in South Africa's history, and he was right. "It doesn't happen often that in one generation a nation gets the opportunity to rise above itself," he said. White South Africa did so that day. But if the referendum marked a positive turning point for South Africa, it proved just the opposite for the career of F. W. de Klerk. His fortunes peaked on the day the results were announced, which was also his fifty-sixth birthday.

De Klerk's harmless delusions of grandeur soon turned to dangerous conceit. Like any gambler on a roll, he began to think he could not lose. The National Party returned to Codesa—where negotiators had been quietly whittling away at the constitutional mountain since the December Codesa I meeting—in far more aggressive mood. De Klerk and his colleagues thought the referendum had given them both the political and the moral right to demand what they wanted.

"The referendum sent inappropriate signals to the government. A week before, they were trying to resolve issues at Codesa," says one senior ANC negotiator. "Thereafter, there was a perceptible change in attitude." This newfound Nationalist arrogance went down very badly in the ANC camp, where the referendum had also, paradoxically, hardened attitudes. The ANC drew from the referendum result exactly the opposite conclusion than de Klerk had drawn: It reasoned that if the white right did not significantly threaten de Klerk's position, the ANC need no longer try so hard to help him pacify it.

Both sides were now playing hardball. They were meeting almost constantly, at the cavernous World Trade Centre building outside Johannesburg. In this squat, gloomy building, with all the charm of an airplane hangar, negotiators from the nineteen Codesa parties spent every waking hour (and some when they ought not to have been awake). They were split up into five separate Working Groups, which struggled valiantly to reach agreements that could be put to a second big Codesa meeting—known as Codesa II—on May 15–16, 1992. There, the leaders of the nineteen parties would be called on to endorse what their subordinates had agreed in the Working Groups.

The pace began to take its toll on the National Party. The government's chief negotiator, Gerrit Viljoen, broke down, resigned his post as minister of constitutional development, and pulled out of the talks. He was the latest in a string of Nationalist casualties; de Klerk had lost Finance Minister Barend du Plessis, a leading *verligte,* in a financial scandal; his ministers of police and defense had been forced to resign over Inkathagate; Minister of Information Stoffel van der Merwe, another de Klerk ally, had left government. De Klerk was left with only a deputy minister, Tertius Delport, to head his team in the most important of the Working Groups: Working Group 2, charged with settling the most important constitutional issues.

Delport was too junior to take decisions on his own, which undermined his forcefulness. He had to withdraw repeatedly to telephone de Klerk for instructions. And the ANC despised him. He did not share the easy bonho-mie that prevailed between rival negotiators at meal and drink times; he was far more conservative than some of his colleagues; and the ANC accused him of constantly shifting his position.

Cyril Ramaphosa, the new ANC secretary general, was Delport's oppo-site number in Working Group 2. He set out to destroy the National Party negotiator. As the group worked feverishly toward their May 15 deadline, Delport began to sicken. Soon, he was exhausted and ill, his voice reduced to a hoarse croak. Ramaphosa moved in for the kill.

"Cyril was really enjoying himself. He loves a scrap," recalls one of Ramaphosa's ANC colleagues from the same Working Group. Ramaphosa would repeatedly push Delport to the limit of his patience on one or another constitutional point, and when the deputy minister exploded, he would in-tervene, in a voice of saccharine concern. "I am really worried about Mr. Delport's health and really, Mr. Delport, you should not get so excited," Ramaphosa would say. "You could just see the pleasure oozing out of him," his colleague recalls, adding, "I can remember thinking, I am damn glad Cyril is on our side."

The job of Working Group 2 was to decide when and how the biggest constitutional question should be settled: Would South Africa be ruled by majority or by power sharing? But to decide that question, Working Group 2 would have to determine how the elected constituent assembly would operate: Would it take decisions simply by a majority vote? Would it need a two-thirds majority some of the time? (Two thirds of the U.S. Congress, and three quarters of the states, are required to pass amendments to the U.S. Constitution, for example.)

This much was already agreed. The nineteen Codesa parties would write an interim constitution, and they would also agree on constitutional principles to bind the elected constituent assembly. That assembly would then rewrite the interim constitution as a final constitution. The battle was over whether the constituent assembly would need to vote by two thirds, or 70 percent, or even 75 percent, to make these changes. Working Group 2 had already agreed that more than a simple majority of 50 percent would would be required. But they had not put an exact figure to it.

All of this was very much to the National Party's liking. It had as many allies at Codesa as the ANC. That meant the two would have equal leverage over the writing of the interim constitution. And once that constitution was on the books, the ANC would need a large majority to amend it—probably larger than its share of the constituent assembly. That meant whites would probably be able to block changes they did not like, simply by voting against them in the constituent assembly.

The day before Codesa II was due to meet, the National Party came up with a new proposal: It suggested that a two-thirds vote would be enough to pass most constitutional clauses in the assembly. But those dealing with a bill of rights, devolution of power, multi-party democracy, and minority rights would need a three-quarters majority. It also proposed that a Senate, representing minorities, should pass the interim constitution by a two-thirds vote. The effect of this would be to give minorities a veto over crucial clauses in the constitution, unless the majority controlled more than three quarters of the assembly (which seemed almost impossible, in view of opinion polls showing the ANC with 45 percent popular support). The National Party's own internal polls showed it might get 26 percent of the vote, enough to block such votes entirely on its own.

This was a trap for the ANC, and Ramaphosa immediately realized it. With percentages set so high, the constituent assembly might take years to amend the interim constitution—or never manage to do so at all. The new South Africa would be stuck with a constitution written by the unrepresentative Codesa, forever.

Ramaphosa and his colleagues took their dilemma to Nelson Mandela. They arrived at Mandela's home in the white suburb of Houghton after eleven o'clock at night, but were unable to get in. While Ramaphosa tried to phone Mandela's secretary on his car phone, the others threw pebbles at the windows in an attempt to wake their sleeping boss. "We only later discovered he thought somebody was shooting at him," says Frene Ginwala, another ANC negotiator who took part in the assault, giggling. "We knew Codesa II was going to fail, and we had to find a way of ending it that was not going to show the ANC in a bad light," she recalls. Eventually, Mandela came down. They explained the problem. "Postpone Codesa II," he told them. The embarrassed negotiators explained that, with the plenary due to open in a few hours, this was not possible.

But Ramaphosa had a plan: he decided to engineer a deadlock. He says he wanted to show the people of South Africa that "we are dealing with an enemy that will not give in easily." Most of all, he wanted to avoid the trap.

At 10:00 A.M. on May 15, two hundred-odd delegates assembled at the World Trade Centre, only to be told that Working Group 2 was still meeting. They sat for hours in the stuffy convention hall, while in another room, Cyril Ramaphosa carried out the final execution. He agreed, cleverly, to a 70 percent majority for passage of all constitutional clauses except the bill of rights, where three quarters would be required. But then, on his own initiative and without consulting senior colleagues, he added a rider: If the assembly could not agree within six months, a referendum would be held. At that point, only 50 percent of the population would be needed to pass a new constitution.

Now it was Delport's turn to claim a trap: the ANC need only twiddle its thumbs for six months, and then rely on the 50 percent support it could almost certainly get, to pass its own constitution. Codesa was deadlocked.

Mandela and de Klerk met that night over coffee. They knew Codesa was a disaster, but they did not dare admit it publicly, fearing the consequences if the peace process was seen to have stalled. They agreed to declare victory, and withdraw. The next day, in his closing address, Mandela praised the "remarkable job" done by Codesa and portrayed the delegates as members of a happy multi-racial family, while de Klerk congratulated the gathering for having turned a crisis into a triumph. Codesa II ended with a vain attempt to trick the general populace into thinking all was well.

Moments later, just after the debacle drew to its close, I and other *Financial Times* colleagues visited de Klerk in his office, only to find him in buoyant mood. There was no hurry to get a deal, he told us. If compromise were required, it must come from the ANC. De Klerk was confident he could get 51 percent of the popular vote by leading an anti-ANC alliance.

Senior members of de Klerk's negotiating team argue today that he should have settled at Codesa II, that the party snatched defeat from the jaws of victory there. Certainly, some of the agreements drafted there but never implemented—including a deal on interim government which would have given the National Party an effective veto—were more favorable than later offers. In the end, even the dreaded percentage question was settled in the ANC's favor. The final deal was a flat two thirds, worse even than what was offered at Codesa II.

De Klerk ought to have known that the deal would inevitably deteriorate over time, as the balance of power shifted inexorably toward the ANC. But he did not then subscribe to the "take what you can get" school of constitutional negotiation.* He was on a roll, he had power, and he was happy to do no more than talk about sharing it. Where he had gambled and won on the referendum, he gambled and lost at Codesa. De Klerk's luck deserted him there; it would never reappear.

In truth, the ANC was no more ready to settle than he was. For Codesa had not succeeded in bridging the biggest gaps between the two sides (in some cases, it had not even discussed them). The National Party still wanted a slow transition to power sharing, while the ANC wanted a quick path to majority rule. There was no basis for a deal.

But then, Codesa II was not really about doing a deal; it was about

* This was Roelf Meyer's argument.

showing how unwilling the other side was to settle. In the end, it gave both sides what they really needed—breakdown. De Klerk needed to be brought back down to earth; and the ANC needed to test its strength, as much to bolster its own confidence as to impress the other side. The government felt too strong to settle and its rivals felt too weak. The ANC set out to reverse that equation, forever.

I ONCE ASKED *Mrs. Anna Bame, the lady who brought me my morning cappuccino in the office, how her life had changed since Mandela left jail. "Since that time, there is no peace at all." That was cheerful Anna's experience of life after apartheid— nothing but violence.*

Anna, twenty-nine, was five months pregnant at the time. And almost every afternoon, she came to me or my journalist colleagues to find out whether it was safe to go home that night to her tiny, spotless house in violent Thokoza. If there was trouble in Thokoza, one of us would have been there to check it out; or the local news agency wire, the radio, or the TV would have tipped us off. So we could warn Anna not to go home, but to sleep at her mother's cramped house in a peaceful part of Soweto, where her three-year-old child had already been sent for refuge.

Far too often, though, the violence caught her unawares, in the middle of the night, and Anna would spend the dark hours hidden in the rafters of her home, listening to gunfire, and wondering whether her husband Paul would come home alive. After two years of this, Anna gave up on Thokoza, abandoning the upwardly mobile bungalow of which she had been so proud. The bank continued to dun her for mortgage payments even so; it was a cruel irony of the township violence that those who aspired to the middle class, and lived in mortgaged rather than state housing, were ruined by it financially.

Eventually Anna's house was taken over by a group of ANC urban guerrillas known as a "self-defense unit." Eight of its members were murdered there, leaving the walls of the house streaked with blood and gore, and a curse over the whole property. After that, Anna could never go home because, in the mysterious way that Africa has, she would have been blamed for the massacre. So the release of Mandela made Anna homeless, and her plight weighed on his mind. By then there were too many Annas for him to bear. . . .

11

The Darkest Hour

IN THE DARK OF a cold winter's night, armed men shot, stabbed, and hacked to death forty-five people in a four-hour orgy of slaughter which set a new standard of South African atrocity. A nine-month-old baby and a four-year-old child were among those murdered on the night of July 17, 1992, at the grim black squatter camp called Boipatong, south of Johannesburg. South Africa was left staring into the abyss of a senseless, ceaseless conflict that promised to destroy it. For Nelson Mandela, Boipatong was the "last straw."

"The police did nothing to stop the criminals, and nothing to find them," Mandela complains in his memoirs; "no arrests were made, no investigation began. Mr. de Klerk said nothing . . . my patience snapped." Pity fueled his anger, as Mandela visited the Boipatong bereaved and watched as forty-five coffins, one of them no more than two feet in length, were lowered into the ground. He had devoted his life to save his people from such agony. The thought that he was powerless to stop it drove him nearly mad with despair.

All the evidence is that Inkatha members from a local migrant workers hostel went to Boipatong, an ANC squatter camp, and carried out the massacre. Local residents claim the police were involved. They refused to give evidence to the authorities, but some told journalists that police had escorted the attackers into the camp, and others said they saw white men directing the carnage. No one will ever know what really happened, because of appalling lapses in the police investigation. An independent inquiry into the massacre, headed by a British police expert, exonerated police of complicity in the attack, but severely censured the police force for its shoddy investigation.

Mandela—and virtually the whole of black South Africa—blamed the de Klerk government for the massacre. "I can no longer explain to our people why we continue to talk to a regime that is murdering our people and conducting war against us," Mandela said at the funeral, his voice shaking with obvious anguish. The ANC pulled out of negotiations, and a grim cloud settled over South African politics.

The abyss was glimpsed at Boipatong, but its depths had yet to be plumbed. For three months, from June to September 1992, South Africa was convulsed by strikes and protests. De Klerk and Mandela—like a couple faced with the irretrievable breakdown of their marriage—communicated only by written insults. Long memoranda were exchanged between them, and each seemed to make matters worse.

The ANC undertook a campaign of mass protest aimed at shaking the white government. For more than two years, Mandela had kept at bay those within the ANC who cherished dreams of insurrection, fantasizing about million-strong crowds in the streets, à la Eastern Europe. After the failure of Codesa II and Boipatong, the insurrectionists captured ANC strategy. The rank and file of the ANC had long been theirs; now they also dominated the executive.

Mandela had no choice but to go along. He supported mass action as a "middle course" between armed struggle and negotiation. "The people must have an outlet for their anger and frustration, and a mass action campaign was the best way to channel those emotions," he wrote in his memoirs. In early August, Mandela led fifty thousand angry ANC supporters in a march on the seat of government in Pretoria, part of a national strike involving several million workers. The symbolism was lost on no one. "Today we are at the door of Union Buildings," said Cyril Ramaphosa, who was a leading populist as well as a negotiator. "Next time, F. W. de Klerk, we are going to be inside your office."

De Klerk was unmoved, so the ANC's insurrectionists planned a dramatic escalation in their campaign. If they could not topple Pretoria, they would try a softer target: one of the shaky black homeland governments, which de Klerk was refusing to abolish. On the morning of September 7, 1992, ANC leaders set off with seventy thousand supporters to march on Bisho, the capital of the Ciskei homeland, hoping to provoke the demise of this remnant of apartheid. At 2:00 A.M. that morning, a local magistrate had granted them permission to march as far as Bisho's Independence Stadium, just over the border from white South Africa, but more than a mile from the town. The Ciskei police and military, commanded by white officers seconded from Pretoria, were ordered to stop marchers there.

Ronnie Kasrils, the leader of the insurrectionists, knew this was the case. But he was unwilling to give up his plan for a people's march on Bisho. He spotted a gap in the stadium fence and led a breakaway group straight through it—into a line of Ciskei Defence Force soldiers deployed there to block the route to Bisho. "One moment I was running, my comrades with me," Kasrils recalls. "The next instant, without warning, the soldiers opened fire." The crackle of gunfire went on, and on, and on. Esther Waugh, a local journalist, hit the ground behind a heap of sand: "There was no other sound, no screaming, just the long death-rattle of the rifles."

Kasrils and other ANC leaders, including Cyril Ramaphosa, survived. But twenty-eight marchers were killed, most shot in the back as they fled. De Klerk was inevitably blamed. But ANC leaders knew it was Kasrils who had led the marchers to the slaughter, and they censured him severely. Mandela has said Bisho was "the darkest hour before the dawn"—for him, for de Klerk, and for South Africa itself. It looked as though the new South Africa could not survive the trauma of its birth.

Even in the dark hours, the ANC and the National Party kept their sights firmly fixed on the dawn. While Mandela and de Klerk were trading insults from Boipatong to Bisho, their two young lieutenants—Cyril Ramaphosa, thirty-nine, and Roelf Meyer, forty-four—were meeting secretly to look for a deal. Between June and September 1992, they met something like forty-three times in what became known as "the channel." More than any other two men—indeed, arguably more than Mandela and de Klerk themselves—it was Ramaphosa and Meyer who opened the road to peace, and kept it open right up until the election.

It is tempting to romanticize the relationship between these two men, who became the true "Siamese twins" of the revolution. All the ingredients are there—each was young, handsome, powerful, charming, and totally dependent on the other for political survival. When news leaked out of an August 1991 trout-fishing trip during which Ramaphosa reversed the usual racial stereotypes by both knowing how to fish and removing an embedded fishhook from the finger of the novice Meyer, the romantic picture was complete. Clearly, South Africa's two chief negotiators were so close that they spent their leisure hours together, bonding over fishhooks. Such friendship could not fail to deliver a deal.

In fact, the two men do not socialize or vacation together, or visit each other's homes. Ramaphosa insists he accepted the 1991 invitation to the trout farm of a Johannesburg stockbroker without knowing that Meyer would also be there; no such outing has ever been repeated.

Sentiment is no guide to understanding their relationship. The image of the trouthook captures it perfectly, not as a tableau of brotherhood and warmth but as a portrait of power: Ramaphosa, with his rock-solid build and ruthless political instincts, administers a glass of whiskey to bolster the courage of the slight Afrikaner Meyer, blanching with pain, and rips the hook from his finger. That image prefigures all that would follow: the strong bond of trust between the two men, but also the imbalance in their power. From Boipatong to Bisho and beyond, the inexorable logic of the revolution weakened Meyer and strengthened Ramaphosa. The National Party was simply on the wrong side of history; nothing Meyer did could change that.

If their relationship was unequal, it was nonetheless immensely effective. The two men seemed to understand each other far better than their bosses. Over the months of their most intensive partnership—June 1992 to November 1993—Ramaphosa and Meyer developed a powerful double act which left opponents struggling to compete. They were both driven by the same need: to deliver the new South Africa, fast. As young, ambitious South Africans, they knew that their political future lay in cooperation.

This was just as true of Meyer as of Ramaphosa. For though he was bred in the traditions of Afrikaner politics—he was chairman of the Afrikaner student union, the Afrikaanse Studentebond, and of the Ruiterwag (junior Broederbond), both breeding grounds for Nationalist politicians—Meyer always knew that the white political road would dead-end soon after he entered it. He says morality prompted him to support reform; but even if it had not, ambition would have been sufficient.

Once morality and ambition had set Meyer on the road to majority rule, he pursued it with a vigor and a commitment not shared by anyone else in the National Party, including F. W. de Klerk. Meyer was the first important party convert to abandon the psychology of ethnic politics in favor of majority rule. As the only conduit to the ANC from Boipatong to Bisho, and the main channel of communication for more than a year after that, Meyer's conversion was crucial.

Like that of F. W. de Klerk, Meyer's political history begins in the land of conservatism. Born the year before the National Party took power in 1948, he started life as a poor farm boy from the eastern Cape, whose family did not even have electricity. Descendant of three centuries of Afrikanerdom—the Meyer family came to the Cape in 1695—he immersed himself in Afrikaans cultural activities. To this day, he speaks English awkwardly, and with a heavy accent.

Meyer describes himself as a "loyalist" rather than a radical. For years, he accepted the wisdom of the prevailing political order, without questioning its justness. But when de Klerk raised the prospect of a new beginning, Meyer reacted with enthusiasm. As he told me in an interview conducted in the study of his luxurious eighteenth-century government residence in Cape Town in November 1994, "I saw it as creating a new opportunity for ourselves. Because it was quite clear that if we had to continue in the same way, we would have lost everything—culture, language, everything. It was as though we had been standing in a corner behind a closed door for decades. The Afrikaner could not play his role from behind a closed door."

While Meyer was learning his power politics in the institutions of the

Afrikaner establishment, Cyril Ramaphosa was attending a far tougher school—and in the end, it showed. Ramaphosa learned about power in the black trade unions, where he worked to build the union movement, only legalized in 1979, into a fearsome political and economic weapon.

Both men are charming, but where Meyer is boyish and direct, Ramaphosa is more calculating. For him, charm is a tool of the trade; it is integral to the way he exerts personal power. Ramaphosa exposes and exploits people's weaknesses in the way that Mandela exploits their strengths. The two men were a formidable combination.

Ramaphosa honed these skills as head of the National Union of Mineworkers, the most powerful black union, after spending a chilling seventeen months in solitary confinement in the late 1970s for his political activities. Ramaphosa says he was first attracted to trade unionism when he saw Sylvester Stallone in the role of a U.S. union boss in the film *Fist*. Soon he was able to play the same role himself in real life—he called the mineworkers out on strike in 1985, and again in 1987, when 340,000 men struck. Though the 1987 strike proved a defeat for the union, Ramaphosa still remembers the thrill of it. "The power that we wielded to be able to bring the mines to a standstill was exciting and intoxicating," he once told me. He never forgot that early taste of power.

Nor did he forget the lesson he learned from the capitalist "bosses" whom he so despised as a young Communist—how to cut a deal. Ramaphosa says the "bosses" outclassed the union. "We were not sophisticated in our approach to negotiations; all we had was just a sense of injustice and a mission to improve the lot of the workers, and the raw power [of a strike]. Intellectual persuasion was not one of our key tools." After being caught a few times "with our pants down," unionists learned to do their homework, "and to present our arguments in a clear, articulate, and sophisticated way."

Meyer reflects on Ramaphosa's background with envy: "These guys had an advantage over us, they'd been through negotiations par excellence in the mining industry . . . while we had to learn through experience on a daily basis—you can't read these things in books." Forty-four years of power had bred complacency in the Afrikaner establishment, while in the tough world outside it, the Ramaphosas were learning to fight and win. And they were fighting for noble ideals, whereas Afrikaner leaders were put in the increasingly uncomfortable position of defending a system they knew to be indefensible. That fact handicapped Meyer, and the whole National Party team. It was far easier to fight from the right side of history.

But within the constraints imposed by history, Meyer played his role with skill and subtlety. His job was to get close to Ramaphosa, and through him to the ANC. His task was to build the bridge of trust needed for a deal.

He could do that, where his predecessor Tertius Delport demonstrably failed, partly by virtue of his personality. Meyer is cool, unemotional, a man who thinks before he speaks; and he had a natural rapport with Africans, from whom he fervently sought acceptance. But it was identity of purpose which bound them, more than personality. Ramaphosa was under pressure from his constituency to deliver a transfer of power, and Meyer was under tremendous pressure to persuade the ANC to settle. Each understood the problems of the other.

Those who watched the two men operate throughout their intimate collaboration say that the dependency was greater on Meyer's part. "Cyril always held the whip hand," says Colin Eglin, chief negotiator for the liberal Democratic Party. "I never once saw Roelf coming out with an initiative which would put the ANC in a tight spot." But Ramaphosa was careful to allow Meyer, too, to score victories. That was one of the lessons he learned in union negotiations, "that you don't rub [the opponent's] nose in the mud. You know when it is time to pull back and let them withdraw or accept the humiliation with dignity."

Then one day, Cyril Ramaphosa decided to put Roelf Meyer "in his place." Both say it was the main turning point in their relationship—a test of strength that distributed power between them for the duration of the negotiated revolution.

"Cyril had been preparing himself for this bust-up," ANC negotiator Mac Maharaj recalls; he says Ramaphosa established a permanent "psychological advantage" over Meyer that day. Participants differ in their memory of exactly what was said. Maharaj insists that Ramaphosa complained Meyer was treating him like a "kaffir" (the crudest term for an African); Ramaphosa recalls accusing Meyer of behaving like a "white man," a slightly lesser category of insult. Meyer does not remember racism being mentioned. But they all remember that Ramaphosa savaged Meyer—that he went too far, that he knew he had done so, that he possibly regretted it, but that he emerged the dominant partner.

The dispute was about power. Ramaphosa complained that Meyer, as National Party minister, continued to behave as though he commanded the negotiation process—the same charge of arrogance Mandela leveled against de Klerk. Meyer reacted with outrage. He stood, gathered his papers, and prepared to storm out. "I said to him, 'I am getting angry now.' And he said, 'Now why is the minister getting angry?', and I said, 'I am getting angry at you,' and then we went on like that and he provoked me," Meyer remembers, saying this was the only time he lost his temper in the countless hours of talks with Ramaphosa. Through all this, Maharaj was frantically kicking Ramaphosa under the table, urging him to stop before Meyer walked out.

But Ramaphosa would not give in. In the end, a colleague mollified Meyer, who sat down. Talks resumed.

It was a trick Ramaphosa says he learned at the union bargaining table, the art of pushing the opponent too far and getting away with it. Meyer sees things slightly differently: He says Ramaphosa embarrassed himself by going too far that day, and never risked doing so again. But Maharaj's judgment is probably more accurate. Ramaphosa remained within bounds after that because he no longer needed to push beyond them. He had established the balance of power in their relationship—and by extension, between the National Party and the ANC.

Meyer does not regret any of it. He insists that the period between Boipatong and Bisho was the most important of the whole time between the release of Mandela and the elections. "Prior to that time, we struggled to trust each other, and that was one of the reasons for the collapse of Codesa II. They didn't trust that we were serious, that we were really moving towards a democratic outcome, they thought we were still on the road to . . . minority rights." The June to September talks in "the channel" made it possible to overcome this distrust. "In the end we could both say, 'It's good to do business with you.' We would not have been so successful in reaching a settlement in the end, and especially having the government of national unity, if it wasn't for that trust-building exercise."

Meyer is almost certainly right that no deal could be done until he and Ramaphosa learned to work together. But they could not succeed by force of personality alone; they needed major concessions to offer the other side. Both sides used the time from Boipatong to Bisho—when formal negotiations were deadlocked, and only the secret "channel" operated—to make serious preparations for compromise.

The ANC began drawing up proposals to soften the blow of majority rule with limited power sharing, and the National Party began tentatively to toy with the idea that majority rule might not be so bad after all. Both sides were desperate to put negotiations back on track, and for roughly similar reasons: the National Party had nowhere else to go, and after Bisho, neither did the ANC. Both were under heavy pressure from the West to return to the table (especially de Klerk, who feared to fail in the eyes of the world which had so eagerly embraced him). Both were appalled by the economic impact of deadlock.

It was the white finance minister, Derek Keys—who also became Mandela's first minister of finance—who did the most to make this reality apparent to the future black president. Keys gave ANC economics head Trevor Manuel a briefing on the economy, and Manuel repeated it to Mandela.

"And I got frightened," Mandela recalls. "Before Trevor finished, I said to him, 'Now what does this mean as far as negotiations are concerned? Because it appears to me that if we allow the situation to continue . . . the economy is going to be so destroyed that when a democratic government comes into power, it will not be able to solve it.' " Mandela made a decision—the deadlock must be broken.

ANC negotiators had already done a lot of work on exactly how to break it. Mohammed Valli Moosa, a leading ANC intellectual and aide to Ramaphosa, takes up the story. While the ANC's mass mobilizers were busy with strikes and protests, the ANC negotiations commission took stock of the failure of Codesa. "We had to ask ourselves, why did the negotiations not work? It wasn't just a case of two thirds, 75 percent, that wasn't the explanation. And the Boipatong massacre wasn't the explanation, nor the fact that the grass roots of the ANC was becoming impatient and wanted to see some militancy. Nor the fact that Madiba [Mandela's clan name] was very angry with de Klerk and the police. . . . None of those individual things could explain why the negotiations were not working.

"What was clear was that the regime was not ready to settle. Why not? Because the security forces were concerned about their future—they were not going to go along with an agreement that would put them before a firing squad; why should they? The civil service would not make the settlement happen if it meant that the day after the elections they would all lose their pensions and walk the streets. The National Party were not philanthropists; there had to be something in it for them . . . and we had to try and understand what it was that they wanted."

The idea of "sunset clauses" began to gain currency. These were measures to protect the vested interests of whites: job guarantees for white civil servants and security force members; pension protection; amnesty for apartheid crimes; and most of all, compulsory power sharing for a fixed number of years after the adoption of the interim constitution, including a coalition cabinet enforced by law.

This was the crucial breakthrough which would permit de Klerk to settle in the end. And it began to take shape just when hopes for a settlement were at their lowest.

But this idea of a "government of national unity"—a multi-party coalition enforced by the law—did not emerge out of thin air. From his earliest days of freedom, Mandela had suggested such a model to help assuage the fears of minorities. Speaking, appropriately, in Afrikaans, he suggested in May 1991 during a speech in Stellenbosch that simple majority rule might not work in South Africa: "it may not be enough to work purely on one-person one-vote, because every national group would like to see that the people of their flesh and blood are in government." Later he elaborated on this thought. "The ordinary man . . . must look to our structures and see that as a coloured man I am represented . . . and an Indian must also be able to say, 'I am represented.' And the whites must say, 'There is Gerrit Viljoen, I have got representation' . . . especially in the first few years of democratic government . . . [we may have to do] something to show that the system has got an inbuilt mechanism which makes it impossible for one group to suppress the other."

ANC leaders had often suggested to me in private conversation that they would voluntarily bring other parties into government in the interests of national unity—especially in the early years of transition. Only days before Codesa II broke down in May 1992, Joe Slovo told me over dinner that he would favor a "government of national unity" to last until the end of the century. And crucially, Thabo Mbeki had already dangled this offer under the noses of government negotiators even before Boipatong—though insisting it was a personal opinion, not the official view of the ANC.

Now the ANC was willing to set the power-sharing principle in stone, for a fixed number of years. But in September 1992, the ANC was not yet ready to make this offer public. Once again it was Joe Slovo—Communist pragmatist—who forced the movement's hand. He administered a bit of what he calls "shock therapy," by publishing his own "sunset clauses" in the October issue of the Communist Party newspaper, the *African Communist.* This was the logic behind his thinking: "De Klerk was motivated by the need to save as much as he could of the old privileges. He knew that he had to give something and quite substantial things, but he fought throughout the negotiation process to ensure that white privileges should not be undermined excessively." Negotiations would get nowhere until the ANC recognized de Klerk's goals and did something to meet them. In the *African Communist,* Slovo suggested how this might be done. He couched his arguments in the kind of revolutionary rhetoric designed to appeal to ANC radicals.

First, he told them a few home truths, which many had yet to accept: That Pretoria was not a defeated enemy, and as such, could not be expected to give up power voluntarily; that they must prepare to accept a deal which was "less than perfect"; that steps should be taken to get white soldiers, police, and civil servants on side, because they might otherwise destabilize the new democracy. He argued that the ANC should seize the initiative—and the moral high ground—with a package of concessions on compulsory power sharing.

The reaction was explosive. The internal debate that ensued was the last, and worst, great debate of the negotiations period. Those who opposed negotiation on the ANC national executive—arguing that the ANC was deluding itself to think that National Party would ever abandon power, no matter what was offered—clashed with those who took a more realistic view of the balance of power. In November 1992, the executive adopted the "sunset clauses" as official policy.

Mandela defended them to me in 1995, when ANC opposition to power sharing had again begun to surface, by saying that they were essential for national reconciliation. "You must understand that there was great opposition even in [the government] to the talks. The sunset clauses won us the support of many people who would otherwise not have been involved in this transformation." Finally, the ANC had provided the nucleus of a deal.

The African National Congress was not alone in having a major crisis of conscience. Between June and September 1992, the National Party's strategy, and its constitutional thinking, both began to shift. For the first time, de Klerk made it his top priority to reach a deal with the ANC—abandoning the idea of an anti-ANC negotiating bloc with Inkatha, which had been rendered impractical by the obstructive behavior of Chief Buthelezi. Buthelezi and the leaders of all the other smaller parties would have to be persuaded to accept the deal in the end, or it would have no legitimacy. But first the superpowers must reach a meeting of minds.

There was another, subtler philosophical shift just beginning to take place. Meyer was urging the cabinet to turn away from the idea of explicit minority vetoes, toward majority rule. Opposition to him was fierce, for Meyer's goals were different from those of older, more conservative members of cabinet. He had the best years of his political life before him; he wanted the best he could realistically achieve under majority rule. They were fighting to preserve remnants of a past that he believed was doomed.

The dispute opened the first serious rift in cabinet since de Klerk launched reform in 1990. Roelf Meyer, representing the *verligte* (liberal) camp, says he often felt that "we were only three and a half in cabinet": Meyer, and *verligte* Ministers Dawie de Villiers and Leon Wessels, plus "all the other bits and pieces together." Ironically, the leader of what became known as the "anti-" or reactionary faction in cabinet was Kobie Coetsee, the man who launched the negotiation decade in 1985, and then found he did not like where it was leading. Even de Klerk himself was often a reluctant convert to Meyer's positions.

Indeed, it would be many months—nearly a year, in fact—before the president would accept Meyer's "democracy or nothing" views. Eventually, he would decide that Afrikaner survival could better be guaranteed under majority rule (with limited power sharing) than by continuing to insist on a political system that would give minorities an effective veto. But in September 1992, de Klerk was still stuck somewhere midway on the path between vetoes and majority rule.

Joe Slovo could hardly conceal his glee. "They caved in on everything." On September 26, 1992, the National Party signed what became known as the "Record of Understanding" with the ANC. The agreement marked a major turning point in the struggle between the two sides. The National Party had blinked.

The deal thrilled the ANC, embarrassed the government, and infuriated Inkatha. In it lay the seed of the final settlement—along with the germ of its near destruction. For the Record of Understanding included measures, such as the fencing off of Inkatha hostels and the banning of Zulu traditional weapons, which were bound to enrage Chief Buthelezi. The Record of Understanding convinced Buthelezi that the ANC and National Party were ganging up against him. On constitutional matters, the Record included no obvious concessions to government—and no hint of the sunset clauses, which would only become official ANC policy two months later. After reading the agreement, I asked Roelf Meyer in some bemusement what was in it for the National Party. He replied with three words from the text: "resumption of negotiations." The National Party was so desperate to see talks resumed that it would do anything to secure that goal.

The Bisho massacre had convinced both sides that it was imperative to return to the table. It had conjured up visions of a future of endless carnage which shocked them back to their senses. But to get talks moving again, the National Party gave up far more ground than the ANC. Six months after peaking at the referendum, de Klerk was reduced to pleading with the ANC to talk. It was partly the ruthlessness of Mandela which had put him in that state. During the negotiations leading up to the summit meeting where the Record of Understanding was signed, Mandela did what Ramaphosa had done before him; he put his opponent "in his place." By then, Mandela knew that the balance of power between the two men had shifted decisively. "De Klerk needed us more than we needed him, he desperately needed that summit," the ANC leader said in a 1995 television interview. Mandela set out to make him pay for it.

The ANC had originally set fourteen preconditions for returning to talks, but after Bisho, these were reduced to three: releasing a number of political prisoners, including three ANC members convicted of terrorist murders (one of whom, convicted of a necklace murder, announced on his release that "I felt happy watching him burn"); fencing in Inkatha hostels;

and stopping Inkatha members from carrying "traditional weapons" in public. For ten days before the September 26 summit, the two sides negotiated night and day to clear these obstacles. Then, late on the Thursday night before the planned Saturday summit, Mandela had had enough.

De Klerk was balking at the release of three particular death row prisoners, including Robert McBride, who had killed three white women when he bombed a Durban beachfront bar. ANC negotiators went to Mandela on Thursday night, and told him this was the only remaining obstacle to the summit. They were willing to back down, fearing the summit would otherwise not take place.

Mac Maharaj, who participated in the negotiations, recalls what happened next: "Madiba just picked up the phone and told F.W., then there is no meeting." De Klerk asked for half an hour. The time expired, the president had not phoned back, and Mandela upped the stakes. "I want McBride released before the meeting," Mandela told him. Again, de Klerk said he needed time. Maharaj then told Mandela, "I think you have gone too far now, you are jeopardizing the whole bloody thing." But Mandela just laughed and said, "This chap, I have had enough of him, we hold the line here today."

And the line held. De Klerk agreed to release the three men; the summit went ahead. But Mandela was not finished with de Klerk yet. At the summit itself, one of the main sticking points was the issue of the fencing of Inkatha hostels (the ANC wanted the hostels fenced off from the surrounding townships). The pro-Inkatha faction in cabinet, led by Police Minister Hernus Kriel, strongly opposed this measure. De Klerk tried to sidestep the issue, claiming that he had not studied the draft agreement on hostels drawn up by the two negotiating teams. But Mandela knew this was untrue, and he had a simple answer to the problem. "He said in that case, when we finish this meeting, I will have to pronounce that it has been a total failure. And F.W. panicked," Maharaj recalls. De Klerk agreed to consider the document over lunch—and then met Meyer and the other young moderates, avoiding consulting the Kriel faction altogether. By teatime, he was ready to sign. The "antis" were furious.

Mandela was still not happy. De Klerk wanted a clause in the Record saying the ANC would curtail the mass action which had kept South Africa in turmoil for months. "F.W. and the old man met one-on-one, and within five minutes—it could have been ten—they scrapped the whole thing," says an exasperated senior member of the government team who does not want to be named. And in exchange for all this, the ANC agreed only to restart talks on the constitution. From then on, the balance of power within the negotiations would always favor the ANC. They had established a psychological ascendency over the National Party that day—and most especially, Mandela now held the whip hand over de Klerk.

Cyril Ramaphosa, who understudied Mandela that day, clearly enjoyed the spectacle. I once asked him what he had learned about leadership from Mandela, and he referred to that summit: "Madiba is a very stubborn man. He has nerves of steel. Once he has decided that a particular issue has to be pursued, everything else matters very little. And he can be very harsh when dealing with an opponent who is unreasonable, very brutal in a calm and collected sort of way."

Ramaphosa recalls that Mandela told de Klerk the facts of political life at that summit. De Klerk had said he would "never" release the three disputed prisoners; Mandela advised him to avoid such positions of intransigence. " 'Because you know in the end you are going to have to give in, and be humiliated, and I am trying to save you from humiliation,' he said." Mandela told de Klerk he was concerned about ensuring that the National Party did not lose support. He had this advice for the white president. "The way to strengthen your party is to work with the ANC, and working with the ANC means giving in to ANC demands. Because if you don't, we are going to humiliate you."

The Record of Understanding was to prove a major turning point on the road to peace. On that day in September 1992, the National Party finally realized it could no longer control the transition, nor count on easily outnegotiating its opponents. When, the next day, Chief Buthelezi angrily repudiated the agreement—enraged that the ANC and National Party were cutting deals without him—it became clear that the National Party's hopes of an alliance with Inkatha had foundered forever. Henceforth, any alliance would have to be with the ANC.

But the Record was not just a triumph for the ANC; it was a triumph of negotiation over conflict. I once asked Joe Slovo when he thought a deal became inevitable, and he replied: On the day the Record of Understanding was signed, "The government realized that there would be no solution without the ANC, that they could take it so far and no further." And, he might have added, so did the ANC.

"WE KILLED HIM *and then we burned his body.*"

Shall I bother to ask why, as though reason can comprehend the primordial hatred that spurred the deed and the bloodlust that carried it through? But I cling to reason in this land driven half-mad by violence. I insist on a rational motive, and it is chillingly simple: The township is at war. The dead man was the enemy.

He was a resident of the local hostel. These youngsters before me are his killers. They tell the tale in the kitchen of a burned-out house, where we use matches for light, fearing that anything stronger will attract enemy fire. I perch on a Formica stool and glance nervously at their AK-47 rifles, and at their eyes.

They are filled with righteousness—and with the unparalleled excitement of violent murder. The young men explain that "hostel dwellers," Inkatha supporters, have killed scores of residents in this, the "Radebe" section of Katlehong. They have burned, looted, and destroyed homes. The local residents have formed a "self-defense unit" to protect Radebe. These young men are its members.

Anyone found on the wrong side of the invisible line that separates "residents" from "hostel dwellers"—or ANC and Inkatha, if you prefer neater, less accurate labels—courts a gruesome death. The dead hostel dweller had to cross enemy territory to get a taxi to work. On his way home, he was caught, killed, and set alight. I ask, who killed him? The reply is obvious: "The community." Individual responsibility, individual guilt are banished by the collective will.

Sipho is the group's leader. Disarmingly shy, with a slow, wide smile and a gentle manner, he tries to put me at ease. It is well after midnight, and we are crouching in a darkened room in one of the abandoned houses the self-defense unit uses as a base. Sipho cautiously shifts the incongruous net curtain at the window, pointing to the row of houses on the other side of the eerily empty street. These are enemy bases.

Sipho is my bodyguard. He stays close to me, with the gun, as we patrol Radebe with the self-defense unit. We follow a maze of paths between houses that crowd upon each other, wall to wall, past malodorous outdoor toilets, under washing lines in backyards crammed with rubble, stumbling in the gloom, taking cover from snipers behind half-demolished walls. The houses are dark: the self-defense unit imposes a nighttime curfew. Windows are blacked out with blankets. Once, Sipho scratches almost soundlessly at a back door, and a resident lets us silently into a warm kitchen.

Then we are out again into the cold night, squeezing through fence gaps, waking up the dogs, sprinting across streets which seem impossibly wide, vulnerable to the guns that lurk in the darkness. A police armored vehicle trundles by, its powerful spotlights trained on the houses. We freeze; a single shot rings out; and then they move on.

These young men have "contempt for death"—the one quality Joe Slovo always said was essential to a revolutionary. But they are not revolutionaries. They are children who walk to school past bodies lying casually in the street, and attend "necklacings" for entertainment. They are the inheritance of the new South Africa.

12

The End of History

IT HAD BEEN A LONG, hard revolution, and the hardest part was yet to come. In September 1992, when the Record of Understanding was signed, South Africa was still several painful battles away from victory.

F. W. de Klerk had decided to do a deal—but to have believed, then, that he would accept majority rule would have required a faith in miracles. Similar suspension of disbelief would have been needed to imagine that Chief Buthelezi would enter the new South Africa on terms laid down by his enemies, the African National Congress and the National Party. Or that the white right wing, which had slowly grown in rage since the March 1992 white referendum, would do the same. Or that the ANC would embrace its old enemy, capitalism, and turn to economic conservatism at last.

To have believed that all this would happen simultaneously, and within nineteen short months of the abyss that was Bisho, would have strained credulity intolerably. That would have required the sort of epidemic of pragmatism of which South Africans no longer seemed capable. They had spent most of the time since Mandela's release fighting and marching and striking and killing; it was hard to believe they would all suddenly decide to be reasonable.

Many parallel revolutions were yet in store, and the first and most important was in the mind of F. W. de Klerk. It was to prove as radical as the transformation of mind that brought him to release Mandela in 1990. De Klerk had to learn to redefine the most basic concept of his political philosophy, the notion of power. His goal had always been to ensure that blacks could not govern without the agreement of whites, but the ANC was refusing to be forced into such an arrangement. So de Klerk began to look for other, subtler means to the same end.

Mandela had rejected outright anything which could be construed as a minority veto—including any of the National Party's various proposals for a revolving presidency, or a kind of "inner cabinet" in which all major leaders would agree jointly on policy. The ANC leader refused to consider any measure that would force him to get de Klerk's approval before he could act. As de Klerk continued his hectic schedule of overseas visits in 1992 and 1993, he heard repeatedly from Western leaders that they, too, would not countenance such a veto. He could call it what he liked—and did, insisting that his proposals for "consensus decision making" did not imply a veto—but the West made clear that it would not endorse a deal unless it was broadly democratic.

De Klerk powerfully craved that endorsement, both to ensure that South Africa took its rightful place in the modern world, and even more important, to guarantee his own personal spot in the annals of history. When de Klerk unbanned the ANC and released Mandela, he became a world figure overnight—and from then on, he felt the gaze of the world heavy upon him. He knew that what the world demanded—a liberal democratic constitution with protection for minorities, but no veto—was not what he had promised his electorate. But he did not dare risk international rejection of the Constitution; that would be a disaster for South Africa, and for his own self-image. Vanity drove him to compromise.

De Klerk, the eternal pragmatist, set out to redefine his goals according to prevailing reality. If he could not have power sharing entrenched in the Constitution forever, then he would take what he could get. He did not seem to have a very clear idea of what that might be, or of how to achieve it, for de Klerk was never strong on creative constitutional thinking, nor was he a great strategist. But he knew, by September 1992, that he wanted and needed a deal. Henceforth, everything else—including the very content of that deal—was subordinate to the goal of getting it signed.

Then Slovo intervened with his "sunset clauses," and de Klerk seized on them. The ANC and the National Party spent the rest of 1992 and early 1993 negotiating a bilateral deal along the lines of Slovo's proposal. In December and January, they retreated to a private game lodge for two "bush summits," or *bosberade*, where, thrown together in the wilderness and forced to share swimming pools and dining tables, they reached a meeting of minds. They agreed on a five-year "government of national unity," to be entrenched in the interim constitution. This would mean Mandela would have to choose a coalition cabinet made up of all parties that passed an (as yet unspecified) electoral threshold. ANC negotiators told me privately that they would make sure de Klerk had "real power" within this government. It was a formula which he could begin to accept as a good second best.

The two sides fudged the important issue of how decisions would be taken in the cabinet, and, crucially, of exactly what power F. W. de Klerk would personally have within it. These were questions that would determine, in the end, whether minority parties had just a presence in the executive, or real power. De Klerk was still insisting on a formula that would give him power equal to that of Mandela himself: a revolving presidency, in which the office would rotate between himself, Mandela, and Buthelezi; or some formula which would ensure that Mandela could make important decisions only with de Klerk's approval.

But he was coming under more and more pressure from the more *verligte* members of his cabinet and government to consider a revolutionary compromise on this question. I remember asking a senior National Party negotiator in February 1993 whether he thought his party would reach its goal of maintaining "a hand on the tiller" of government well into the new era. "That depends on how well we do in the elections," he said. "If we win 40 percent, we'll be powerful; if we get only 25 percent, we'll be in trouble."

That sounded suspiciously like democracy to me—and seemed to bear little resemblance to the artificial formulas favored by de Klerk. I knew that his chief constitutional thinker, Fanie van der Merwe, a senior civil servant, had long argued that these formulas were impractical and would paralyze government. Now his political allies were also urging the president to make his peace with democracy.

Chris Hani lay dead in a pool of blood in his own driveway, and again, the abyss beckoned. Hani was one of the ANC's most charismatic populist leaders, and a hero to the radical youth. He was assassinated on a sunny Easter Saturday morning in April 1993, gunned down as he returned home from buying a newspaper. His young daughter, alerted by the sound of gunshots, discovered her father lying dead in the drive.

South Africa held its breath, terrified of the explosion of anger that might follow. For Hani's assassin was a member of the white right wing, a Polish immigrant, Janusz Waluz, who had conspired with a senior official of the white right Conservative Party. Visions of a race war loomed large in the national imagination.

Mandela went on television to appeal for calm. "A white man, full of prejudice and hate, came to our country and committed a deed so foul that our whole nation now teeters on the brink of disaster," he said. "But a white woman, of Afrikaner origin, risked her life so that we may know, and bring to justice, the assassin," he continued, referring to the white neighbor who noted the assailant's license-plate number and ensured his arrest.

"Tonight I am reaching out to every single South African, black and white, from the very depths of my being," Mandela pleaded. "Now is the time for all South Africans to stand together against those who, from any quarter, wish to destroy what Chris Hani gave his life for—the freedom of all of us."

For the whole of the long Easter weekend, and in the week of mourning and funeral rallies to follow, we all held our breath. When I drove with colleagues to a massive rally in Soweto, we three whites were the sole available target if the crowd sought revenge. When police opened fire on the rally, killing four and injuring many more, I could not believe we would escape unharmed. But the marchers steadfastly refused to indulge the racist anger which would have been so much more rational than tolerance. One ANC marshal, seeing my frightened face, even sought to reassure me. "This is Africa. It's our land. You don't worry!" he told me with a broad smile. The ANC's long tradition of non-racialism, its forgiveness and its compassion, triumphed that day. South Africa had survived yet another crisis.

No other single event proved so conclusively that, whatever the traumas yet to come, South Africa's center would hold. Within minutes of the murder, ANC officials announced that negotiations would not be called off. The days when progress was held hostage to violence were firmly at an end.

The crisis clarified, once and for all, the balance of power. Symbolically, de Klerk was all but unseated by it. He contented himself with issuing a statement on the murder from his Cape holiday home, while Mandela dominated the TV screens. De Klerk was still president; but Mandela was the nation's leader. He shouldered the task of racial reconciliation shirked by de Klerk, who showed little understanding of the anger and loss felt by the black majority.

It also raised the specter of a serious threat to peace from the white right wing. The radical right were a motley crew, composed mainly of splinter groups numbering only a few men. Even the *Afrikaner Weerstandsbeweging* (Afrikaner Resistance Movement) or AWB, the largest group of paramilitary white supremacists, scarcely raised visions of Bosnia. Its fiery leader, Eugene Terre'blanche, rode to battle on a large black horse—from which he regularly tumbled—not on a tank.

The white right had no heavy weaponry, no planes, no armories. But the unknown factor that terrified the ANC was the extent of right-wing support in the security services. Many whites in the army and police had conservative sympathies, including many senior officers; and among part-time, locally based forces and reservists, totaling as many as 450,000 men, right-wing support was strong.

These were the people who were almost certainly behind the third force. They had already seriously destabilized South Africa by fueling the fighting between the ANC and Inkatha. They probably masterminded many of the drive-by shootings and train massacres which made daily township life such a nightmare. If they now undertook a campaign of selective assassination of ANC leaders, they could derail the whole process. With Hani's murder, they had struck at the very core of the ANC leadership. What if Mandela were next?

Black South Africans obeyed Mandela when he urged them not to avenge Chris Hani's death. But he knew that their obedience was not automatic. Anger was building again at the slow progress of negotiations. Multiparty talks had begun once more shortly before Hani's death, but the public had little tolerance for their interminable debates, which could not even yield agreement on what to call the talks—the name "Codesa" was disgraced—let alone on anything more substantive.

The ANC used Hani's assassination to force the pace of those talks—which never were given a name—and to maneuver the National Party into a trap from which it would never escape. ANC negotiators insisted that the talks should set a date for the first all-race elections. Agreement on a constitution to govern the elections then seemed impossibly distant, but the ANC did not care. Joe Slovo argued eloquently in the negotiating chamber that a date was needed to send a signal to South Africa that negotiations were on the "last mile." The National Party gave in, perhaps thinking it could change the date later, if more time were needed to complete the interim constitution. They ought to have known this would be impossible. Once fixed, the date was set in stone. As one disgruntled Afrikaner commented to me at the time, it was like handing over the title deeds to your farm without first agreeing the price.

Mandela forced de Klerk into this trap by exploiting the president's passion for international kudos. The two men were due to travel to the United States to receive the Liberty Medal jointly in Philadelphia on July 4, 1993. Mandela said he would not attend unless the election date had been set, and without him, de Klerk could not receive the award that meant so much to him. The two men set off for the States while their negotiating teams faced off over the issue. In the end, the ANC forced through agreement that elections would be held on April 27, 1994—only hours before Mandela and de Klerk were to see President Bill Clinton (separately) at the White House.

The setting of the election date was to prove an important turning point in two very different ways. Inkatha and the Conservative Party, which had been participating in the talks, walked out in protest when the date was set. They were never to return. The isolation of the right would have serious consequences in the future, but in the short term, it was good news. Progress at the talks (which came to be known by the name of the venue, the World Trade Centre) was rendered that much easier by removing any need to accommodate the right.

Fixing the date also proved momentous for de Klerk. Just over nine months remained until election day, and in a country where most blacks had never voted before, preparations would take months. So the negotiators had only a few weeks to agree on a new constitution. Time was not on the National Party's side.

Meanwhile, back at the World Trade Centre, the ridiculous vied daily with the sublime. Debates went on interminably, and seemed to get nowhere. One day debate would have to be suspended because a female was missing from a particular delegation (each was meant to be a man-woman team). It could not resume until women were found to warm all the required seats. Another day, delegates would spend three hours debating whether they had time to listen to a twenty-minute statement from one of the parties.

The talks were fractured into an array of committees and groups baffling to the outside eye. There were "technical committees" to deal with specific issues, a ten-man "management committee" to steer the process, and the fifty-two-person "negotiating council." This structure was to prove crucial to the eventual deal: the existence of "technical committees" meant that even the toughest and most basic disputes about power could be treated as technical problems, susceptible to solution by experts in an atmosphere of rational discourse. Members of these committees were not exactly impartial (in the polarized politics of South Africa, such people do not exist), but they were at least unemotional. They were problem solvers, and with their technical language, legalistic ponderousness, and aura of almost scientific expertise, they managed to disguise a blunt transfer of power as a fair and mutually agreeable trade-off.

The chief politicians at the talks were Cyril Ramaphosa and Roelf Meyer, who carried on their earlier double act. But when they could not agree, which was often, they turned to the two men who became their deal brokers: Mac Maharaj, the Operation Vula terrorist; and Fanie van der Merwe, Mandela's interlocutor in prison. They were charged with overall management of the talks.

Both had the unquestioned trust of their principals. Maharaj and Mandela had spent many years together on Robben Island, and van der Merwe was de Klerk's chief constitutional adviser. Both enjoyed the role of éminence grise, and played it well. And they understood one another perfectly. "You could throw anything at them, and they would look at it objectively and find a compromise," National Party negotiator Leon Wessels recalls. "They were a very exceptional combination." Van der Merwe was especially crucial in ensuring that F. W. de Klerk was on board. He proved a far more liberal thinker than almost any of his colleagues, championing democracy long before de Klerk or even Meyer.

Larger than the personalities was the process itself—the rules of behavior set down at the World Trade Centre. All the parties to the talks accepted that reason was their best weapon. Each learned to present an argument for sectional interests in the language of universal, and overwhelmingly liberal, values. They learned that they must appeal to the overall public good, if they wished to win concessions for their own party. So black South Africans did not just come to the talks and say, in the words of Anglo American Corporation's Bobby Godsell, "we are the majority, give us the tanks, the planes and the chequebooks please, or we will take them." South Africans learned how to do what they had never had a chance to do before: to solve political battles through rational debate, rather than fighting.

But both sides say the toughest battles were not those at the World Trade Centre but those which took place within the rival camps. "There are two aspects of negotiation—negotiating with the enemy, and negotiating with yourselves. The latter is ten times more difficult," ANC negotiator Mohammed Valli Moosa once told me. "A camaraderie develops where your constituency is seen as your enemy, and the enemy is your ally," says his colleague, Frene Ginwala. Negotiators were reduced to speaking "the language of the enemy" with their own people.

If this was difficult for the ANC, it was even harder for the National Party, where Roelf Meyer came to be seen almost as an enemy agent by the conservative faction in the cabinet. The de Klerk cabinet was deeply split between those—like Meyer, Leon Wessels, and Dawie de Villiers—who were on first-name terms with their ANC counterparts, and outsiders who were not subjected to the atmosphere of the talks. The negotiators were by then spending almost every waking moment with the enemy, under conditions of sleep deprivation, heavy alcohol consumption, and the absence of almost all contact with the outside world. So when Meyer and his colleagues appeared at cabinet meetings, they were treated like so many Trojan horses sent by the ANC.

Then, at the beginning of September 1993, came the first public signal that de Klerk might opt for majority rule: he agreed to the installation of a multi-party interim government to rule until the April elections. And, crucially, he accepted that the National Party would have no veto in that government.

At Codesa II, it had been agreed that the interim government, known as the Transitional Executive Council, or TEC, would need an 80 percent majority to take decisions—a figure which would have given the National Party and government, each separately represented, dominance. But in the end, de Klerk compromised on a lower majority, which denied him an automatic veto; if he wished to prevail in the council, he would have to secure allies from other parties. It was the first public sign that de Klerk was ready to play the democratic game of persuasion, rather than relying on a rigid veto entrenched in law.

There was no hint yet that he would be so flexible when it came to the government of national unity, which would rule for five years after the elections. For the ANC and the National Party were avoiding the issue of power sharing in the government of national unity, knowing that it would be the most difficult of all. There was tacit agreement to put off that battle until everything else was resolved.

In the meantime, they went about the business of writing a classic, liberal democratic interim constitution for South Africa. It broadly incorporated the principles of separating power between the three branches of government (executive, legislature, and judiciary), spreading it from the center to provinces, and preventing the misuse of power. It included a bill of rights enforceable in the courts, to protect human rights and individual property (the liberal Democratic Party, tiny but influential, was instrumental in ensuring agreement on a powerful bill of rights); a constitutional court to resolve disputes and ensure that the constitution reigned supreme in the new state; and it assigned some limited powers to provinces. For de Klerk, these constitutional checks and balances were all part of power sharing.

Many of the central issues in this constitution were fudged—especially the issue of devolution of power, which the National Party failed to exploit as a forceful tool of power sharing. Hasty compromises were reached, which only deferred battles to the (post-election) constituent assembly, where they would be reopened all over again. And had the National Party spent less time looking for convoluted forms of power sharing, and focused on fighting for democracy from the beginning, South Africa might have emerged with a stronger constitution in the end. But however flawed, the general outline of the constitution was clear; it would protect liberal democratic values about as well as those of most Western nations. And that was broadly what both the National Party, and the ANC, had intended.

The constitution also included other provisions aimed directly at appeasing the National Party: guarantees for the jobs and pensions of white civil servants (though these were later proved to be less than watertight); and provisions for the first local government elections, which would give white voters in conservative rural areas a heavier weighting in the poll. But the main area where de Klerk was demanding appeasement—power sharing in the executive—remained unresolved. This problem was two-fold: What position would F. W. de Klerk occupy in cabinet? And how would that cabinet take its decisions?

Joe Slovo had a plan for dealing with the first problem. He told his colleagues, "We must think about de Klerk, his personal position, and if we can find a solution to that, the National Party will just collapse." Meyer had made clear that de Klerk wanted a position of personal power within the new government. He was insisting on being the deputy president—deputy to Mandela.

Cyril Ramaphosa sweetly agreed that this could be so, but there must be *two* such deputies. The first deputy president would come from the majority party (the ANC), and the second from the runner-up National Party. De Klerk was furious. He would hold only a poor third position in cabinet. But there was worse to come. Meyer had frequently raised the question of how decisions would be taken in cabinet, where parties with over 5 percent of the national vote would be represented proportionally. De Klerk was insisting that important decisions be taken by consensus—meaning everyone must agree—or at the very least by special high majorities (this would give de Klerk a blocking vote). But Ramaphosa had always deflected discussion of this issue.

Toward the end of October 1993, both sides knew the problem must be resolved. Officially, government was still insisting that most cabinet decisions be taken by something like a two-thirds majority, and decisions on security matters by three quarters. But privately, men like Meyer and his close colleague Leon Wessels knew this battle was lost. Several weeks before, they had begun to argue that it was unwise to insist on a figure at all, on the grounds that a figure of two thirds in cabinet would simply mean that the other third could be permanently ignored. With opinion polls showing the ANC likely to score more than a two-thirds vote, this would mean oblivion for the National Party.

Meyer and Wessels began to argue for percentages to be dropped in favor of a commitment from the ANC that it would take decisions "in a spirit of national unity." They wanted to create a moral obligation on the part of the ANC to listen to the National Party. According to their proposal, blacks would no longer be forced to get the agreement of whites in order to govern—they would just feel morally obliged to do so. The most central tenet of the National Party policy on power sharing was about to be abandoned.

De Klerk had not yet come round to this view. At the height of the campaign to persuade him, Leon Wessels outlined to me the argument for doing a voluntary deal: "The ANC *knows,* as we do, that South Africa can only be governed by a government of national unity. They *know* they need us or there will be no stability. Those of us who have grown up with the process don't fear the risk [of a voluntary arrangement]. But those who haven't, do. What is the alternative? Constitutional entrenchment won't be achievable, and fighting over it will divide the parties further. A meeting of minds is the only way."

Cyril Ramaphosa had caught the strong scent of capitulation from the rival camp, and he was delighted. When, toward the end of October, I wrote an article in the *Financial Times* suggesting that de Klerk was about to accept majority rule, he congratulated me for "rubbing salt in their wounds." But Meyer genuinely did not feel that his side was capitulating; this was not a case of Ramaphosa wielding "the whip hand." Meyer fervently believed the National Party would have more power under a voluntary arrangement than under a compulsory one. Forty-five years of apartheid had showed him the folly of relying on laws to protect culture. He felt convinced—on the basis of his experience at the World Trade Centre—that the ANC was more likely to obey the spirit of national unity than it was to obey a constitution which it resented.

South African realities would force the ANC to share power, far more effectively than any constitution, he argued. The real centers of power—in the civil service, the security forces, the business community—still owed allegiance to de Klerk. "The country will grind to a halt without National Party cooperation," he told me late one night over drinks. Mandela would have no choice but to rely on de Klerk to govern.

Meyer could argue that the long delay in reaching agreement—which had so weakened his party's negotiating position—had actually created the perfect conditions for a reasonable deal. The two sides had grown together during their long courtship, building bonds of trust that would not have existed had they settled earlier. The culture of consensus which grew between them would protect the Afrikaner more powerfully than any law could ever do, Meyer maintained. For his eye was always on the future be-yond the first post-apartheid constitution; however secure its protections, they could not last beyond the end of the century. After that, the Afrikaner would have to prove his worth to the ANC, to secure influence where he no longer had power. Meyer became quite passionate on this theme, stressing, "The choice is between merely surviving, and making ourselves *indispens-able* to them." And that, after all, had been the Afrikaner's larger goal all along, not merely to live on, but to secure a new base of power under black rule.

Meyer was not indulging an impossible dream of being needed by the ANC. Senior ANC leaders like Slovo firmly believed that de Klerk's cooperation was vital to ensure stability. He said as much to Meyer. "All we will achieve when we have won the election is to gain political office. We would not gain state power in the sense of having a complete transformation on day one of the police, the armed forces, the judiciary, and the civil service," he once told me.

Mandela was sending the same message to de Klerk. At about the time of the final battle over power sharing, Mandela told guests at a private dinner party, "My worst nightmare is that I wake up one night and de Klerk isn't there. I need him. Whether I like him or not is irrelevant, I need him." When Mandela speaks from the heart, he can be a very persuasive man.

"I genuinely believe that at one of their endless meetings at the Union Buildings, they slit wrists and made a blood promise that they would make this thing work," says Richard Carter, who was then spokesman to the president. And members of cabinet remember de Klerk returning jubilant from a meeting with Mandela, about a month before the eventual deal, telling them Mandela had agreed that the two men must govern the country together.

De Klerk says that nothing so dramatic happened, but that Mandela assured him of his commitment to consensus "more than once." Still, on the very eve of the deal, the matter remained unresolved. Political leaders were due to adopt the new constitution at the World Trade Centre the next day, and still there was no deal on power sharing. So, late on the night of November 17, 1993, de Klerk and Mandela met for one last time.

Maharaj was there waiting when the two emerged, sometime in the dark hours of that interminable night. "Mandela charged de Klerk with clinging to the vestiges of white minority power," Maharaj says, reconstructing the meeting which only the two presidents plus Ramaphosa and Meyer attended. "But then Mandela just told him, 'I've always acted on the basis that you're needed and that you have a role to play.' "

ANC negotiators had not believed this would be enough to placate the president, so they had prepared other offers; they were prepared to agree that, say, a 60 percent vote would be required to take decisions in cabinet. But Mandela was adamant—the majority (50%) would decide. He could not run a cabinet any other way, he told de Klerk, who had to acknowledge that this was probably true. "Madiba went there not to give an inch, and he just hammered him," says Maharaj. "And in the end, he cracked him." That was the moment when de Klerk accepted majority rule, finally and forever.

The wording of the interim constitution left room for dispute on exactly how the cabinet would make decisions. The clause eventually inserted read, "The cabinet shall function in a manner which gives consideration to the consensus-seeking spirit underlying the concept of a government of national unity as well as the need for effective government." Fanie van der Merwe insisted that this clause, taken together with another saying the president must act "in consultation with the cabinet," meant that Mandela must govern by consensus. But the ANC said the majority would rule, and they turned out to be right.

"We won the battle for an executive based on majority decision making—something I thought we would never win. None of us thought, even a week [before], that we could win that," a jubilant Joe Slovo told me late that night. Mandela's judgment was the same, though more subtle: "Majority rule will apply—we just hope we will never have to use it." But he left no doubt that, if de Klerk got in the way of any ANC program, "the majority will rule."

"What have you done? You've given South Africa away!" Tertius Delport grabbed de Klerk by the shirt front and shrieked in the exhausted and bewildered president's face. De Klerk had just finished outlining the final deal on power sharing to an emergency cabinet meeting, held at 7:00 A.M. on November 18, 1993, the very day the constitution was due to be adopted at the World Trade Centre.

Delport and three colleagues had met at five-thirty that morning to decide whether to launch a mutiny.° The others balked—no doubt judging that it was far too late by then for a rearguard action. Delport, who was then local government minister, was left to oppose the deal in cabinet. He listened as Meyer outlined yet another agreement which fell below the party's bottom line. Patiently, Meyer explained why percentage voting in cabinet would handicap the National Party; he argued the case for letting a "convention" of power sharing develop naturally; and he stressed the (minor) concessions included in the package (vague safeguards for provincial powers, and ANC agreement that a 60 percent, rather than 50 percent, referendum vote be required to pass the new constitution if parties deadlocked in the elected constituent assembly). Then the group broke for tea, and Delport's anger and frustration overcame him. He pursued de Klerk into his office, where they had their angry confrontation.

Eventually, de Klerk succeeded in mollifying Delport, persuaded him to stay on in the party, and got the deal through cabinet safely. When he did, he thanked his collegues with tears in his eyes. He had managed to keep his party together, with no significant defections, from the day he unbanned the ANC to the day he agreed to hand over power. He had dragged his party from the backwater of ethnic politics into the modern world. It was an extraordinary achievement.

° Law and Order (Police) Minister Hernus Kriel, Minister of Home Affairs Danie Schutte, and Minister of Regional and Land Affairs Andre Fourie were also there.

But how would he defend to his constituents a deal which could only honestly be described as majority rule—the very thing he had so long opposed? Why did he accept it?

The reasons are as varied as those which pushed him to make his first great "leap" in 1990. In part, de Klerk was merely outmaneuvered: he let the ANC use its natural advantage, time, to defeat him. He waited to do a deal until the pendulum of power had swung so decisively in the ANC's favor that he was left with little alternative but to accept whatever Mandela offered. Vanity was another factor; de Klerk was desperate not to fail, in the eyes of the world. And, closely allied to it, the arrogance of power: the personal arrogance of believing that he could influence debate in the cabinet, by sheer force of personality; and the institutional arrogance of believing that the National Party would do well enough in the elections to give him a moral and political right to the powerful position denied him under the constitution. Perhaps, in the end, de Klerk also succumbed just a little to the great seducer. Mandela assured him he was needed, and de Klerk desperately wanted to believe that would be so.

In November 1994, well into his tenure as second deputy president, I asked de Klerk why he had done it. "Well, I think as we went along, all of us realized that we'd have to take greater risks than we had originally planned," he replied. That was the true test of his greatness—that he repeatedly took such risks, without hesitation, from the moment he released Mandela to the day he accepted majority rule. That he constantly redefined the conditions necessary for Afrikaner survival, in the light of prevailing reality. That he never turned back, even when he knew his path would take him well beyond his original destination, to a new South Africa where he and his people would have far less power, and far fewer guarantees, than he could ever have imagined. De Klerk accepted the democratic revolution, in the end, not because he was "converted" to democracy but because he had no choice. He was a man of the system, who destroyed that system from within, and celebrated when he had done so. It took courage to launch that process. But it took far greater courage to see it through.

At midnight on November 18, 1993, the new constitution was passed at the World Trade Centre. That was the moment when white hands truly let go their 350-year grip on the baton of power. The rest of the National Party team retired exhausted, but Roelf Meyer stayed on. In the bowels of that grim building, he and Cyril Ramaphosa joined exhausted delegates and journalists to dance for hours, waltzing in the new South Africa.

But the World Trade Centre peace would soon take the new country as close as it had ever come to civil war. To make a deal between them, the

ANC and the National Party had had to force out all those who would not agree. They had cemented a powerful core at the center of South African politics, hoping that it would give critical mass to the deal. But when it was signed, Inkatha and the white right wing were not there. That meant millions of potential dissidents were dangerously left out. Already they were preparing to fight back.

WHEN IT CAME TO *the revolution—the revolution of right-wing whites against black majority rule, that is*—Sakkie van der Schyff was going to be a general.

The new South Africa might be fine for Roelf Meyer, with his middle-class values and his sophisticated black friends, but van der Schyff lived in a different world. He lived in Koppies, once part of the Boer Republic of the Orange Free State, where fifteen thousand blacks—mostly poor, ill-educated, rural people—were about to take over the government from one thousand whites. Roelf Meyer could talk about power sharing, but in Koppies, numbers told the story.

I met van der Schyff in the bar of the Friesland Hotel, which I entered with trepidation. I had come to know and dread these grim platteland hotels—the musty scents, the bone chill, the forty-watt gloom. But the bars were worse. The conversation was always a depressing cocktail of lewdness and racism, and the wine was undrinkable. I was tired of right-wing Afrikaners acting out their stereotypes for my benefit.

Van der Schyff did just that. He told me a joke about a black and a dog. I struggled for the right response. To splutter in outrage would be to fall into the trap deliberately set for the foreigner. I played dumb and changed the subject, to the issue which had brought me to see him: the Koppies blockade.

Van der Schyff had commanded a paramilitary group of whites who penned the black residents of the Koppies township, Kwakwatsi, inside their "location." They shot at anyone who tried to leave (no one was hit). Van der Schyff said the blockade was no more than reciprocal. Blacks had boycotted white shops in Koppies off and on for the better part of 1993; they had stayed away from work, burned down a warehouse, refused to pay for electricity, water, or sewerage. They had exhausted the patience of white Koppies.

All of that was fairly predictable, almost a cliché of platteland life. Then van der Schyff told me another story. One day, squatters from Kwakwatsi stole the fencing from his farm, which borders *directly on the township, and began to graze their cattle in his field of young sorghum. Farmer van der Schyff could simply have shot them, in the time-honored tradition of the old South Africa. Instead, he made a deal. They could graze their cattle in his winter fields (at the cost to him of thousands of Rands he could otherwise earn by selling the fodder). In return, Kwakwatsi would keep its stock out of the fields during the summer growing season, and save his crop. General van der Schyff was learning to fight the real revolution.*

13

Battling for the Right

A MAN WITH a rocket-propelled grenade launcher sat in the seat normally occupied by Roelf Meyer at the World Trade Centre. The negotiating chamber was filled with such men (and women), dressed in fatigues, carrying assault rifles and crossbows, some wearing masks. Right-wing whites had invaded the World Trade Centre, driving an armored personnel vehicle through its plate-glass front windows, and chasing black delegates through the corridors screaming. They beat up several female black delegates and black journalists, all to dramatize their demand for a white homeland, or *volkstaat*. Negotiating with such people was not going to be easy.

But that became the next priority after the peace deal signed at the same World Trade Centre on November 18, 1993. That deal bound only the ANC, its allies, and the National Party. Now the white right wing, and Inkatha, were demanding a separate peace.

The ANC was terrified that the white right, with its strength in the police and army, would sabotage the transition to majority rule. Mandela had visions of right-wing Afrikaners—heavily armed, trained, and already organized in local militia units of the South African Defence Force—rising up to prevent the elections. Mandela knew de Klerk could not stop them: right-wing whites despised their president even more than they hated Mandela. They believed de Klerk had betrayed the Afrikaner nation. If anyone could make peace with them, Mandela would have to be the one.

The ANC would need to act in secret. Most ANC members, not to mention most right-wing whites, would be outraged at the idea that the racist murderers and godless terrorists of their political mythology should meet. In the middle of 1992, in conditions of strictest secrecy, *Umkhonto we Sizwe* chief of staff Joe Modise approached the South African Defence Force second in command, Lieutenant General Pierre Steyn, a known moderate, to establish the first direct contacts between the two rival armies. According to Steyn, they met for "drinks and snacks" and the occasional *braai* (barbecue), at a secret army safe house. The talks continued through late 1992 and 1993, involving even the most conservative officers, and proved a major factor in ensuring that the top army leadership supported the elections. Senior military officers had an interest in making peace with the ANC: as professional soldiers, they would soon find their salaries paid by Joe Modise.

Next, Mandela spread his net wider, to try to bring in the rest of the white right, ranging from the official parliamentary opposition, the Conservative Party, which gained 800,000 votes in the 1992 white referendum, to neo-Nazi splinter groups of the lunatic right. For that, he turned to retired General Constand Viljoen—the man who had headed the South African military in the days of the total onslaught.

Viljoen had emerged from retirement to lead the far right in May 1993, when he and other retired generals formed the *Afrikaner Volksfront* (Afrikaner People's Front), an umbrella grouping of the white right. Viljoen gave the right a new, more pragmatic leadership. He had valiantly tried to prevent the World Trade Centre attack, and was the only right-wing leader to intervene when the neo-Nazi storm troopers attacked blacks caught in the building. But he was having trouble uniting the right wing behind the cause of negotiating, rather than fighting for their *volkstaat*. He had difficult relations with Eugene Terre'blanche, the leader of the *Afrikaner Weerstandsbeweging*, the largest of the paramilitary white supremacist groups. And the general's relations with the Conservative Party, which represented by far the largest number of conservative Afrikaners, were strained.

Viljoen had entered the political fray to try to prevent a war he knew his people could not win. Mandela wanted to talk to him. They both believed a way could be found for Afrikaners to live with Africans. But Viljoen wanted Afrikaners to live *alongside*, not under a black government. He disparaged the idea that the ANC could create a new nation "like you make instant coffee—a little bit of coffee, a little bit of milk, a little bit of brown sugar." He wanted a geographically separate peace for the Afrikaner, in his own homeland. Mandela was willing to discuss anything, however far-fetched, to stop Viljoen going to war.

Viljoen's twin brother Braam had close links with the ANC. At his instigation, the two leaders met for the first time on August 12, 1993. The idea of it was as shocking as Mandela meeting P. W. Botha—a conference of sworn enemies. Constand Viljoen's people were white supremacists, ready to fight and kill blacks; they were not the modernized Afrikaners Mandela had grown used to dealing with in the National Party. But the two men clicked immediately, just like Mandela and the Groot Krokodil. Ironically,

Mandela and Viljoen—both nationalist leaders, both men of principle as much as politicians—almost immediately found the closeness that had always eluded Mandela and de Klerk. By then, Mandela was fed up with de Klerk, accusing him of fighting for white jobs and privilege, not for the public good. But he felt genuine sympathy for Viljoen's fears, which focused on culture, religion, and language, not privilege. Mandela's aides put it simply. General Viljoen won the old man's heart; he was to become just about the only opposition politician whom Mandela trusted.

The ANC leader gave talks with Viljoen a high priority, and carefully chose a team of moderate Africans (not the Indian and white Communists whom the Afrikaners distrusted) to run them. The amiable Jacob Zuma was one of them. He explained to me why the ANC pursued them. "We said to them, 'We can't go for war, we are from war already! We thought we could destroy one another, we couldn't! Why can't we talk?' "

As Thozamile Botha, another member of the ANC team, explained, "Our approach was that we needed stability after the elections, that was the motivating factor. It was not enough to say, we have got the numbers on our side—experience in Africa and elsewhere has shown that you can win the elections and still not be able to govern." So the talks began, and once again, it was Thabo Mbeki (who was involved only peripherally in the World Trade Centre talks, but continued to be a major ANC strategist) who won the day. Mbeki's strategy was simply to keep the Afrikaners talking. That way, they would remain under the seductive influence of himself and Mandela; they would be kept away from their war councils; and they would be exposed continually to a barrage of reasonable questions which might in the end make them doubt the viability of their own *volkstaat* demands.

General Viljoen's insistence on a separate territory for the Afrikaner was demonstrably unrealistic. In no significant part of South Africa were Afrikaners in the majority; to create a *volkstaat* would mean deporting blacks, or denying them the vote—neither of which the ANC could countenance. Mbeki did not tell Viljoen he thought his idea was crazy; he just kept asking him questions which he could not answer. Viljoen had promised that his *volkstaat* would not be based on racism. Well, if not, Mbeki would ask, how do you ensure Afrikaners are in the majority? Where will your *volkstaat* be? How will it operate? The ANC never had any intention of giving Viljoen his homeland—but they managed to make him think they were seriously considering it. They hoped to keep him talking right through the elections and beyond, certain that the demand for a *volkstaat* would diminish once Afrikaners had seen that they would not be victimized in the new South Africa.

The onus was on the general to produce a rational proposal for a *volkstaat,* and he did his best to comply. He sent delegations to study the communal systems of Belgium and Switzerland, and they came back with flexible proposals for limited Afrikaner autonomy—a sort of "*volkstaat* of the mind," rather than a territorial homeland. Viljoen knew that the vast majority of his supporters were not prepared to give up their comfortable lives to emigrate to some far-flung *volkstaat.* They just wanted to feel a minimum of security, in an uncertain future.

Then suddenly, in December 1993, the ANC and the Afrikaner Volksfront announced they were going to sign a deal on a *volkstaat.* The news came as a shock to both sides, but especially to ANC supporters. They were prepared to give their wily old leader considerable latitude, but a deal on a white homeland? For many, that was a step too far. Yet he persisted. The deal was extremely vague, and represented primarily a statement of intent to keep looking for a solution. But it was a stroke of strategic genius from the ANC, designed to give Viljoen the political ammunition he needed to keep his supporters away from the warpath, and to help isolate the violent right at its own extreme end of the political spectrum, where it could more easily be dealt with by force.

At 1:00 A.M. on December 21, 1993—the day the deal was to have been signed—Viljoen was forced to back out. The agreement fell victim to a wider crisis in the negotiations. General Viljoen was part of a negotiating alliance known as the Freedom Alliance, which grouped together his Afrikaner Volksfront, the Conservative Party, Inkatha, and the conservative governments of the Bophuthatswana and Ciskei homelands. While he was talking about Afrikaner self-determination with the ANC in the Transvaal, his allies were carrying on parallel negotiations with Cyril Ramaphosa and Roelf Meyer in Cape Town. They were talking about the related issue of federalism, which was Inkatha's main concern. On the night before the so-called Volkstaat Accord was to be signed, those Cape Town talks deadlocked. To maintain the solidarity of the Freedom Alliance, Viljoen had no choice but to pull out.

Constand Viljoen immediately accused Ramaphosa and Meyer of sabotaging the *volkstaat* agreement. Certainly, there was circumstantial evidence for this charge. Ramaphosa had said privately that the Mbeki-Viljoen talks were "a sideshow," and Meyer did little to further them. The two men had forced the Freedom Alliance talks to deadlock at exactly the most crucial point for Viljoen, but their actions had nothing to do with the *volkstaat.* They were gunning for a different foe—Inkatha. Spoiling the *volkstaat* agreement was just a by-product of their long campaign to outmaneuver Chief Buthelezi.

That campaign had been going on for years. While ANC and Inkatha members fought each other in the streets of Katlehong and the villages of Natal—leaving over twenty thousand people dead by the end of 1993—the rival parties had also fought brutal political battles at the negotiating table. And from the very beginning of the negotiations, the ANC and the National Party had made sure that the cards were stacked against Inkatha. Before Codesa had even begun, during the talks preparing for its commencement, the two super-parties had concluded a little known and poorly understood deal which cut Inkatha definitively out of the negotiating process. They thrashed out a formula for how Codesa's nineteen parties would take decisions: Codesa would decide by what was termed "sufficient consensus." Officially, this was defined—by a process of circular reasoning—to mean the agreement of all those who needed to agree, to avoid a breakdown. But Cyril Ramaphosa gave me a far more blunt and accurate definition, only minutes after the deal on "sufficient consensus" was struck. "It means that, if we and the National Party agree, everyone else can get stuffed." Specifically, Inkatha could get stuffed.

Ramaphosa was clearly elated at the thought that the National Party and the ANC could carve up power without worrying too much about anyone else's claim to a share of it. But the decision had ominous consequences. It was used several times during the negotiations to overrule Inkatha. On occasion, it seemed to be wielded deliberately to enrage the Inkatha delegates. In the end, Inkatha rebelled and left the World Trade Centre process altogether.

The rift between Inkatha and the others was fundamental. Inkatha wanted the new South Africa to be a federal state, one where regional governments would have strong powers, as strong (or stronger) than those of the American states. Under such a system, Inkatha, as a regional party, would have a chance to rule in Natal. But for the ANC, federalism was "the 'f' word": four decades of apartheid—itself a demented form of federalism— had discredited the concept forever. The ANC feared that by devolving power to regions, it would lose the ability to control government at the centre. ANC officials argued that federalism would create chaos and constrain development.

These positions were, at least, understandable. Inkatha wanted a federal South Africa to give it more power, and the ANC wanted a unitary South Africa exactly to prevent that. The National Party's position was more confused. As a minority party, with a strong base in the Western Cape (the only major region where Africans do not have an overwhelming majority), it might have favored federalism. As a way of limiting the power of the central state—surely the goal of power sharing—devolution would be a powerful tool. But after forty-five years of ruling a highly centralized old South African state, the National Party seemed to have little idea what federalism meant, and only a weak inclination to fight for it. The party failed to press hard for devolution while it still had the power to do so.

The constitution that emerged from the World Trade Centre did provide for some devolution of power. It was so vague that it was hard to characterize, and left many important decisions on the division of powers between center and regions to the Constitutional Court, which would rule where the constitution was unclear. But it appeared closest to the German model of federalism, in which the central government has broad powers to override the regions on most issues. The National Party claimed this made South Africa a federal state; but Joe Slovo, speaking freely out of exhaustion and drink on the eve of the deal, insisted the new state would be "not *remotely* a federation. . . . We've managed to give them devolution, without losing control," he told me, with considerable satisfaction.

Slovo's was far from the last word on the subject. As soon as the new constitution was adopted, the ANC and National Party took it to Inkatha— which had not attended the World Trade Centre talks for months—to try to strike a deal that would bring Chief Buthelezi into the elections. The debate on federalism began all over again. By that time—the end of 1993—the bitterness and frustration built up over years of abortive talks made rational discourse difficult. Theirs truly was a dialogue of the deaf: neither side seemed able to appreciate, or even to understand, the viewpoint of the opponent. The paradox never ceased to baffle me—the constitutional gulf between the ANC and Inkatha proved harder to bridge than that between the ANC and the National Party itself.

Too often, the talks had nothing at all to do with issues of substance. Buthelezi was intransigent, Ramaphosa uncompromising, and each seemed more intent on casting blame on the opponent than on finding a solution. The ANC did not really think it needed Buthelezi. Ideally, Inkatha's participation was needed to give the elections broad legitimacy, especially in Natal. But with something like 80 percent of voters nationwide backing either the African National Congress or the National Party, many in the ANC did not think his participation essential. They blamed the Zulu leader personally for the violence, arguing with justification that his constant veiled threats of civil war were seriously destabilizing Natal. And they believed he was directly involved in masterminding the activities of hit squads operated by his Kwa-Zulu police. Many in the ANC preferred force to negotiation in dealing with Buthelezi—and that inevitably undermined their desire to settle.

Quite apart from calculations of raw power, ANC leaders genuinely believed they could do nothing to satisfy Buthelezi, however hard they tried.

They thought that he would boycott elections no matter what they did, because he did not dare to run for election and risk losing power. ANC leaders also suspected the Zulu leader's commitment to federalism, convinced that his real goal was to secede from South Africa altogether. When Buthelezi published a draft constitution for the state of KwaZulu-Natal, which would take it close to secession, they became convinced that what he really wanted was a separate kingdom for KwaZulu. While they were trying to build a modern, color-blind nation, Chief Buthelezi wanted a tribal kingdom with a state ideology of Zulu ethnicity. He wanted to restore a feudal oligarchy to Zululand; the ANC would never accept that.

Buthelezi fueled these suspicions by dragging the Zulu king, Goodwill Zwelithini, a weak and inarticulate man whom he had always dominated, into his campaign for federalism. The king—who as monarch had wide support among Zulus, far wider than that for Buthelezi—was produced, dressed in leopard skins and carrying traditional clubs and spears, to demand the restoration of the Zulu kingdom. This tactic angered the ANC, which was further enraged by Buthelezi's reliance on foreign advisers—mostly radical right-wing Americans, obscure constitutional lawyers—to draw up his constitutional proposals. Both the ANC and the National Party had always insisted that South Africa's problems be solved by South Africans. They deeply resented Buthelezi's reliance on foreigners.

Perhaps as much as anything, the ANC simply found Buthelezi infuriating. They were not alone; his own envoys to the talks (which he did not attend) were reduced to spluttering rage by his habit of reneging on deals they had struck. His deep paranoia made him explode at slights where none were intended, and generally rendered him incapable of rational debate. No one found it easy to talk to Buthelezi: not de Klerk, who had wrecked their relationship forever when he signed the Record of Understanding without the agreement of Buthelezi (even though it included several provisions aimed only at Inkatha); not the white businessmen who had long been his friends (when top businessmen offered him millions of Rands in election funds in December 1993, he accused them of being agents of the ANC). Even Mandela lost all patience with him. Those who tried to persuade the ANC leader to be more flexible were treated to a tirade on the past wrongs done to him by Buthelezi. "It's amazing how much the two are alike in that regard," commented one frustrated diplomat. "They never forget a slight."

Still, Buthelezi was hardly the first irrational South African the ANC had learned to deal with. Yet they never found a way around him. All sweetness and subtlety when handling Constand Viljoen, ANC leaders chose frontal confrontation when dealing with Chief Buthelezi. It was a strategy designed to fail, and it never disappointed. The breakdown of talks on the eve of the Volkstaat Accord was a case in point. The Inkatha delegation had brought a compromise proposal which would have given provinces stronger powers, but which was far from secessionist. By that stage, Inkatha was asking for a weaker form of federalism than in the United States. The proposal was scarcely unreasonable.

Cyril Ramaphosa blocked discussion of it altogether. He insisted that Inkatha commit itself to participate in the elections before anything else could be discussed. This would be to admit defeat before the battle: the threat to stay out of elections was Inkatha's only tactical weapon. Buthelezi would have to be mad to give it up for nothing, and Ramaphosa must have known that. But he was looking for the public relations advantage, not for a solution. He offered to let Inkatha make its participation "conditional" on constitutional agreement; but this, too, was just a ploy. In the real world of politics, once Buthelezi had said he would join the elections, he would pay dearly for backing out.

The talks deadlocked, only to resume after Christmas, and drag on through January and February 1994. By then, the elections were perilously near. Yet there could be no polling in Natal, South Africa's most populous province, or in many townships around Johannesburg, unless Buthelezi could somehow be persuaded to participate. If he could not, fighting would almost certainly prevent the voting. That would be a disaster for the new South Africa. But by February, the ANC and National Party had more or less abandoned any hope of doing a deal with Buthelezi. They made various small improvements to their offer on regional powers, and amended the constitution to include them. But their intention was to win the public relations battle against Buthelezi more than to entice him. They prepared for a show of force.

The Transitional Executive Council (the multi-party interim government in which Inkatha did not participate) sent troops to Natal, and Kobie Coetsee, then minister of defense, let Buthelezi know that "the guns are trained on Ulundi," Buthelezi's capital. Many ANC leaders began to relish the idea of crushing their hated enemy once and for all. Buthelezi seemed to do all he could to invite such an outcome. At a base outside Ulundi—a spot easily visited by journalists—he used right-wing whites to train so-called self-protection units, the mirror image of the ANC's self-defense units. But where the ANC units were largely formed spontaneously at local level, the Zulu units were created deliberately by Buthelezi. At one camp in Northern Natal, raided just before the elections, evidence was found of guerrilla training of some four thousand men.

The Inkatha guerrillas' access to arms was limited—but as their commander Philip Powell once told me, "Vietnam was won by people on bicycles who made their own grenades." Buthelezi could not hope to resist invasion, as he had no army. But he could cause lasting havoc in KwaZulu-Natal. As the poll drew near, ANC leaders began to fear that he would join forces with the racist right, militarily as well as politically. With the white right to provide the military skills and weapons, and thousands of Zulus as cannon fodder, such a force could make a peaceful election impossible.

Then, on March 1—a scant eight weeks before the election—came the first tentative sign that disaster might be averted. Mandela promised to "go down on my knees to beg those who want to drag our country into bloodshed and persuade them not to do so," and that was what he did. He went to Durban and did what other ANC leaders could never bring themselves to try—he "stroked" Chief Buthelezi.

"Buthelezi is very strange, he is like a child in front of Mandela," one participant in the meeting recalls. "And he was just overwhelmed." Mandela offered Buthelezi a tactical concession. He would submit the constitutional dispute to "international mediation," a process from which the ANC, with its positive international profile, would have little to lose. In exchange, Buthelezi agreed to register Inkatha for the elections "provisionally." The Zulu leader continued to insist he would boycott the poll unless his constitutional demands were met. But he had left the door open to participation. Impossible as it then seemed, there was a chance that Inkatha might be in the elections after all.

Three white men lay in the dust of an African street, watched over by black men with guns. One was dead; the other two were bleeding and begging for mercy. Suddenly, without warning and with no perceptible increase in the tension in the air, one of the black men turned toward the wounded whites, pointed his rifle, and fired. There was a *pop,* another *pop,* and then two more, kicking up a puff of dust. Three white men lay dead in the street, staining the earth with their blood.

The power of that tableau—the vision of groveling white men executed by blacks, replayed incessantly on South African television—seared the imagination of white South Africa. The illusions of 350 years of white domination, and the myths of racial superiority which attended it, had been disintegrating for years. But that stark picture made the transfer of power an emotional reality at last.

Alwyn Wolfaard and Fanie Uys had been members of the *Afrikaner Weerstandsbeweging*, and they were executed on March 11, 1994, by a paramilitary policeman in the black homeland of Bophuthatswana. Their deaths helped turn the tide of right-wing emotion against resistance, and marked perhaps the most decisive moment in the revolution which brought the white right into the new South Africa.

Few episodes in the history of South Africa can have been more surreal. Early on the morning of March 11, 1994, I stepped outside my hotel in the Bophuthatswana capital, Mmabatho, to find armed white men in the street. The AWB had invaded Mmabatho. Bophuthatswana was one of the nominally independent black states created by apartheid, and Mmabatho was an African capital, where only a handful of whites would normally be seen. But that day, white men dressed in khaki controlled every road junction.

Mmabatho had been in turmoil for several days already. Civil servants, employees of the Bophuthatswana government which would cease to exist under the new constitution, were striking to demand back pay and pensions; students had revolted when homeland leader Lucas Mangope announced there would be no elections in the homeland; police later joined them; and through the night, Mmabatho residents had looted the local shopping center, carrying out major appliances and entire living-room suites, under the watchful eye of police.

During the night, I was awakened by a particularly loud burst of gunfire—the looters were storming the back door of my hotel. The hotel's heavily armed white security guards fought them off. And I went back to sleep—until a colleague phoned to tell me that armed right-wing whites were on their way to Mmabatho. That seemed the kind of tale which was too improbable, even for South Africa. Again I went back to sleep.

But there they were, outside the hotel, which had just announced it was closing its doors and evicting all guests. Somehow, I and a black American colleague would need to get past an AWB roadblock directly in front of the hotel. The AWB do not like journalists at the best of times, and a white woman in the company of a black man risked provoking their ire. So we took an armed member of hotel security along with us, and he talked his way through. Then we went to try to find out what was going on.

That only became clear much later. The homeland's leader, Lucas Mangope, had appealed to General Constand Viljoen to send armed men to prevent his overthrow. Drawing his precedent from tribal history, Mangope told Viljoen that the Boer people had helped his ancestors defend themselves against the alien raider Mzilikazi in the nineteenth century; now they must do the same. Viljoen and Mangope were allies in the Freedom Alliance. The general agreed to cooperate.

Mangope insisted there must be no forces from the AWB—they were ultra-racists, and their presence would provoke the Boputhatswana Defence Force to mutiny. Viljoen agreed, and mobilized a force of 4,000 men which did not include the AWB. He kept 2,500 in reserve, and sent 1,500 into Mmabatho, bearing only sidearms. They were to rally at the airport, where Mangope's soldiers would give them weapons.

But the AWB's leader Eugene Terre'blanche had ignored the plea to stay away, and he and his men arrived before Viljoen in Mmabatho. They had removed the swastikalike insignia which normally identified the AWB, but it was not hard to recognize them. They drove through the streets of Mmabatho and its twin town Mafikeng, shooting at bystanders, leaving dead bodies strewn along the streets. Afrikaans newspapers called it a *kaffirskiet-piekniek*—"a nigger-shooting picnic." The Bophuthatswana army revolted.

Viljoen ordered his men to withdraw and the AWB men followed them. But they went out shooting, and local police and soldiers returned their fire. That was how Uys, Wolfaard, and their colleague Nic Fourie were captured. In their elderly Mercedes, they were the last in a convoy. They were executed in the presence of journalists, cameramen, and rolling TV cameras. Within hours, all of South Africa knew how they had died—including Wolfaard's own wife and daughter, who unwittingly watched the execution on the nightly news.

Bophuthatswana succeeded where Mandela had so far failed. It persuaded Constand Viljoen to drop any remaining dreams of armed resistance and participate in the election. "On the light plane out of Mmabatho that evening, I finally decided, there's no way out," he told me. "With the AWB and its ill discipline, I just cannot—I dare not—undertake military action. And if I did, what would be the result? We would not be able to maintain a *volkstaat* financially, and politically it would be completely isolated in the world. I decided to go for a negotiated settlement. And that gave me only one choice: to go through with the election."

Viljoen registered a list of candidates for a breakaway party, the Freedom Front, only minutes before the midnight deadline on March 11, the day of the Bophuthatswana debacle. Terre'blanche denounced him, as did the Conservative Party. The ANC had engineered a white right split, at last.

Bophuthatswana proved a turning point for Viljoen, but also for the South African Defence Force. They moved into Mmabatho, as the right wing moved out, to depose Mangope. De Klerk had opposed this move, mounting a rearguard action to protect the spurious independence of this unsavory ally. But Mandela forced him to back down. The chief of the South African Army, General Georg Meiring, was ordered to oust Mangope; when he obeyed that order, it marked a decisive psychological break with the past. The army had chosen sides. It would not support Viljoen—and without the South African Defence Force, he could do nothing. The threat of organized right-wing resistance was no more.

The election juggernaut, fortified by the fall of Mangope and the capitulation of Viljoen, was now bearing down on Buthelezi. The broad right alliance had crumbled, leaving him in splendid isolation. Meanwhile, his position seemed to have hardened. Although he had "provisionally" registered Inkatha for the election, he failed to lodge a list of candidates in time for the March 11 deadline which had galvanized Viljoen. It looked as though he would boycott, after all.

Infuriated by Buthelezi's intransigence, and excited by their triumph in Bophuthatswana, ANC leaders began making plans to topple him. Their campaign was bolstered, a week after Mangope fell, when Judge Richard Goldstone announced that he had found a "horrible network of criminal activity" linking the South African and KwaZulu police, and Inkatha. Police were involved in manufacturing, smuggling, and supplying weapons to Inkatha, he said (see page 168). When the Ciskei government followed Bophuthatswana into oblivion on March 22, the anti-KwaZulu campaign gathered pace. An obviously delighted Joe Slovo commented, "Two down, one to go." He wanted to crush Buthelezi then, and be done with him. Many of his colleagues still regret that this was not done.

Every day now seemed to bring a new rise in the political temperature. The head of the Independent Electoral Commission, charged with running the poll, called for direct intervention in KwaZulu. He said there could be no voting in Natal without it. Voter educators from the ANC were murdered; electioneering in the province became a life-threatening activity.

On the morning of March 28, 1994—exactly a month before the planned election—Inkatha said it would stage a demonstration in Johannesburg. The day that ensued was to prove the bloodiest the white city had ever seen: thousands of Inkatha supporters marched through the modern business center, their spears, shields, and clubs in stark contrast to the glass-fronted skyscrapers of this American-style city. They were gunned down by snipers, in the large square in front of the public library, and outside ANC headquarters at Shell House. ANC security officers killed eight demonstrators, claiming Inkatha had tried to storm the building; eyewitnesses disputed this. After a day of appalling carnage, of the kind that had previously been confined to distant townships, fifty-three people lay dead, most of them from Inkatha. South Africa was shocked, not least by the fact that Mandela personally prevented police from searching Shell House after the massacre. Prospects for a peaceful election had never seemed worse.

With the elections now a month away, the ANC had largely concluded that force was the only way. Moderates within Inkatha had long been pressuring Buthelezi to participate—but by then, even they had despaired. Meanwhile, the Zulu leader continued to insist that the election be postponed. But Mandela had made a promise: international figures would be invited to mediate the constitutional row. Exactly two weeks before the poll, former U.S. Secretary of State Henry Kissinger and former British Foreign Secretary Lord Carrington arrived to do just that.

They never got to square one. The ANC and Inkatha could not even agree on the terms of reference for mediation. Thabo Mbeki had agreed on draft terms with Inkatha's Joe Matthews, a leading moderate. Their draft agreement tactfully avoided the contentious issue of the election date. But when Cyril Ramaphosa saw the terms, he exploded. Rather than merely leaving the issue unstated, as Mbeki had done, he tried to force Buthelezi to commit himself in writing to the poll. Such a frontal attack on the Inkatha leader had never worked in the past, and it did not work now. No terms could be agreed upon; the international mediators left in disgust. It seemed that the last chance for peace had finally passed.

Enter the deus ex machina. Sometime on the afternoon of April 15, according to the account given by Chief Buthelezi, God chose to interfere with the engine of the aircraft in which he was traveling, setting off a chain of events which led to Inkatha participating in the elections after all.

The way Buthelezi tells it, the chain reaction went as follows: On April 15, Kenyan mediator Washington Okumu, who had arrived with the Kissinger/Carrington team but had not left with them, summoned him to a meeting. Buthelezi was airborne, and would have missed the meeting, but his plane developed engine trouble and he had to turn back. He met Okumu, a friend of twenty years standing; the Kenyan talked him into participating; the Inkatha central committee endorsed the decision. On Tuesday, April 19—exactly a week before the first day of polling—Buthelezi became the last major South African leader to throw in his lot with democracy.

Perhaps Okumu, and the deity, did have a role in persuading Buthelezi. Perhaps he simply faced the reality of exclusion from the election, and let reason be his guide. Maybe he intended all along to participate, and just took brinkmanship a bit far. For within hours of the decision to participate, Buthelezi launched a fully fledged election campaign, with a vigor his exhausted competitors could not rival. Thousands of election posters went up overnight, and Inkatha advertisements flooded the media. Members of Inkatha's election committee claim they ran an "underground" campaign, making these crucial preparations without Buthelezi's knowledge. But given his dominance of the party, that seems unlikely.

No one, even in Buthelezi's inner circle, claims to understand the workings of his mind well enough to know what really happened. It seems likely that, like F. W. de Klerk and Constand Viljoen before him, Buthelezi simply calculated his options and chose the least costly one. The attack of rational behavior had become an epidemic. Not everyone was delighted by Buthelezi's arrival on the ballot: Joe Slovo told me candidly he would have preferred to see the Inkatha leader crushed. And Roelf Meyer clearly felt the same. Both the ANC and the National Party were enraged that Buthelezi had blackmailed them into concessions on provincial powers—less than he had hoped for, but more than they felt he deserved—by threatening the legitimacy of the first election. Now he seemed to have been rewarded for his behavior.

Their bitterness could not obscure the central fact. Buthelezi's decision to participate was impossibly, almost miraculously good news, for the fate of the first election. Three days before the poll, the Volkstaat Accord was finally signed, sealing the participation of Constand Viljoen. Every significant political group in South Africa had now agreed to contest the poll: the ANC and the National Party; the radical right Freedom Front and the radical left Pan Africanist Congress; and now Inkatha. Only the rump of the ultra-radical right—the Conservative Party and the AWB—were left out.

United by a common danger—the risk of a descent into barbarism—the soldier and the statesman, the politician and the chief had finally chosen a future based on broadly common values. Each had demonstrated that essential attribute of the reasonable man: that if the price was right, he would compromise. They had compromised on a new South Africa which none of them really liked—and then decided they were stuck with it. Three hundred and fifty years of South African history had taught them that they could not live without each other. Now they would no longer try.

"I WANT A BIG CAR. I want a posh house. I want to be rich." Ntsiki Mbundu is a member of the ANC. When he spoke those words, the ANC was an avowedly socialist organization. But he is not interested in dogma. Like most black South Africans, Ntsiki is a born capitalist—he is interested in making money.

With his sculptured haircut, stylish dark glasses, and expensive clothes, Ntsiki is clearly a big-man-around-Soweto. He is a successful black entrepreneur—an endangered species under apartheid. Ntsiki meant to be a doctor. But the Boers put him in jail, and when he came out, he decided to get rich instead of getting educated. As a child he had worked for $2 a day, blacking out the windows of Soweto churches to turn them into movie houses (Soweto has only one cinema). He reckoned he had a knack for business.

We are touring Ntsiki's empire: a network of tiny Soweto grocery stores known as "spaza shops." Spaza means "hidden"—from the days when it was illegal for blacks to run such shops. Soweto was supposed to function as a labor camp, not a permanent suburb. So this city of 2 or 3 million people has no major shopping center and only a few, recently built retail outlets. Residents buy basic necessities in the spaza shops, and they are very basic—a candle, two or three cigarettes, a packet of sugar.

When he left jail, Ntsiki wanted to get into the spaza trade. But there are virtually no business premises in Soweto. He heard that the township council planned to demolish disused electricity substations—small brick structures a few yards square. He went along, with a bottle of whiskey, to the electricity department, where he befriended an Afrikaner engineer. Soon, Ntsiki had converted eighteen of the stations to miniature shops, and was making $1,000 profit a month, a fortune by Soweto standards.

Has he got any message for the ANC? "I want a big car. I want a posh house. I want to be rich." The mantra of the new South Africa.

14

Bake Bread Not Slogans

POLITICAL POWER—South Africans had spent decades fighting over it and years talking about it. But it was not an end in itself. The subtext of the negotiated revolution was always economic.

De Klerk was struggling to find a way to end white rule without surrendering white prosperity, while Mandela was determined to redistribute wealth along with power. That battle could not be settled just by a new constitution. Business and labor and government and institutions of civil society would be fighting over how to distribute economic power for years to come. But by the end of the negotiated revolution, consensus had at least begun to emerge on the ground rules for that battle. That involved another, quieter revolution—in the economic thinking of the ANC.

The African National Congress of 1985—the year when Mandela and Coetsee started their tentative dialogue—planned a simple handover of economic power to match the political one. ANC economic thinking was dominated by the South African Communist Party; the party believed it had to control economic production, in order to redistribute wealth. The ANC's policy in 1955—when it published its economic blueprint, the Freedom Charter—had been the nationalization of mines, banks, and "monopoly industries." It had changed little since. That, as much as anything, was what terrified South African whites. Surrounded by failed socialist experiments in the rest of Africa, they feared that if the ANC came to power, it would destroy Africa's only functioning economy. ANC economic policy might have been designed to ensure that whites would never hand over power.

Then the world changed, Slovo changed, and so did the white view of an economic future under ANC government. Within months of the fall of the Berlin Wall, in January 1990, Slovo published his *Has Socialism Failed?*, asking the question Afrikaners most wanted to hear. He concluded that, though socialism was the ideal solution for the problems of human society, it was an ideal which had not been made to work. He still believed it could succeed, if it were run under democracy and not bureaucratic oligarchy. But the East European model was dead, and he acknowledged that. It was good news for the Boers.

Old commandist habits die hard, however, and the ANC changed its rhetoric more quickly than its true beliefs. So banks, mines, and monopoly industries might not be nationalized, Slovo told me, but they must be "taken into public control." "The real question will be whether a particular sector is run in the interests purely of profit, or whether it is run in the interests of people," he said. "If control remains in private hands, it will be run predominantly in the interests of profit."

Slovo, as a committed Marxist, did not speak for the whole of the ANC, which included many leaders who were not Communists, Mandela among them. Still, a deep suspicion of capitalism and "big business"—which were viewed as the handmaidens to apartheid—pervaded all ranks of the ANC. This was ironic, given that the National Party was itself a late convert to capitalism: it ran a heavily interventionist economic policy, including nationalization, until the end of the 1980s. Still, capitalism and apartheid were equated in the popular mind. Capitalism was blamed for the gross racial disparities of wealth which made South Africa one of the most starkly divided societies on earth.

The ANC in exile never articulated a clear program for economic change. Slovo had always stressed that change would not come overnight. "The economy of South Africa, the day after the ANC flag flies over the Union Buildings, will be exactly the same as the day before," he told me just before returning from exile. "You can't transform it by edict unless you are prepared to risk a complete economic collapse. We can't just bake slogans— we've got to bake bread."

The intention at the time of Nelson Mandela's release, however, was that an ANC state would control, if not own, much of the economy after liberation. Yet four years later, Mandela took office armed with an economic policy indistinguishable from that of any other liberal democratic leader on earth: nationalization was out, privatization was on the horizon, capitalism was to be encouraged and nurtured to provide growth, fiscal and financial discipline were dogma.

What had wrought that revolution?

Primarily, it was the collapse of the socialist ideal in Eastern Europe: "We all grew up on Marx and Lenin, we believed in socialism," says Jay Naidoo, who as general secretary of the Cosatu union federation was the top trade unionist in the old South Africa. He went on to hold one of the most important economic portfolios in Mandela's government—minister for the Reconstruction and Development Programme, the ANC's anti-poverty plan (described in chapter 15).

When the Wall fell—revealing not the just and democratic society of South African Marxists' dreams but authoritarian regimes in an advanced state of industrial decay—Naidoo and his fellow leftists were shocked. They were jolted out of the intellectual time warp in which apartheid had trapped them, and forced to elaborate a new economic vision. That took shape in a world where there was suddenly overwhelming consensus on what constituted sensible economic policies. For four years, ANC economic policy makers—chief among them Nelson Mandela himself—were bombarded by the new conservative orthodoxy.

The ANC underwent a crash course in reality. There had been little enough of that in exile. Guerrillas had lived in a kind of mini-socialist state known as the ANC; it provided for their needs, in exchange for total commitment to the cause. Many were educated in Eastern Europe or Cuba, and had deep emotional ties to the countries that had succored them in their distress. The rest had spent their exile in underdeveloped African countries like Zambia, Tanzania, and Angola. They had no experience of a sophisticated modern economy like South Africa's.

For some, the new realities were clearly a shock. Tito Mboweni, head of the ANC's economics department before the election, and labor minister afterward, returned to South Africa from exile in July 1990. He told me of his grand plans to dismantle the six giant conglomerates which dominate the South African market. He showed me a diagram of the structure of the local market, with its tight pattern of cross-shareholdings between the large companies, and said all of this would be unwound. I asked who would buy the assets that conglomerates were forced to sell, and he suggested the state might have to do so. I asked where the ANC state would get the funds for such a massive nationalization program, and he said it would find them. I asked what effect this would have on business confidence and growth; he implied that sacrifices would have to be made. Mboweni's approach seemed more emotional than rational. He despised and resented the white businessmen who invested money on the Johannesburg Stock Exchange rather than in building houses for the poor. He would find a way to make them do less of the former and more of the latter.

In less than a year, reality had begun to tame Mboweni's fury. He remained convinced of the need for an active anti-trust policy to promote competition—a policy that the ANC would promote vigorously once in government—but it was no longer a matter simply of the forced breakup of conglomerates. Nine months after our first meeting, he gestured at the same chart of tangled cross-shareholdings and said: "The process of democratizing the economy will be complex. It's clear you need large companies to compete internationally. We're concerned that whatever policy we adopt should not destroy the productive capacity of the private sector." The process of consensus building was under way.

Consensus was pursued through many different channels, formal and informal. Within the ANC alliance, union leaders had a more sophisticated understanding of the South African and world economies than exiled politicians. They had spent the past decade getting to grips with South African capitalism around the negotiating table, and had even agreed to a new, more liberal Labour Relations Act, in tripartite negotiations with government and employers. They had also spent years visiting trade unions around the world, and studying the impact of modern capitalism on production. Unionists were a major force in providing a more nuanced economic vision for the ANC.

ANC economic policy makers were in constant contact with businessmen, both local and foreign. After the Anglo American Corporation's high-profile visit to Zambia in 1985, low-level contacts were maintained. In the late 1980s, Anglo director Clem Sunter was summoned to Nelson Mandela's prison cell to give him a briefing on the politico-economic scenario for South Africa which Sunter had recently published. And in 1990, Thabo Mbeki celebrated the news of Mandela's imminent release from prison by drinking champagne with top Afrikaner businessmen whom he was then meeting in exile—including Marinus Daling, who would go on to become the head of Sanlam, the Afrikaans insurance giant, one of the conglomerates targeted for dismemberment by Mboweni.

Mboweni himself was bombarded with invitations to conferences, cocktail parties, and dinner engagements with local and visiting businessmen, all of whom delivered impromptu lectures on market economics. ANC officials were sent to Washington, D.C., for a familiarization course at the World Bank, and returned without some of the baggage of suspicion and hatred which cripples African relations with that institution (though Mboweni himself remained suspicious of both the World Bank and the International Monetary Fund, and often sent a junior official to meet their representatives, refusing to attend himself). Everywhere, they heard the same message: Generating economic growth is the biggest priority. Nothing must be done to jeopardize that.

Mandela was getting the same treatment. He listened attentively as British Prime Minister Margaret Thatcher told him a few economic home truths, soon after his release from prison. He constantly sought the views of international businessmen and bankers on South Africa's future. And he cultivated close relationships with top local businessmen—he spent holidays with the head of one of the country's leading mining families, the late Clive Menell; he entertained at the home of one of Johannesburg's most ostentatious businessmen, insurance magnate Douw Steyn, where guests were met in the driveway with champagne on silver salvers; and he dined regularly with Anglo partriarch Harry Oppenheimer and participated in his "Brenthurst Group" (named after Oppenheimer's Johannesburg estate) of leading businessmen and opinion formers.

Oppenheimer recalls the first time Mandela came to dinner. "When you talked about the future of the country, particularly on the economic side, he said a great many things that seemed to me very silly, but he says many less of them now, and even when he said [them] . . . you never got a feeling of ill-will from the man. Even if he felt that capitalism should be destroyed, it wasn't out of hatred for capitalists. He was just doing his best as he saw it for the country."

For the first two years of his freedom, Mandela carried on saying things which not only Harry Oppenheimer thought were silly. Chief among them was his continued defense of nationalization. Though ANC policy on the subject was fluid—Mandela often even contradicted himself on the subject—he maintained, until well after he became president, that he still believed in nationalization.

He believed in it, as he told an investment conference in 1994, but business had persuaded him to forget about it. The turning point, Mandela said, was the 1992 World Economic Forum Conference at Davos in Switzerland. "Nationalization is our policy, but there is a shift in our thinking," he commented after the conference. "We have observed the hostility and concern of businessmen toward nationalization, and we can't ignore their perceptions . . . we are well aware that if you cannot cooperate with business, you cannot succeed in generating growth."

It soon became clear that Mandela was using the royal "we" in his comments; the ANC was far from unanimous on the question. Alec Erwin, a leading trade unionist who became Mandela's deputy finance minister, recalls a critical debate on the issue, at the ANC's economic policy conference in May 1992, just after Davos. Mandela, the supreme pragmatist, argued: "Even if we leave aside the merits of the economic debate, there is a political reality facing us. The business community worldwide is not going to have any truck with a government that wants to nationalize; it's a reality. Do you want to fly in the face of this reality? You can't do it," he told the conference. The argument continued. Mandela urged his colleagues to remove the word "nationalization" from their policy; they refused. In the end, he suggested a compromise. Everyone agreed that not only nationalization but privatization were possible policy options. So the document would refer to both of them. Mandela had lost his battle to get the "n" word removed; but at least investors could see that the ANC was not dogmatic about it.

Soon, Mandela would get some help in the struggle to bring his colleagues round to reality—from de Klerk's new finance minister, Derek Keys, a former businessman who became a great favorite with some top economic thinkers in the ANC. He had the clarity of vision to see what needed to be done, and the political skill to persuade the ANC and the trade unions that they saw it first themselves. He spent endless hours listening to the ANC, and stroking its leaders. "Alec Erwin was sent by God; Jay Naidoo, I embrace him," Keys used to tell everyone who would listen. After the adversarial relations of the past, the ANC welcomed his positive approach.

Erwin pays the highest tribute to Keys, who stayed on as finance minister for a few months under Mandela. Keys formalized the process of economic consensus building when he agreed to the launch of the National Economic Forum—bringing together business, labor, government, and the ANC—in August 1992. It was a kind of "economic Codesa," and Keys took it very seriously.

It was at the National Economic Forum, says Erwin, that South Africans finally bridged the reality gap. "Rather than debating our paradigms, we learned to debate the realities facing us," he remembers. "We came from two different starting points. My argument was, I am a socialist, I still believe that a society where collective rights and individual rights are in harmony is a better society. A businessman would say, 'I still believe that if markets were allowed to operate with no interference by the state, we would have a perfect world.' We could both continue to hold those paradigms, while being ready to reach pragmatic solutions to current problems." South Africans were willing to adjust their ideology to reflect changing realities. This was just as true in the economic sphere as in the world of politics.

Keys ran a coalition economic policy well before the formal interim government, the TEC, had been formed. Erwin says this vastly reduced conflict around economic questions, but also gave the ANC a chance to face the grim realities of government before taking office. Keys brought home to the ANC the extent of the fiscal crisis they would inherit from the previous government: the high level of government debt and the bloated civil service. Servicing the one and paying the other would consume 91 percent of the government budget, leaving only 9 percent for development expenditure. Spending on social services like education and health was already high by international standards (though inefficiency, corruption, and overstaffing meant that service provision was poor). Keys confronted ANC policy makers with the unpleasant reality that they were not taking over a rich country with lots of surplus cash to spend on black economic upliftment. They would have tragically limited room for economic maneuver.

From that crash course in fiscal reality, the ANC emerged with as powerful a commitment to budgetary discipline and fiscal conservatism as white South Africa could have wished. Fiscal discipline was no longer an ideological weapon used to cheat the poor; it was an economic instrument needed to ensure that government could deliver development without stifling economic growth. Keys's all-party economic team, the Economic Technical Committee, even agreed to commit the new orthodoxy to paper. As a condition for a loan from the International Monetary Fund (IMF) in 1993, the committee sent a so-called letter of intent on economic policy to the IMF. It committed South Africa to hold its budget deficit to 6 percent of gross domestic product—a figure that would force a real reduction in spending. The ANC had finally bought into the world consensus on good economic government, and was applauded internationally for so doing.

Back in South Africa, De Klerk and the National Party could not believe their luck at the economic transformation of their adversaries (though Keys ensured that they judiciously avoided crowing about it, which might have jeopardized the conversion). For though he could claim little credit for it, de Klerk had secured his goal of preventing immediate economic trauma for whites. The bill of rights, agreed at the World Trade Centre with the help of powerful arguments from the Democratic Party, prevented summary expropriation of land or property. The ANC understood that there could be no quick economic revolution to match the transfer of political power. The battle had begun, but at least the ANC knew it could not afford a bloodbath.

Soon, big business was in Mandela's pocket. He told the *New York Times* in 1995 that he had approached twenty top businessmen for at least R1 million each to help him in the 1994 election, and all but one had complied. The last, improbable rapprochement of the old South Africa had finally taken place: the ANC had made its peace with Inkatha, the Freedom Front, the National Party, and now with business. In the world of economics as much as politics, the negotiated revolution had reached its conclusion. Nothing was left but the voting.

"A black person entered the voting booth one person, and emerged on the other side a different, a transformed person. He entered the booth weighed down by humiliation and he exited saying, 'Hey, I'm free, my dignity has been restored.'

"A white person entered the booth burdened by guilt and emerged on the other side a new, a transformed person, 'Hey, I'm free, the weight of guilt has been lifted off my shoulders.'

"It really was heady stuff."

Archbishop Desmond Tutu was reflecting on the day South Africa stepped through the looking glass. It was a magical moment for all concerned. South Africans did their civic duty that day with a reverent solemnity which citizens of older democracies could only envy. In their millions, they stood for hours in the dust and heat of township streets, and on city pavements multi-racial lines stretched for over a mile. The sense of interracial goodwill was spontaneous and overwhelming.

Everyone had expected the worst. The days before the poll were filled with carnage, as right-wing car bombs left dismembered bodies strewn across the streets of Johannesburg and the television screens of the nation. But April 26, 1994,* dawned clear and cold, and blacks and whites waited calmly at the polling stations, hardly bothering to worry that they were easy prey to drive-by snipers. In almost every line, voters drew on the vocabulary of faith to explain what had happened; many said it was simply a miracle.

Outside the Soweto Home for the Aged, where the elderly and infirm were allowed to cast their poll in a special, first day of voting reserved for them, Mrs. Lena Tshabalala was waiting to vote for the first time in the eighty-five years of her life. Asked whom she thanked for the privilege, she said, "First, Jesus. Second, Nelson Mandela." And F. W. de Klerk? "We shall pray for Mr. de Klerk," she said in a tone of steely Christian charity. Behind her, bent and hobbled by a lifetime of poverty and humiliation, Soweto's elderly knew dignity that day. Again and again, Sowetans and South Africans voiced the same wonder. "We never thought this day would come," said Mrs. Tshabalala. "It's a miracle."

Unfortunately, the miracle did not extend to election logistics and planning. From the first day of voting—which was eventually extended to four days in Natal, to compensate for the late arrival of ballots showing the tardy entrant, Inkatha—chaos reigned. After a last-minute flurry of extra printing, the Independent Electoral Commission did not even know how many ballots existed or where they were. It had no way of controlling fraud, especially in rural areas, where some essential ingredient always seemed to be missing. Either there were no ballot papers, or none of the special Inkatha stickers printed to append the party's name, or none of the invisible ink used to mark voters' hands, or no electricity to run the machine used to detect the ink and prevent multiple voting.

In the KwaZulu homeland, elections were held at schools, with electoral officials drawn from the teaching staff; as teachers at KwaZulu schools were forced to belong to Inkatha, they were hardly impartial. With no voter rolls to use to verify authenticity, there was nothing to stop Inkatha electoral officials—or ANC officials in the Transkei and other ANC strongholds—from stuffing ballot boxes. Some seventy thousand election monitors, includ-

---

* Election day was first fixed for April 27, 1994. Later, it was extended to three days, beginning April 26, with a special day of voting for the elderly and infirm. Eventually it was extended another day in Natal.

ing five thousand from overseas, were deployed at polling stations around the country. But in the deep rural areas which I visited, none were present. Hundreds of boxes duly arrived at counting stations with broken seals, or no seals at all, or filled with grass, or with ballots neatly stacked by illegal hands. The election process was a mess.

Counting the votes was even worse. Results were due out within less than twenty-four hours of the close of polling; in the event, the count was not completed for a week. There were scores of disputed returns, and all the major parties were threatening to challenge results in the courts. South Africa's transition was again under threat: If the election were declared invalid, it would be a disaster.

The politicians fell back on their trusted remedy, compromise. If they could not have a free and fair election, they would have a negotiated one instead. F. W. de Klerk, whose National Party claimed it lost something like 8 percentage points in the poll due to fraud, was under severe pressure from his party to declare the election invalid. De Klerk's press secretary, Richard Carter, recalls the president's reply. "He said, 'Gentlemen, there is one way out of this, I must concede. Once I concede, nothing else really matters . . . the result can take six months for all I care, but once I concede, this thing is over.'

"I didn't start this to stop it now," he told them. So at 6:00 P.M. on Monday, May 2, 1994—three days before the results were announced—F. W. de Klerk addressed the nation, with a catch in his voice and a tear in his eye.

> I shall lay down my responsibilities as State President, secure in the knowledge that we have achieved what we set out to achieve four years and three months ago. . . . I shall be surrendering power, not to the majority of the moment, but to the South African people. . . .
>
> A power greater than man has given South Africa the spirit, the chance to go forward in peace. God almighty has been kind to us. God bless South Africa. Nkosi sikeleli'Afrika.

And then, as he had done the day he became president nearly five years before, de Klerk shed a private tear for all he had lost, and for all his country had gained.

Later that night, Nelson Mandela celebrated victory. Echoing the words of Martin Luther King, Jr., whose widow was present at the ANC victory party, he said with joy and emotion, "Thank God almighty, we are free at last!" It was a "joyous night for the human spirit," he said, and none present could have disagreed.

Three days later, the Independent Electoral Commission was finally able to declare a result, after the parties agreed amongst themselves simply to ignore all the many disputed returns. It was a quintessentially South African compromise. Rather than insisting on the principle that voting must be free and fair, they chose to take what they could get: an election that was manifestly flawed, but better than no election at all.

Luckily, the result conformed broadly to both polls and expectations (except in Natal). The ANC got 62.7 percent of the vote, short of the two-thirds majority it would have needed to write a new constitution on its own. Mandela immediately declared his delight that the ANC had not passed the two-thirds threshold, risking his colleagues' ire, but sealing his reputation as a remarkable statesman. "Ironic as it is, I was very much relieved when we failed to get a two-thirds majority," he later told the Senate. Rival party leaders had warned him they would challenge the result in court if the ANC got more than two-thirds. Mandela realized that, "if we wanted stability, cooperation and the smooth functioning of the government of national unity, we should not get that two-thirds majority." Without it, minority parties would be confident "that they can prevent us from writing our own constitution." And the ANC would be satisfied, "because we do not rely on laws, we rely purely on persuasion."

If Mandela was satisfied, the result was a severe disappointment to de Klerk. The National Party got 20.4 percent of the vote, just above the important psychological barrier of 20 percent, but well below its hopes. De Klerk's gamble on democracy had backfired. He told his brother Wimpie, only three days before the poll, that he would not be surprised if the National Party won 35 percent of the vote. The actual result, a scant 20 percent, was not enough to make him indispensable to Mandela. De Klerk had done a deal based on a very different electoral outcome. That deal looked even worse after the election than before it.

But crucially for peace, Inkatha was satisfied. It won KwaZulu-Natal Province. Mandela publicly accepted that victory, infuriating the local ANC and Cyril Ramaphosa, who wanted the result challenged. Mandela said in his autobiography that the ANC had underestimated Inkatha's strength in the province. His colleagues simply believed Buthelezi had cheated.

It may not have been an accurate result, but it was a designer outcome. The African National Congress got just enough of the vote to exercise real power, without dominating. The National Party gained enough to avoid humiliation. The Inkatha Party got control of its home base, newly christened KwaZulu-Natal. The Freedom Front got 680,000 votes in the provincial ballots, out of a total Afrikaner electorate of 1.8 million—enough to be taken seriously in its demands for self-determination. The radical left, the

Pan Africanist Congress, got almost nothing (1.25 percent), proving once again that the vast majority of South Africans eschewed political extremes. It was the perfect end to the negotiated revolution—a negotiated election.

My vision blurs when I recall the days that followed: the image of Nelson Mandela, elected president by the first all-race Parliament, standing to attention, hand over heart, as the Afrikaner anthem *die Stem* was played by a police band. Another image, just as unlikely, of a security policeman proudly saluting the African anthem, *Nkosi sikelel'iAfrika*. And the vision of Archbishop Desmond Tutu, singing *die Stem* with gusto and exuberance, and declaring South Africans "the rainbow people of God."

But nothing could compare with that inaugural flypast, the moment when apartheid's bombers dipped their wings to the new commander, Nelson Mandela, as he declared, "What's past is past," appropriately, in Afrikaans. That snapshot will never fade—the moment that white power ended forever. The day the Boers gave it all away—and discovered they were glad to have done so. One of the great psychological transformations of the twentieth century was complete; a strange but wonderful tale of mutual liberation. As Nelson Mandela said: "free at last, free at last!" South Africa was indeed free at last.

PART THREE

LIFE AFTER APARTHEID

I have discovered the secret that after climbing a great hill, one only finds that there are many more hills to climb. I have taken a moment here to rest, to steal a view of the glorious vista that surrounds me, to look back on the distance I have come. But I can rest only for a moment, for with freedom come responsibilities, and I dare not linger, for my long walk is not yet ended.

Nelson Mandela, 1994

NOSIPHO MLANGENI *is a child of the new South Africa. She was born on the eve of Nelson Mandela's release from prison, at a time when her mother was living in the maid's quarters of my house. Her grandmother, Elsie, was my maid, and Elsie's daughter, son, and two other grandchildren were living with us when Nosipho was born.*

She very nearly entered the world in the back seat of my car. For at the time of her birth on December 28, 1989, South Africa's hospitals were still legally segregated. When Elsie came frantically to shake me awake in the middle of that night, I debated whether to try taking Nosipho's laboring mother, Maureen, to the white Johannesburg hospital for the delivery. The law still forbade the hospital to treat her, but in practice, black patients were usually admitted in emergencies. I thought the hospital would treat Maureen, but she did not want to risk it.

We could not call a blacks-only ambulance; they were criminally slow. I considered calling a white ambulance and making a scene if they would not take her. But this was hardly the time to make gestures of anti-apartheid defiance. So Maureen, Elsie, and I climbed into my Volkswagen and headed for Baragwanath, the black hospital in Soweto, more than twenty-five miles away. We sped through the midnight streets of Johannesburg's white suburbs, running every red light and breaking every speed limit as Maureen moaned in the back. But Nosipho, whose name means "Gift," had the good sense to wait until we reached Baragwanath, where she was born soon afterward.

Today, Nosipho is a second-grade student in what used to be an all-white school, in the all-white suburb where we went to live when she was two. Unlike her siblings and cousins, she speaks perfect English, because she went to nursery school with white children. Her best friend was the little white boy across the street. Nosipho's class at Melpark Primary School is a rainbow mixture of the races.

But this is not a new South African fairy story. When I left South Africa, Nosipho lost her automatic right to attend Melpark Primary because without me, her mother, who is a nurse's aide, cannot afford to live anywhere near the school, in any of the posh white suburbs that feed it. If she did not have help with rent and accommodation, Nosipho would be back in a black township school with fifty other children in the class.

Apartheid has never held Nosipho back, at least not since the day of her birth. But the legacy of apartheid—the appallingly low educational qualifications that prevent her mother from getting a well-paid job, the grinding poverty that afflicts her family, and the threat of unemployment that always beckons—could prevent her from becoming whatever she wants to be. It will be a hard life for Nosipho, even after apartheid.

15

Now for the Hard Part

THE HUGE BLACK MAN in the brightly colored shirt beamed down at the tiny, white-haired lady dressed in pink. The frail ninety-four-year-old had just handed the elderly man a cup of tea and *koeksisters*. Now she was preparing to read out a letter, written in her uncertain childlike hand, to thank him for coming.

Anxiously clutching the two-page missive, she became more and more upset as she found she could not read it without her glasses. The gentle black man peered over her shoulder and began softly prompting her in Afrikaans. The letter was addressed to State President Nelson Mandela. The signature at the bottom was that of Mrs. Betsie Verwoerd, widow of the architect of apartheid, Hendrik Verwoerd.

Mandela had gone to visit the widow Verwoerd at her retirement home in the empty vastness of the Northern Cape province, at the town of Orania. There, she lives with 460 other Afrikaners in a private colony where blacks are not allowed, her own personal *volkstaat*. President Mandela visited her for the excellent reason that he was invited. He had asked Mrs. Verwoerd to take tea with him in Pretoria, but she declined on grounds of infirmity. So she wrote to thank him, and threw in a pro forma Afrikaans phrase of the "do drop in if you're ever in the neighborhood" variety. He took her up on it.

Soon, he was helping her read out a letter calling on him to "dispose of the fate of the Afrikaners with wisdom." When she had finished, she looked up to where he towered above her, with a radiant smile of thanks. She packed Mandela off to visit the statue of her husband that stands on a hill above the town. The new president commented that the statue looked very small. Verwoerd would cast no shadow in the land of Mandela.

Hendrik Verwoerd decreed certain truths to be self-evident: that race was bondage; that ethnicity was fate. Nelson Mandela's mission was to set South Africa free from that color-coded prison.

That mission did not end on the day apartheid ceased to exist. Mandela vowed to dedicate the rest of his life to completing the unfinished business of liberation—the psychological, economic, and social emancipation of South Africa. He would preach his religion of non-racialism to all his countrymen. He would create powerful symbols of a single nationhood, to unite the many peoples of South Africa in one rainbow. And he would tackle the toughest challenge of all: the battle for economic equality and prosperity, which would determine the fate of democracy itself.

By the end of the negotiated revolution, this divided nation—a land fractured not only by race, ethnicity, and culture, but by a yawning gulf of wealth—had chosen a common destiny. But there was no iron law of nature to decree that South Africans would continue to choose unity. Mandela set out to do what he could to prevent his nation from choosing to self-destruct rather than co-exist. He launched a drive for racial reconciliation that would set the tone of his presidency, and create race relations precedents that his successors would violate at their peril.

His campaign fell on inherently fertile ground. Despite apartheid's best efforts, South Africans were not terminally polarized by race. The color-blind camaraderie of the workplace had long begun to undermine racial stereotypes, at least in urban areas. In rural areas, a kind of feudal paternalism survived, based on a peculiar intimacy and interdependence, not on fanatical aversion. Throughout the country, the pathological hatred so common in other divided societies was a rarity. Racism was certainly a problem; but in the afterglow of the miracle election, it seemed far from intractable.

The will to reconcile had to come from the victors, and black South Africa readily supported Mandela's project. Africans are not a vengeful people; the guiding principle of their traditional culture is *ubuntu,* a concept only roughly translatable into English, but one that embodies charity, forgiveness, generosity, and an essential humanity. Archbishop Desmond Tutu, a great proponent of *ubuntu,* once explained it to me like this: "We say that a human being is a human being because he belongs to a community, and harmony is the essence of that community. So *ubuntu* actually demands that you forgive, because resentment and anger and desire for revenge undermine harmony. In our understanding, when someone doesn't forgive, we say that person does not have *ubuntu.* That is to say, he is not really human."

Mandela made non-racialism the new civil religion of South Africa. He spoke of giving nervous minorities a "silver bridge to cross" to the new South Africa, and he began to trace its path from the moment he was elected.

The politics of reconciliation reigned supreme in those early days, and every ANC politician did his bit to contribute. ANC provincial premiers went out of their way to speak Afrikaans, the hated "language of the oppressor," one of eleven new official languages. Ordinary people showed no desire to rock the boat: they left statues of Verwoerd and Vorster carefully on their pedestals, and street signs in place. The vast majority of politically inspired place names remained unchanged; when they were altered, neutral replacements were chosen. Reconciliation began to seem almost a cliché of the new South Africa.

Until Nelson Mandela discovered rugby.

With his deft feel for the politics of symbolism—and his total disdain for political correctness—Mandela chose rugby, high totem of Boer nationalism, to buttress his silver bridge. Rugby was a sport which apartheid's architects had embraced with a passion they reserved for nothing else but religion and politics. If the Dutch Reformed Church was the National Party at prayer, rugby was the National Party at play. For blacks, the sport came to symbolize the arrogance of Afrikaner power, and the brutality and aggression that went with it.

The Afrikaner government took the sport deadly seriously. In 1961, Verwoerd banned dark-skinned Maoris from the visiting New Zealand rugby team, sparking a process that led, more than twenty years later, to South Africa's expulsion from world rugby. For many Afrikaners, rugby isolation was the harshest cut of all: they could survive economic sanctions, the cultural boycott, the arms and oil embargoes, but they could not live without rugby. So the arrival of the world's top teams to contest the World Rugby Cup in South Africa in May 1995 was an occasion for white jubilation. Afrikaners had swopped apartheid for rugby, and there was every sign they thought it a fair deal.

Blacks ignored the event; they played soccer, not rugby. Apartheid had kept them separate, even in sport. Mandela could not accept that. He was the president of all South Africans, and he could not discriminate, in sport or in politics. Support for the national rugby team, the Springboks (the squad was all-white, after its lone coloured player was sidelined due to injury), was one of the patriotic requirements of citizenship in the new South Africa. Mandela, the first citizen, was going to make that point.

He did so in spectacular fashion, turning up to celebrate the quintessential black public holiday, Sowetoday (which marks the 1976 massacre of schoolchildren in Soweto), wearing a green rugby supporter's cap, complete with the hated Springbok emblem, symbol of apartheid sport. "You see this cap I am wearing?" he asked his bemused supporters. "This cap does honor to our boys who are playing France" (in the World Cup semi-final). "I ask you to stand by them, because they are our kind," he said. Fifteen Afrikaner boys, raised on apartheid and drawn from the most conservative circles of Afrikanerdom. Finally, they were Africa's kin.

Over the week leading up to the June 24 final, Mandela fueled a national hysteria which transcended race. His boyish enthusiasm was infectious as he visited the team on their practice fields and in their dressing rooms. He won the devotion of Springbok Captain François Pienaar, who said he would "play his heart out" for the president.

Then, as the team took the field for the final, Mandela emerged on the pitch wearing the green and gold, number 6 jersey of Captain Pienaar, and the overwhelmingly white crowd went wild. Afrikaans accents chanted, "Nel-son, Nel-son," a sign of intimacy and approval that would have been unthinkable only days before. In the stands, thousands of white faces were painted with the garish colors of the new South African flag, and thousands of white hands waved it, acknowledging, for the first time, their loyalty to this most central symbol of the new nation. White Springbok lips stumbled through a rendition of the national anthem, *Nkosi sikeleli'Afrika.* White spectators bellowed out the new Springbok theme song, "Shosholoza," a traditional African work song that had become a favorite of the banned ANC in the 1980s. The cultural crossover was dizzying.

The "Bokke," as they were affectionately known, desperately wanted to win, and they did, after the almost intolerable excitement of extra time. Their victory proved to be the most potent political event since the release of Mandela. Nothing could compare with it—not the muted festivities of an exhausted electorate after the April 1994 elections; not the solemn emotionalism of the inauguration. This was pure, non-racial joy of a kind South Africa had never seen in 350 years of shared history. Crowds danced in the streets of Soweto, chanting, "*Viva, Amabokoboko!*" (the African version of the team name), while black youths waltzed with life-sized replicas of a blond François Pienaar in central Johannesburg. Police armored cars, symbol of apartheid brutality, used their loudspeakers to broadcast renditions of "Shosholoza." And seeing my white face in the street, black, brown, and Indian South Africans congratulated me on the victory of the Bokke as though I had personally won the trophy myself.

With two small gestures, and a huge dose of enthusiasm and patriotism, Nelson Mandela had provoked an orgy of national reconciliation. For the first time in history, blacks had a chance to be proud of their white countrymen, to share their feelings in a way never possible before. Whites were hugely grateful to Mandela for that—and for restoring their national pride. But he could not have succeeded unless millions of other black South Africans willed it so.

And in the street, a small black boy imitated a springbok, the antelope with the vertical springing gait after which the team was named. So far, the future was doing a valiant job of defeating the past.

Mandela had not yet finished with his campaign to prove that, as he said in Afrikaans at his inauguration, *"Wat verby is verby"* ("What's done is done"). Again and again, his actions spoke of a triumph over bitterness. He built a retirement home identical to his prison bungalow. He was shown on South African television signing letters of congratulation to retiring members of the security forces, thanking them for their dedicated service—to the cause of suppressing the ANC.

He invited the wives of all South Africa's past political leaders, white and black, to lunch (this was the invitation Betsie Verwoerd had to decline). The widow of Steve Biko, the black-consciousness leader murdered by police in 1977, lunched with the widow of the prime minister in whose jail he died, John Vorster. Elize Botha, wife of P.W., was seen helping Mrs. Urbania Mothopeng, widow of the former leader of the ultra-radical Pan Africanist Congress, to her feet in the presidential garden. Mandela complimented Mrs. Botha on her attire: she wore a black jacket bordered with the intricate beadwork of the Ndebele tribe, her own tribute to Africa. The widow of ANC leader Oliver Tambo exclaimed with delight on meeting Mrs. Botha, "I've seen you on TV!" Mandela said the gathering was "a practical way of forgetting the past."

Through all that, his housekeeper made it known that he still made his own bed. It was hard to imagine a politician, anywhere in the world, with a more positive public image.

Such gestures gave Mandela a direct line to the heart of the Afrikaner nation. Ordinary Afrikaners, even conservative ones, prayed nightly for his safety. Many said simply that he was a "gift from God" (including one who told me Mandela was like the crooked stick in the Bible—God could do much good with it, though it be flawed).

Afrikaners, pragmatists as they are, made their peace with the new South Africa with extraordinary rapidity. Theirs is a political culture based on an obedience that borders on obsequiousness, so they easily made the transition from obeying the National Party to obeying the ANC. Even the Afrikaner-dominated civil service and security forces—groups that the ANC had feared would undermine black rule—swiftly fell into line. They knew that the ANC had assumed the power of patronage, along with political office; there was nothing to be gained by fighting it.

All of this surprised the African National Congress, which had expected far greater resistance. Indeed, the "sunset clauses" were offered precisely because the ANC feared it could not rule without the National Party to guarantee civil service and security force cooperation. So the ANC had agreed to protect the jobs and pensions of white civil servants, and had included F. W. de Klerk in government as a deputy president.[*] But within months of the election, senior ANC figures were asking whether these gestures had been necessary.

"The ANC discovered quite late that we had made a mistake. None of us really factored in the dynamism of what was going to happen. We didn't factor in the speed with which they [Afrikaners] would shift, recognize the fact that here is a majority party, here is a new government and we have got to define a relationship with that majority." That was Deputy President Thabo Mbeki's view, within months of taking power.

"The notion of a government of national unity," he went on, "derived precisely from the understanding that the National Party would be the political representative of the army, the white police, white business, the white civil service, that it would have a hold on very important levers of power. When we came into government, we would come in with the numbers, they would come in with the power, and we would need to work together for a certain period instead of saying to those power centers, you are the opposition."

But almost overnight, in the time-honored tradition of political transition in Africa, the National Party lost its hold on those levers of power. Political power, and patronage, had made them gatekeepers to the civil service, to the army, to the police, to business, for nearly fifty years. With sickening speed, the party sank to a position of weakness unthinkable only weeks before. The monolith seemed to crumble in an instant. What was left was a party which continued to command something like 20 percent popular support, and which controlled one provincial government, in the Western Cape. But it lacked the electoral or institutional power to form any serious opposition to the ANC.

Mandela paid lip service to the government of national unity. Most of the time, he genuinely tried to take decisions (as the interim constitution bade him do) in a "consensus-seeking spirit." But if de Klerk had influence in the new cabinet, he had almost no power. His preelection dreams of power sharing—of making all the important decisions in concert with President Mandela—were dashed within weeks. The last-minute compromises he made at the World Trade Centre had left him with nothing more than a presence in cabinet.

Tensions quickly emerged within the new thirty-member coalition cabinet, which included de Klerk as second deputy president, six other National

---

[*] A position from which he has since resigned.

Party ministers (including Roelf Meyer), Inkatha leader Chief Buthelezi as minister of home affairs, and two other Inkatha ministers. Relations between de Klerk and Mandela reached a new low.

Mandela's animosity toward the former president erupted in cabinet, and once even on the streets of Johannesburg, when the two men were caught by cameramen publicly arguing after a formal dinner. Part of the problem was Mandela's continuing suspicion that de Klerk had been involved with the third force. They argued bitterly in cabinet over the issue of whether former security force personnel should be given amnesty for apartheid crimes.

The clash was also personal. De Klerk remained aloof from his new black colleagues, and they complained of his arrogance; some accused him of racism. Mandela complained, in one particularly acrimonious cabinet meeting (described in chapter 9), that de Klerk was still acting "like a white man talking to a black man." And de Klerk often proved blind to ANC sensitivities, looking at his watch, or speaking to his wife, during the singing of *Nkosi sikeleli'Afrika*. But anger mostly focused on Mrs. de Klerk, who provoked a major diplomatic incident when she fought with the new president over his request that the de Klerks move out of Libertas, their presidential home, in favor of Deputy President Thabo Mbeki. Mrs. de Klerk's tone in describing the incident reflects the attitude of mind which the ANC found so offensive. When President Mandela came to inspect Libertas, she said, "he looked into everything, he even looked into our bathrooms and our dressing rooms." The ANC was quick to pick up such subtle hints of racism. Several friends of de Klerk were asked by ANC envoys to intervene with the former president, and tell him to reprimand his wife, who regularly snubbed Mandela in public and criticized him in private.

Despite all this—despite the animosity of his cabinet colleagues, and the painful fact of his diminished status—de Klerk seemed unaccountably pleased with the revolution he had wrought. He spent large amounts of time traveling the world's capitals as an economic ambassador for the new government, and obviously enjoyed the international accolades he received. Whenever asked, he passionately and convincingly defended his new role.

"We could have clung to power for another five to ten years, I could have remained president of South Africa until the end of my political career. But it was a way towards destruction," he said a year after the election. He admitted that the psychological adjustment had been painful. "But what I am doing now is *as important* as what I did when I was president, and I find it fulfilling." It was clear from his tone of voice, and the gleam in his eye, that he meant it. As de Klerk's brother, Wimpie, put it in late 1994, "F.W. is heart and soul committed to the new dispensation. He is a full hundred percent converted, now, that everything that happened was good, that we must continue with it, there's no turning back, there's no regret."

De Klerk, like the nation itself, had undergone a remarkable psychological transformation. He wept when he was inaugurated in 1989, and he wept again when he conceded defeat to Mandela in 1994. But in between, he never let emotion get the better of him. And in the end, he had reason to feel satisfied with the result. For in the broadest terms, the new South Africa was a place where F. W. de Klerk and his nation could feel comfortable: religion, language, and prosperity were protected; the values of the new nation were liberal democratic; life went on, much as before.

The main difference, for whites, was the surge in violent crime, which took the murder rate to ten times the U.S. level. Whites felt politically secure, but physically threatened. The violence was not racist—black township dwellers were victims just as often as white suburbanites—and it was less a product of black rule than a legacy of poor policing bequeathed by the old government. Poverty drove the criminals, who found automatic weapons easy to come by once township political battles had largely ceased. The new government found it difficult to reestablish respect for the law, undermined both by apartheid and by the ANC's own ungovernability campaign of the 1980s.

Still, the big picture was that South Africa's had been, largely, a revolution without change. De Klerk was glad of that, and so were most of his white countrymen. Overwhelmingly, throughout the country, Afrikaners made the shrewd calculation that they had gained more than they had lost in giving up power. This was what the ANC had always assured them would happen. Thabo Mbeki had been peddling that message since he first met Broederbond chairman Pieter de Lange in 1986. Early in 1995, he outlined for me the fruits of his long struggle to convert the Afrikaner to South African nationhood:

"There are certain things that they have not lost, and some things they have gained. They have not lost whatever prosperity they had, they haven't lost their language, so change has not been threatening in that sense. And they have gained a lot, they have rediscovered their South Africanness, and that is a very powerful thing among whites in general. They are very proud to be South African. It has to do in great measure with acceptance by the rest of the world. They are human beings again."

Even the right wing was pacified. Mandela had made his own separate peace with the right, both by carefully nurturing the symbols of reconciliation, and by cultivating a close personal relationship with General Constand Viljoen, gatekeeper to the white right. Viljoen's demand for a *volkstaat* was debated within the so-called Volkstaat Council, a statutory body set up to deal with Afrikaner fears of domination. This—and the fact that power had changed hands without the slightest sign of victimization of the Afrikaner— kept the white right silent. Their bloody preelection bombing campaign ceased on the day of the poll.

No one could tell whether the pacification of the white right was permanent, for in the years to come, they would be at the front line of change. Their members, drawn mostly from the white working class, would be hit hardest by the ANC's policy of affirmative action, especially in the old Afrikaner preserve of the civil service. Their economic prosperity was most directly threatened. But the majority of Afrikaners appeared to have made a permanent peace with black rule. For them, apartheid had served its purpose, and they were ready to discard it: white rule had raised the Afrikaner people from a poor and ill-educated mass in the 1930s to create a nation of architects and lawyers, academics and administrators, businessmen and bankers.

Marinus Daling, chairman of one of South Africa's largest companies, the Afrikaans insurance giant Sanlam, commented that "loss of political power has freed us. . . . Politics can never be the real and lasting source of our Afrikanerdom." Afrikaners were already economically strong, and faith, hard work, and courage would make them stronger in future.

It was time for the Afrikaner to think beyond politics, to other forms of power, Pieter de Lange told me in 1995. "Afrikaners are convinced they have a role to play, they have a stake in this country, they are people of Africa, and they want to provide service to their society. There are so many examples in history, especially Jewish history, of minorities developing alternative power bases, in the media, in the world of learning, in the arts, in the economic life of a country. Those are all areas of vital activity and essential power."

De Klerk, too, began to think long term. The Afrikaner was stuck with democracy, a system that would doom him to permanent political opposition unless his countrymen could rise above the politics of blood and race to the politics of values. So de Klerk announced he would try to build a multi-racial alliance around "core values" such as belief in God, traditional morals, and free enterprise economics.

Toward that end, de Klerk pulled the National Party out of the government of national unity altogether in June 1996. The announcement of his intention to withdraw provoked a severe drop in the value of the Rand, but it need not have done. De Klerk had been virtually powerless within cabinet from the day Mandela was inaugurated; the fact that he would no longer sit at the cabinet table could make little practical difference in the way South Africa was run.

Before pulling out, de Klerk endorsed the new Constitution adopted in May 1996 by the constituent assembly—a majority rule constitution which abolishes all lingering vestiges of enforced power sharing, but is otherwise broadly liberal democratic like its predecessor, the interim constitution. He cast his departure as a sign that the new political system was coming of age. "First we brought you democracy—Now we bring you multiparty democracy," the National Party proclaimed in a nationwide advertising campaign. De Klerk's argument was that his party could exert more influence as a traditional opposition party within Parliament (where the party continued to be represented) than as a partner, silently fuming, in a cabinet of national unity.

Someday, that may prove to be true. But it may take a decade or two before de Klerk's dreams of a new Afrikaner powerbase—as part of a multiracial, centrist coalition—will come to pass. For though South Africans do not, in general, hate each other by race, they do not take tolerance as far as voting non-racially. South Africa's first elections in 1994 were the equivalent of a racial census—South Africans voted by race, almost to a man. In the local government elections of November 1995, voters again made their choices on strictly ethnic lines. To change that would require the ANC itself to split into different value-based parties—say, a Social Democratic one, and a Christian Democratic one—which seems unlikely to happen as long as the ANC can unite behind the fight for economic equality.

The ANC is likely to dominate South African politics for a long time to come. South Africa will be what political scientists call a "one-party-dominant state"—a state that is democratic, but where there is only a weak opposition. That is perhaps the most worrying fact about the new South Africa, that demographics will deny an effective opposition to the ANC. Parties that rule unchallenged are tempted to abuse their power. That is politics.

It is people like Sipho Maduna who made reconciliation real. Sipho was the leader of the ANC self-defense unit in the Radebe section of Katlehong township which had so chilled my soul with its acts of collective execution. About eighteen months after the election, I returned to Radebe to see how Sipho was coping with the future. I found him thinking about the past. He was thinking about the so-called Truth and Reconciliation Commission, then being set up by the Mandela government to try to heal the wounds of the apartheid past by exposing the crimes hidden by the white government. It was a quasi-religious idea: that members of the security forces (and others) must confess their crimes before the commission, which would have the power to grant them amnesty. Families of victims would then have the satisfaction of knowing what was done to their loved one, and by whom. But the perpretrators would not be prosecuted.

The ANC felt that the alternative to such a commission—Nuremberg-style war crimes trials—would tear South Africa apart. They counted on black South Africans to demand knowledge but not revenge. ANC leaders argued that South Africa could not heal itself until the criminals had admitted that, though they believed they were right at the time, they now knew they were wrong.

I asked Sipho about revenge. He was the young man who had been tied up in a canvas bag and dropped in the river; the one taken to the graveyard for a bit of target practice. I wanted to push him beyond the stock ANC line on revenge. He told me quietly that God had exacted revenge on his behalf. Why, I asked; were his tormentors dead already? He laughed. The "revenge" he spoke of was the ANC's victory in the elections. "We were fighting for Madiba, and today Madiba is free, we are all free." And that, for Sipho, was the sweetest revenge of all. It was a matter of *ubuntu*, he said; in giving up power the white government had implicitly admitted that it was wrong. Free and fair elections were their apology for apartheid. "And if people apologize, we Africans must accept their apology," he carefully explained, aware that this philosophy was alien to my culture. "That is *ubuntu*."

Sipho went on to say that, though he did not want his torturers to suffer as he had done, he would like to see their superiors—the head of the police, the head of the army, F. W. de Klerk himself—pay at least a symbolic price. Tentatively, he suggested that each of these men should go to jail for a year . . . or well, maybe six months. And after thinking about it for a while, he decided that de Klerk might need to be exempted from this sentence. Arresting him would destroy the government of national unity (of which de Klerk was still, then, a member), and Sipho did not think that worthwhile.

If I had not heard the same remarkably generous views expressed by scores of black South Africans over the years, I would have thought Sipho was either fooling me or fooling himself. I do not believe he was. With few exceptions, black South Africa thinks revenge is pointless. Blacks are immensely proud of their struggle. Whatever the many and complicated reasons for white South Africa's capitulation, Africans believed in a simpler truth: They won; and as victors, they can afford to be magnanimous.

Sipho knew, better than anyone, that whites and blacks were not the only ones in need of reconciliation. For the bitterest battles of his life had not involved white police, but black members of Inkatha. And for his role in that fighting—in which he estimates that his self-defense unit killed hundreds of Zulu hostel dwellers—Sipho himself may be expected to appear before the Truth and Reconciliation Commission, or face prosecution. The commission is charged with reconciling not just apartheid belligerents, but all belligerents. And the vast majority of deaths during the liberation struggle were caused not by whites killing blacks, but by blacks killing other blacks (with or without white "third-force" collusion).

Reconciliation within the black community is, if anything, an even more sensitive matter than reconciling across the color line. Partly, it is a matter of expectations. Blacks can more easily understand why whites would fight to protect the power and privilege of their own racial group; but how blacks could fight other blacks, when they ought to have been struggling jointly against apartheid, is something ANC-aligned Africans have never been able to accept.

This habit of mind continued even after the liberation struggle was won. Even then, the ANC could not countenance opposition from other black groups—and especially not from Chief Buthelezi. Ironically, the new government seemed to find it easier to heal the wounds of 350 years of white domination, than to resolve its ten-year-old dispute with Inkatha.

In some areas, mostly outside Natal, peace was achieved between the two groups. Katlehong was one. So, on a sunny Sunday afternoon in November 1995, Sipho was able to show me the houses where we spent our 1993 vigil—their net curtains repaired, their owners returned, loud music blaring from the open doorways. We visited the forward bases of Inkatha, which we had watched so carefully that night; now, ANC families lived in them, and the Inkatha fighters had returned to live peacefully in the nearby Buyafuthi hostel. And best of all, he took me to watch a soccer match on the sports ground outside the hostel. Two years before, had we tried to cross this bit of open ground in full view of hostel residents, we would both have been killed. Now they ignored us.

Both sides were obviously delighted and relieved at the peace. But it was achieved on one condition: That Inkatha accept the dominance of the ANC in the area. In the local elections of November 1995, no votes were cast for Inkatha there—because the Zulu party did not put up a candidate. As Sipho pointed out, hostel dwellers were vastly outnumbered by the residents in surrounding houses. He reckoned that, now that the ANC controlled the police, hostel residents would no longer dare to mount any opposition.

Unfortunately, in the new province of KwaZulu-Natal, where the opposing forces were more evenly balanced (Inkatha won 41 provincial seats in the 81-member assembly, to the ANC's 26) and where there is a longer history of conflict, no such easy solution was found. Political violence in the province dropped off sharply after the election, but remained unacceptably high. During the first eighteen months of black rule, thirteen hundred people died in political unrest in KwaZulu-Natal.

The election had resolved the largest question of race and power, but it had left the central problem of black politics untouched. Whites and blacks had spent four years getting used to each other, in a kind of long dress rehearsal for the government of national unity. But in KwaZulu-Natal, where the ANC, Inkatha, and the National Party were represented in a "government of provincial unity," there was no such heritage of preexisting consensus to draw on. Given the accommodating personalities of both the ANC and Inkatha leaders in the province—Jacob Zuma and Frank Mladlose—there seemed a good chance the two men could reach a modus vivendi. But they never really had a chance to try.

Immediately, the two parties resurrected their old preelection battle, over the power of provinces in the new South Africa. The ANC had promised to submit this question to international mediation after the election; it reneged on this promise. Chief Buthelezi pulled Inkatha out of the constituent assembly, which was charged with writing a final constitution to replace the document from the World Trade Centre. The two belligerents found themselves, again, in their respective corners: the ANC argued for a constitution that would reduce the powers of provinces further, in the interests of what it called "cooperative governance." Inkatha fought for greater devolution. In the meantime, the two sides battled over the power of patronage in KwaZulu-Natal. The ANC tried to introduce legislation which would allow traditional chiefs—the backbone of rural power—to be paid (and controlled) by central government. Buthelezi fought to preserve that right for the (Inkatha-controlled) provincial government.

The rhetoric got worse and worse. Buthelezi demanded virtual autonomy for KwaZulu-Natal, including a separate provincial police force and militia—something he knew his opponents would never concede—while the ANC accused him of trying to set up an ethnic dictatorship based on violence. Passions ran high. ANC officials, capable of being rational about the worst apartheid excesses, became enraged at any suggestion they should make concessions to Buthelezi. He became ever more irascible and unreasonable as time went on.

Both sides seemed to lack the political will to compromise. The new South Africa was left with a low-level civil war in its most populous province. Mandela's policy of reconciliation had done much to defuse the ethnic threat from the white right. But the same could not be said of the conflict in KwaZulu-Natal, where the battle was not between different ethnic groups, but over the very question of ethnicity itself. As always, the ANC insisted ethnicity did not matter and Buthelezi fought to prove that it did. The real test of reconciliation in years to come will be whether Africans can reconcile with Africans.

Ultimately, even if both racial and political reconciliation can be achieved, a huge task of economic reconciliation will remain. Unless the haves and the have-nots can be reconciled, nothing else will matter. For South Africa finds itself in the middle of a revolution, not at the end of one. The inauguration of Nelson Mandela brought about political liberation. But in the economic sphere, it was largely a revolution without change. That cannot remain true if the ANC is to retain its popularity—and if racial reconciliation is to endure.

Deputy President Thabo Mbeki argues that reconciliation must, in the end, mean more than "a newfound ability between black and white to share a pot of tea." It must involve a transfer of wealth. "Reconciliation that merely sought to reassure the former rulers by forgiving them their sins and legitimizing their position of racial privilege could never be sustained," Mbeki says, asking the obvious question: "Can you carry out a process of transformation in which nobody loses anything? Is that possible?"

Mbeki, who is overwhelmingly likely to become president of South Africa after Mandela retires in 1999, outlines an ambitious program for removing racial disparities in all spheres. He argues that stability—and racial harmony—demands such action. "Durable national reconciliation requires . . . the fundamental transformation of the patterns of ownership of wealth, the distribution of income, the management of society and the economy, and the skills profile," he insisted in a 1995 speech.

"But it's a very delicate thing, to handle the relationship between these two elements—it's not a mathematical thing, it's an art," Mbeki admits in another speech. If change is used as a stick to beat former opponents, reconciliation will be destroyed. "But equally, if you handle transformation in a way that doesn't change a good part of the status quo, those who are disadvantaged will rebel, and then, goodbye reconciliation!" Somehow, the new government will have to find a way to impose a "balance of sacrifices" on all its people, if the new South Africa is to thrive.

The issue of economic inequality, which had never been central to the liberation struggle, has become the focus of the post-apartheid government. But the ANC knows that the war against poverty cannot be won by revolution. Revolutionary change would destroy South Africa's functioning market economy (its most positive inheritance from the apartheid state); it would cripple the country's efforts to attract foreign investment; and it would abort the improvements in quality of life that have always been the ANC's ultimate goal.

Black South Africans are not demanding revolutionary change; opinion polls consistently reveal relatively moderate expectations. My private, unscientific inquiries always yield the same response—overwhelmingly, black South Africans want jobs, not handouts. Their reasonable expectations of what government can achieve are pitifully limited. They have so little that any improvement—the grading of dirt roads in the township, for example, or access to electricity—makes a huge difference. Patience is not unlimited; but it is considerable.

The development task is huge, however. Though the incomes of black South Africans have risen rapidly since the 1960s—the share of whites in the country's total personal income dropped from 70 percent in 1960 to 53 percent in 1994, while black South Africa's share rose from 22 percent to 35 percent—the gap remains wide. In 1995, at the dawn of the post-apartheid era, whites still earned on average eight times more than blacks. An estimated 45 percent of the economically active population (mostly non-whites) were either unemployed or worked in the so-called informal sector (hawking a handful of vegetables on the street, or doing other odd jobs). With some 400,000 new job seekers coming onto the labor market each year, and only around 30,000 finding new formal-sector jobs, the problem just gets worse and worse.

Some 2.3 million Africans were estimated to be suffering from malnutrition in 1994, 30 percent of the population was illiterate, only 13 percent of people in rural areas had running water in their houses, and in Gauteng, the richest province around Johannesburg, nearly a quarter of the black population lived in shacks. The ANC estimated the need for new housing at 3 million units.

Just prior to the April 1994 elections, the ANC launched a grand plan to deal with these problems entitled the Reconstruction and Development Programme (RDP), the ANC's blueprint for economic development and social change. It promised to build 1 million houses in its first five-year term of government, and electrify 3.5 million homes.

The ambitions of the RDP—the acronym became almost a mantra of the new government—went far beyond bricks and wiring. Its goal was the grand one outlined by Mbeki: Total transformation of South Africa. Once again, as in the apartheid era, South Africa was to be the object of a major project of social engineering. But the world had changed since then. The new government's actions, however noble, would be constrained by many factors it could not ignore: the huge debt burden inherited from previous governments (which consumed—at the time Mandela became president—92 percent of the budget, leaving only 8 percent for capital spending on development); the powerful private business sector, which would oppose revolutionary change; and world opinion, which always mattered greatly to the ANC. Under those conditions, transformation would take time.

The RDP got off to a very slow start. Large sums of money were voted for RDP spending in the government's budget—R2.5 billion in the first year alone—but delays in putting programs in place meant much of this was not spent. Housing construction—the most politically sensitive of all the RDP's projects—was especially slow. The ANC had promised to build 1 million homes by 1999, yet by the end of its first twenty months in power, only a paltry 10,000 had gone up.

The ANC had far more success in the field of electrification, where some 375,000 homes were electrified in the first year of the new government. But this was, ironically, a legacy of the old government. The electricity utility, Eskom, had a rapid electrification program in place long before the elections. Provision of clean water to rural areas was another example of rapid growth. But for normal people, the main impact of the RDP during the first couple of years of Mandela's government was more limited: free peanut butter sandwiches for black children at school; and free health care for pregnant women and children under six.

Economically, the main beneficiary of the early years of Mandela's rule was undoubtedly the black middle class. The affirmative action policy of the new government meant blacks were rapidly promoted to senior positions in the civil service (where, despite pre-election guarantees, half of the directors general inherited from the old regime were replaced within eighteen months). Private-sector business followed suit, appointing blacks to prominent positions to avoid coercive action by government. Major corporations, eager to create black vested interests in capitalism, sold off parts of their businesses to black entrepreneurs who became millionaires overnight. Through the trade unions and pension funds, ownership trickled down to the black community, but very slowly. Overwhelmingly, control and ownership of the economy remained in white hands.

In the long run, the prospects for stability and democracy in South Africa will depend on efforts to bring prosperity to ordinary blacks. That will not mean abolishing racial inequalities of wealth all at once—or even for many many years to come—but a steady reduction in inequality. And it will mean getting people back to work. It will be a tall order for a country with a high population growth rate, a low skills base, low productivity, and—in both the white and black communities—the absence of the kind of work ethic that propelled Asian countries to high growth.

It will require competent and efficient government of a kind that other newly independent African states have woefully failed to provide. The new South African government started well enough. Mandela's politics were reassuring, and the ANC's economics were as well. But in future, it will not be enough for the ANC simply to avoid making socialist mistakes. It must tackle the country's economic problems with vigor, and there was little sign of that in the first two years.

Somehow, even with only moderate growth, a way will have to be found to give black South Africans hope that their lives will improve—a sense of progress, however slow. The ANC must prove that democracy can be made to pay. Otherwise, pressures will build to dispense with it altogether.

When South Africa stepped through the looking glass, it did not emerge in Wonderland. It emerged in the real world, where poverty is the biggest challenge to all democratic governments, and where there are tougher problems to solve than apartheid.

The new civil religion, racial reconciliation, rapidly came under strain, as competition increased between the races for jobs, resources, and wealth. This raises the prospect that blacks may cast off racial tolerance in time, as they throw away the habits of dependency and submission bred by centuries of white rule. Still, with luck, the demographics of South Africa and the culture of Africa may continue to favor black magnanimity. Africans outnumber whites by eight to one—almost exactly the reverse proportions as in the United States—and a powerful majority may be less tempted to aggression than a weak minority.

Overall, the skills and strengths that South Africans evolved in the battle against apartheid have so far served them well in the new order. The democratic center—constructed so painfully over those years of negotiated revolution—continues to hold.

Hopefully, the same factors that brought South Africa together for the 1994 election will keep it together: the realities of economic interdependence; the expectations of the outside world; and above all, the essential pragmatism of South Africans. Before the election, they were repeatedly and temptingly faced with the chance to destroy their country to further their own sectional interests. They always refused, and there seems at least a chance that they will continue to do so.

No one, of course, can be sure of that fact. But then, again, no one could ever have predicted that the South Africa I first visited in 1985—a land of intolerance, and despair—would, a decade later, deliver itself of a miracle. Like every miracle, it had its antecedents; it was less a gift from God than a gift from men to other men. Perhaps there is a chance—just a chance—that such a man-made miracle can endure.

Nowhere will that be harder than at Koppies, the little town at the front line of all the new South Africa's many revolutions.

Koppies was the Orange Free State town I visited in 1993, when right-wing white farmers penned blacks into the township. Koppies was the home of farmer Sakkie van der Schyff, with his racist jokes and his pragmatism. Koppies was a world where fault lines ran deeper than almost anywhere else in South Africa. When I went back there at the end of 1995, reconciliation was proving difficult. Transforming Koppies looked well-nigh impossible.

First, the numbers gap—whites were outnumbered by more than fifteen to one. The wealth gap was even greater: of the fifteen thousand blacks living at Kwakwatsi, Koppies' dependent black township, an estimated 80–90 percent were unemployed. Despite a recent extension of waterborne sewerage, one quarter still used buckets as toilets, placing the malodorous contents outside for collection every morning. The streets were not only unpaved but ungraded. Many residents lived in shacks.

White Koppies—a town of absurdly broad streets and absurdly narrow politics—was scarcely rich itself. But its residents enjoyed all the trappings of "platteland" prosperity: modest bungalows with luxuriant gardens, tended by cheap black help; membership in the local golf and tennis clubs; a good school, clean streets, and reliable municipal services. They were not rich in the absolute, but in the relative terms of Kwakwatsi. The two were different worlds.

Politically, they became one world on November 1, 1995, when democratic local government elections were held throughout South Africa for the first time. Previously, the tax bases of the two areas had been separate; now they were one, and the local budget—funded almost entirely by the taxes of white Koppies—was controlled by a black-dominated local council. This was a real transfer of power, of the kind that did not occur in such stark terms at central government level. This was where racial reconciliation would face its toughest test, where not just power but money was at stake.

In Koppies, I found a world where the happy non-racialism of the rugby pitch had given way to economic hostility. I found a white community which held its citizenship of the rainbow nation under protest. I found a huge backlog of racism, far bigger than any I had experienced elsewhere in the new South Africa. And as always, I found a determination from black South Africans to defeat that racism, not with force but with generosity of spirit, and with patience.

I started in the white town, where the shelves of the hardware store—

owned by the outgoing mayor, Pierre de la Harpe—said it all. Kerosene lanterns were stocked next to pool chlorine: two worlds, one tax base. De la Harpe outlined the central problem facing the new Koppies council, composed of seven blacks from Kwakwatsi and three whites from town. (The local government system negotiated in the dying days of the old government gave whites representation in rural local councils out of proportion to their numbers.)

The new council's problem was that Kwakwatsi residents were refusing to pay for water and other municipal services. They had started boycotting such payments as an act of protest against the white government. Payments had never resumed. As long as Kwakwatsi would not pay, neither would the whites, de la Harpe said. Whites could bankrupt the council within months by withholding payments. The battle lines were drawn, like everything else in Koppies, along racial lines.

So I went to Kwakwatsi to find the new mayor, high school principal Samuel Khote, and Johannes Tladi, the brains behind the ANC in the township. On my previous visits, we had sat in some dreary township room, on broken chairs at empty tables, and perhaps sent out one of the ubiquitous township children to buy us a bottle of Coke. This time, I decided, it was a new South Africa, and I was going to take the two men to lunch.

I proposed it; Samuel looked away, and Johannes looked at Samuel. They seemed to be holding their breath. With the natural delicacy that is so much a part of African society, they did not want to tell me that there was nowhere two black men and a white woman would be served lunch in Koppies. I had suspected this was so, but then dismissed the idea; Samuel was, after all, the mayor of the town. But Johannes (who had been deputy mayor under the transitional council that governed Koppies after the April elections) had recently been refused a drink in the local hotel. It was the only luncheon venue. None of us wished to risk the humiliation of a second refusal.

So we drove some twenty-five miles to a Wimpy bar on the main highway to Johannesburg, and had our meal there, in neutral territory. I was ashamed, for my skin and for the people of Koppies. But Johannes and Samuel were more realistic than emotional. They would use the new constitution to force the hotel manager to change her racist habits; Samuel was looking into withdrawing her municipal licence. Over time, they assured me, such things would come right. The habits of mind which fostered racial separation had formed over 350 years, and changing them might take a generation. As thirty-three-year-old Samuel told me, "People grow up to be what they are taught to be." The only solution is to change the teaching.

Whites could change, they both assured me. And then, to my great surprise, they said, "Look at Sakkie van der Schyff." Sakkie, the farmer who led the Koppies blockade; Sakkie, who commanded the armed white right in Koppies during their preparations for the *volkstaat* war which never began. Why single out Sakkie?

So Johannes told me the story of his sister's graduation party in Kwakwatsi. He wanted someone to record it on video. Sakkie had a video camera, so he asked Sakkie to do the job. "I thought I'd test the waters," says Johannes, who admits he was nervous but thought the gesture was worth the risk. The lanky blond van der Schyff arrived with his camera, was treated like royalty by the hosts, plied with cold drinks and given an umbrella to shield his head from the hot African sun. A narrow, fragile basis for reconciliation was finally laid. Johannes is confident that he will convert Sakkie to membership of the new South Africa, if not of the ANC. Then he will be an example to all the people of Koppies—for if Sakkie van der Schyff can change, surely anyone can.

Sakkie is already making his own kind of peace: he has built up a good business videotaping township weddings and funerals, which supplements his income as a farmer. And at the film-developing studio he runs in Koppies, he is training ten blacks from Kwakwatsi, issuing them with cameras and film, and setting them up in their own photographic businesses. They will take snapshots in the township, repay his investment from the proceeds, and substantially increase the turnover of his developing business.

Sakkie van der Schyff needs black South Africa, and black South Africa needs him. Africa and the Afrikaner, at peace in the same fatherland. Africa and the Afrikaner, free at last.

Postscript

Since this book was written, South Africa's euphoria has faded, leaving South Africans with a massive post-liberation hangover, and a painful case of depressed spirits. They have awakened to a world where Nelson Mandela has begun to lose his aura of sainthood; a world where corruption and incompetence have emerged to taint the new administration; where fear of crime and violence is a constant companion; and where the arrogance of power has begun to claim its victims. (They even lost at rugby.)

But this book has tried to paint on a larger canvas: to put aside, where possible, concerns for the future in favor of an accurate rendering of the immediate past—not just the facts, which endure, but all those feelings which have now faded. It aims to be a first draft of history; one that, like all histories, will change as the times change, and as perspectives shift and moods alter. It is history untainted by too much hindsight, for hindsight will write an entirely different story. The death of apartheid is one of the great tales of twentieth-century politics. And that will remain so—whatever the sequel.

Notes on Sources

1 *The Myth of the Monolith*

This chapter draws heavily on personal interviews, as well as on the written works of historian Hermann Giliomee and philosopher Andre du Toit. I have used some material from F. W. de Klerk's speech to top businessmen in Cape Town on November 19, 1994; from Willem de Klerk's biography, *F. W. de Klerk: The Man in His Time* (Johannesburg: Jonathan Ball, 1991); and from Tom Lodge and Bill Nasson, eds., *All, Here, and Now: Black Politics in South Africa in the 1980s* (New York: Ford Foundation/Foreign Policy Association, 1991). The Kissinger quote comes from National Security Study Memorandum no. 39: Southern Africa, December 9, 1969. The extracts from Mandela's *Long Walk to Freedom: The Autobiography of Nelson Mandela* (Johannesburg: Macdonald Purnell, 1994), are at pp. 448, 617, 239, and 20–21. The story about Mandela and General Steyn was told to me by Mac Maharaj.

2 *The Age of Contradictions*

Professor Pieter de Lange, formerly chairman of the Afrikaner secret society, the *Broederbond* (Brotherhood), told me the story that precedes this chapter (in 1994). The farmer was his wife's uncle, and the events took place in the late 1960s near the Western Cape town of Somerset West.

This chapter has been shaped by interviews with a number of politicians including former President P. W. Botha and former South African Defence Force Chief Constand Viljoen, as well as a number of political analysts, chief among them Hermann Giliomee, Andre du Toit, and Helen Zille of the University of Cape Town; Bobby Godsell, Harry Oppenheimer, and Michael Spicer of the Anglo American Corporation; Chester Crocker, former U. S. Assistant Secretary of State for Africa; Steven Friedman of the Centre for Policy Studies in Johannesburg and F. W. de Klerk's brother, Wimpie de Klerk. Merle Lipton's *Capitalism and Apartheid: South Africa 1910–86* (Cape Town: David Philip, 1985) provided essential research material, as did Robert M. Price's *The Apartheid State in Crisis* (Oxford: Oxford University Press, 1991), a fascinating account of the political and economic strains on apartheid in the late 1960s and 1970s. The writings of John Kane-Berman, head of the South African Institute of Race Relations, also influenced my thinking.

The account by a black journalist of the June 16, 1976, Soweto riots is quoted in Hilda Bernstein, *The Rift: The Exile Experience of South Africans* (London: Jonathan Cape, 1994), p. 66. Merle Lipton's discussion is in her *Capitalism and Apartheid: South Africa 1910–86* (Cape Town: David Philip, 1985).

Anthony Sampson's remark comes from his book *Black and Gold* (London: Hodder & Stoughton, 1987), p. 113. F. W. de Klerk's comments on the homelands were made to a seminar audience at the Center for Strategic and International Studies in Washington, D.C., on November 8, 1994. They are reproduced in the CSIS publication, *A Conversation with F. W. de Klerk.*

The quote from "Dawie" is from the "Dawie" column in the Afrikaans newspaper *Die Burger,* November 13, 1976. It is cited in an unpublished manuscript by Hermann Giliomee, "A Question of Survival: A History of the Afrikaners," University of Cape Town, 1995. Pik Botha's 1978 interview was recorded by Anna Starcke and published in her book *Survival* (Cape Town: Tafelberg, 1978), p. 66.

3   To the Rubicon, and Beyond

I am indebted to P. W. Botha and the Institute for Contemporary History at the University of the Orange Free State in Bloemfontein for the opportunity to consult the former president's personal papers, which are lodged there in a closed archive, as is Dr. Daan Prinsloo's unpublished 1993 biography of Botha, " 'N Stem Uit die Wildernis" (A Voice from the Wilderness), which includes detailed documentary records of Botha's presidency. The episode involving U.S. Ambassador Heiman Nickel is quoted from " 'N Stem Uit die Wildernis," p. 1301. The handwritten notes of Botha regarding the Rubicon Speech are from File PS/13/21/2 (1985–86). I have also drawn on research by Professor Tom Lodge, the foremost expert on ANC politics, published in his essay "State of Exile: The African National Congress of South Africa: 1976–86," in P. Frankel, N. Pines, and M. Swilling, eds., *State, Resistance and Change in South Africa* (Johannesburg: Southern Book Publishers, 1988), and from "Rebellion: The Turning of the Tide," in Lodge and Nasson, eds., *All, Here, and Now.* Howard Barrell's unpublished doctoral dissertation, "Conscripts to Their Age: ANC Operational Strategy 1976–86," Oxford University, 1993, provided valuable insights, as did the published and unpublished writings of Professor Hermann Giliomee, including "The Last Trek? Afrikaners in the Transition to Democracy," *South African International,* South African Foundation (January 1992), and the manuscript, "A Question of Survival: A History of the Afrikaners."

The account of the Mxenge murder is taken from a chapter written by Dirk Coetzee, in A. Minnaar, I. Liebenberg, and C. Schutte, *The Hidden Hand: Covert Operations in South Africa* (Pretoria: Human Sciences Research Council, 1994).

4   The Great Seduction

The Paton quote in the epigraph to this chapter is from an address to the South African Institute of Race Relations on July 3, 1979.

This chapter draws heavily on personal interviews with leaders of the ANC in exile, conducted over many years beginning in 1984 when I was based at ANC headquarters in Lusaka for the *Financial Times*. I frequently discussed ANC strategy with exiled leaders Joe Slovo, Mac Maharaj, and Thabo Mbeki. ANC officials Mohammed Valli Moosa, Joel Netshitenzhe, Thozamile Botha, and Parks Mankahlana also offered invaluable insights into this period of ANC policy, as did the transcripts of broadcasts by the pirate ANC radio station, Radio Freedom, as well as official ANC publications, including the in-house magazine *Sechaba,* and official reports of the Kabwe ANC Conference of 1985. Mandela's autobiography also provided some material.

Gavin Relly, former chairman of Anglo American, spoke to me of his experiences at the first meeting between businessmen and the ANC, in Zambia in 1985. The quote from Tony Bloom is taken from his notes of a meeting with the ANC at the Mfuwe Game Lodge in Zambia on September 13, 1985. Vernon Webber, formerly MD of Anglo American in Zambia, offered insights. Colin Eglin, participant in one early Lusaka meeting, also contributed. Three former advisers to Zambian president Kenneth Kaunda provided invaluable information on contacts between South African intelligence and the ANC in exile—they are Milimo Punabantu, Mark Chona, and Wilted Phiri.

Historian Tom Lodge's essay "Rebellion: The Turning of the Tide," in Lodge and Nasson, eds. *All, Here, and Now,* provides essential background on the effect of states of emergency on the black population.

Many Afrikaner participants in the early talks have spoken to me of their experiences. Pieter de Lange, Willie Esterhuyse, and Frederik van Zyl Slabbert have been particularly helpful; they have spent hours, over the years, helping me to understand Afrikaner politics. Kobus Jordaan, involved in early talks with UDF leaders, spoke to me at length, as did Dakar participant Theuns Eloff and participants in the Mells Park talks, including Wimpie de Klerk, Mof Terreblanche, and Marinus Daling. Sam de Beer and Mark Swilling, both of whom were involved in early contacts between the UDF and government, were also very helpful. The American network PBS filmed parts of the Dakar meeting, including a fascinating debate between Thabo Mbeki and other Afrikaners.

Oliver Tambo's promise of "more bloodshed than ever before" comes from the minutes of evidence Tambo gave before the Foreign Affairs Committee of the House of Commons, London, on October 29, 1985. The remark about the ANC being "an organisation on its knees" is taken from "ANC Shifts Strategy in South Africa," *Washington Post,* March 7, 1986. The quote from Willem de Klerk's biography, *F. W. de Klerk: The Man in His Time,* is at p. 55.

5 *Secret Mission*

This chapter draws on interviews with the main participants in the early phase of secret negotiations, including Mandela himself, as well as on the detailed accounts of the period given in his published memoirs, *Long Walk to Freedom,* particularly pp. 507–540. Botha's unpublished autobiography, *A Voice from the Wilderness,* also provided some material from pp. 1188–1191, as did a BBC television documentary, *The Death of Apartheid,* screened in 1995. Allister Sparks's excellent book, *Tomor-*

row Is Another Country, published by Struik in Johannesburg in 1994, provided insights and information, though the accuracy of all information was confirmed in interviews with the principals.

Mandela's tribute to Coetsee as his "hero" was made on South African comic Pieter-Dirk Uys's television programme *Funigalore,* screened on South African television in 1994. The Eminent Persons Group's visit to South Africa in 1986 is chronicled in *Mission to South Africa,* a report published by Penguin for the Commonwealth Secretariat in 1986. The quote from warder Aubrey du Toit comes from Jurgen Schadeberg, ed., *Voices from Robben Island* (Johannesburg: Ravan Press, 1994), p. 47. David Ottaway's study of Mandela and de Klerk, *Chained Together* (New York: Times Books, 1993), provided further insights into Mandela's character.

6 *Why the Boers Gave It All Away* / 7 *The Great Leap*

This chapter and the next draw mainly on personal interviews with de Klerk's friends, family, legal associates, political colleagues and opponents. But the judgments in it are mine, based on seven years of seeking the answer to the question, why did F.W. do it? Wimpie de Klerk's biography of his brother, *F. W. de Klerk: The Man in His Time,* was very helpful, as was Professor de Klerk himself. Quotes are from pp. 544, 547, 569. The account of the January 1990 cabinet meeting in chapter 6 was provided by a minister who was present but who wishes to remain anonymous. The account of the January 1986 Botha cabinet meeting is drawn from Dr. Daan Prinsloo's " 'N Stem Uit die Wildernis," pp. 985–986. The section on the effect of sanctions draws on the writings of economic historian Merle Lipton, especially her 1990 paper *The Challenge of Sanctions,* published by the Centre for the Study of South African Economy and International Finance at the London School of Economics, as well as on Robert Price's *The Apartheid State in Crisis,* especially p. 274. I have also consulted Chester A. Crocker's excellent *High Noon in Southern Africa: Making Peace in a Rough Neighborhood* (New York: W. W. Norton, 1992). Information is drawn too from interviews conducted by Allister Sparks and broadcast in the BBC documentary *Death of Apartheid* (1995), and from Sparks's book *Tomorrow Is Another Country,* though this was also confirmed by those involved.

De Klerk's comments about the failure of apartheid come from a BBC interview with David Frost, February 14, 1993, quoted in Hermann Giliomee, "Survival in Justice: An Afrikaner Debate Over Apartheid," (University of Michigan), vol. 36, no. 3 (July 1994). F. W. de Klerk's comments to a seminar audience at the Center for Strategic and International Studies in Washington, D.C., on November 8, 1994, are reproduced in the CSIS publication, "A Conversation with F. W. de Klerk." Joe Slovo's *Has Socialism Failed?* was published by the South African Communist Party in London in January 1990. The quote from Henri de Villiers of Stanbic is reproduced in Price, *The Apartheid State in Crisis,* p. 274.

8 *Siamese Twins*

This chapter is based on interviews with participants, as well as my notebooks of the period.

9 The Third Man . . . and the Third Force

The massacre of the lady in the bathrobe and fifteen others took place at Henley, Natal, on March 29, 1990. I visited the Njilo brothers at Patheni and Ndaleni in March 1994. My interviews with Jacob Zuma were conducted in 1992 and 1995. Material on Zulu history was drawn from Donald Morris's book, *The Washing of the Spears: A History of the Rise of the Zulu Nation Under Shaka and Its Fall in the Zulu War of 1879* (London: Jonathan Cape, 1966), and from numerous interviews with prominent Zulus in Natal, including Harriet Ngubane, Prince Vincent Zulu (then KwaZulu minister of culture), senior *Natal Witness* editor Khaba Mkhize, former Inkatha official Oscar Dhlomo, and many Zulu chiefs and ordinary residents of ANC areas near Durban.

The interview with Mandela is Bill Keller's "A Day in the Life of Nelson Mandela: Charm, Control, a Bit of Acid," *New York Times*, September 12, 1994. The extracts from *Long Walk to Freedom* are at pp. 579–580. The letter from the former "foot soldier" of apartheid, Greg Deegan, was published in the *Johannesburg Mail and Guardian* newspaper, in the edition July 14–20, 1995.

I interviewed numerous individuals on the third-force question, including Lieutenant-General (rtd) Pierre Steyn, now defense secretary to the new government, who conducted an inquiry in 1992 into third-force activities in the military, as well as numerous members of the former cabinet, who preferred to remain nameless, and of the new government.

10 Rollercoaster Revolution / 11 The Darkest Hour

These two chapters are based primarily on personal interviews with the negotiators from both sides, including Roelf Meyer, Cyril Ramaphosa, Mac Maharaj, Fanie van der Merwe, Niël Barnard, Mohammed Valli Moosa, Fanus Schoeman, Tertius Delport, Leon Wessels, and with former Finance Minister Derek Keys, as well as on my personal notebooks from 1990 to 1993. I also consulted two excellent studies of the Codesa process, by Johannesburg's Centre for Policy Studies: *The Long Journey: South Africa's Quest for a Negotiated Settlement,* edited by the Centre's director, Steven Friedman (Johannesburg: Ravan Press, 1993), and *The Small Miracle: South Africa's Negotiated Settlement,* edited by Friedman and Doreen Atkinson (Johannesburg: Ravan Press, 1994). Martin Meredith's *South Africa's New Era: The 1994 Election* provides an excellent account of the negotiation period (London: Mandarin, 1994). As an overview, Heribert Adam and Kogila Moodley's *The Negotiated Revolution: Society and Politics in Post-Apartheid South Africa* (Johannesburg: Jonathan Ball, 1993) is extremely thoughtful and well argued.

The extracts from *Long Walk to Freedom* are from pp. 588, 595, and 596. Cyril Ramaphosa explained his rationale for precipitating deadlock at Codesa II when he addressed a closed meeting of trade unionists the next day; I consulted one participant's notes of that meeting. The comments of Ronnie Kasrils are taken from his book *Armed and Dangerous: My Undercover Struggle Against Apartheid* (London: Heinemann Educational, 1993), p. 354. Esther Waugh's article on the Bisho massacre appeared in the Johannesburg *Saturday Star* on September 12, 1992. The television interview with Mandela was part of the 1995 BBC documentary *Death of Apartheid.* I have also drawn from an interview with Mandela published by the *Johannesburg Star* on September 15, 1992.

12 The End of History / 13 Battling for the Right
14 Bake Bread Not Slogans

These chapters are based almost entirely on many hours of personal interviews with those involved, both in the heat of the negotiations and during the eighteen months that followed the peace deal. Many of those involved gave generously of their time: from the National Party, Roelf Meyer, Leon Wessels, Dawie de Villiers, Fanie van der Merwe, Rina Venter, Gerrit Viljoen, Tertius Delport, Fanus Schoeman, Richard Carter, and F. W. de Klerk. From the ANC: Mac Maharaj, Thabo Mbeki, Frene Ginwala, Essop Pahad, Aziz Pahad, Cyril Ramaphosa, Mohammed Valli Moosa, Joel Netshitenzhe, Parks Mankahlana, Thozamile Botha, Jacob Zuma, Zola Skweyiya, and Nelson Mandela. General Constand Viljoen and his associates General Tienie Groenewald, Koos Reyneke, and Pieter Mulder from the white right. From Inkatha, Joe Matthews, Mario Ambrosini, Ben Ngubane, and Chief Mangosuthu Buthelezi. Hermann Giliomee, Andre du Toit, Pieter de Lange, Willie Esterhuyse, and Wimpie de Klerk were all extremely thoughtful commentators on the period. On economic matters, Derek Keys, Alec Erwin, Tito Mboweni and his ANC colleagues Max Sisulu and Trevor Manuel, as well as Anglo American's Harry Oppenheimer, Bobby Godsell, and Michael Spicer, Clive Menell of Anglo-Vaal, and Brian Gilbertson of Gencor, were particularly helpful. My notebooks of the period were also invaluable.

Mandela's comments on nationalization after the Davos conference were reported in the *Financial Times* on February 5 and 7, 1992. Archbishop Tutu's reminiscences on voting were made at a dinner of the Foreign Correspondents Association in Johannesburg on November 13, 1995. Mandela's comments on the election results were made in the Senate in Cape Town, and reproduced in *Hansard,* the official parliamentary record, No. 1, May 20–27, 1994.

15 Now for the Hard Part

The Mandela quote in the epigraph to Part Three is from *Long Walk to Freedom,* p. 617.

Thabo Mbeki's comments are taken from an interview with me, and also from public speeches he delivered after becoming deputy president in 1994. I also drew on interviews with Archbishop Tutu, F. W. de Klerk, Wimpie de Klerk, Marike de Klerk, Pieter de Lange, Mof Terreblanche, Willie Esterhuyse, and Fink Haysom.

Marinus Daling's comment on Afrikanerdom was made in a speech to the Afrikaanse Sakekamer—The Afrikaner Chamber of Commerce—on September 22, 1995.

Acknowledgments

I HARDLY KNOW WHERE TO BEGIN. So many people contributed in different ways to the preparation of this book that it will be impossible to list all of them here. The endgame of apartheid was an extraordinary period, and it threw up extraordinary people to match. The thoughts and insights included in this book are theirs far more than mine. I owe to all of them a debt I can never repay.

But some debts must be acknowledged. To Michael Holman, my friend and mentor, the man to whom this book is dedicated and to whom I owe my career. To Philip Gawith and Mark Suzman, who were so much more than colleagues. To Anna Bame and Anna Maleka, who buoyed me up with their unaccountable good spirits. To Elsie Mlangeni, who looked after me so well, and especially to Abdul Bemath, my assistant, whose faithful, diligent, and excellent service was wholly undeserved.

My fellow foreign correspondents were always a source of insight and entertainment: John Carlin, David Beresford, John Battersby, Paul Taylor, Phillip van Niekerk. Corinne Moutout, my constant companion and fellow explorer, taught me to be brave.

Many South Africans helped to shape my thinking over many years. The hospitable folk of the townships and of the platteland invited me into their homes and into their minds. I will omit many names from this list, but I turned most often to the following when seeking answers to South Africa's mysteries: to the late Joe Slovo and to Pieter de Lange; to Mac Maharaj and Cyril Ramaphosa and Frederik van Zyl Slabbert; to Willie Esterhuyse and to Michael Spicer; to Fanie van der Merwe, and Mohammed Valli Moosa, and Aziz Pahad; to Franklin Sonn and Joe Matthews and Oscar Dhlomo; Tony Leon and Derek Keys, Tertius Delport and Sam de Beer and Con Botha, Zach de Beer and Helen Zille, Alan Fine and Mike Robertson; to Ann Bernstein and to Moeletsi Mbeki, who had an uncanny knack for putting things in perspective; to David Unterhalter, who took the liberal view; and most recently, to Hermann Giliomee and Wimpie de Klerk.

Martin Meredith encouraged me to write the book and kept my spirits up throughout. My *Financial Times* editors gave me generous leave to work on it, and cheerfully took me back at the end. Duncan Randall valiantly transcribed hundreds of hours of interview tapes, and provided valuable research assistance. Wayne Fredericks has been, as always, a tireless supporter.

I must thank especially those who read chapters, corrected errors, and provided advice: Martin Meredith, Mark Suzman, Michael Holman, Ann Bernstein, and Professor Hermann Giliomee of the University of Cape Town, whose insights were invaluable. My editor, Starling Lawrence, had excellent ideas for improving the manuscript, and Patricia Chui was a cheerful presence throughout. Stephen Robinson deserves the greatest thanks: he fought with me over every comma, but proved himself an excellent reader.

In the largest sense, my late mother, my father, and my brother made all of this possible. They gave me the confidence to wander so far from Tiger Stadium—with the security of knowing I could always come back home.

Index